COLLEGE

WITHDRAWN FROM
THE LIBRARY

UNIVERSITY OF
WINCHESTER

D1429501

KA 0010468 X

THE VICTORIAN PUBLIC SCHOOL
A SYMPOSIUM

THE VICTORIAN PUBLIC SCHOOL

Studies in the Development of
an Educational Institution

A SYMPOSIUM EDITED BY
Brian Simon and Ian Bradley

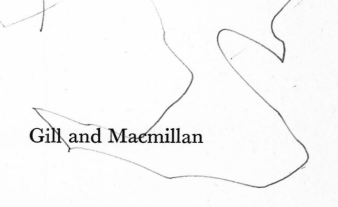

Gill and Macmillan

First published in 1975

Gill and Macmillan Ltd
15/17 Eden Quay
Dublin 1
and internationally through
association with the
Macmillan Publishers Group

© T.W. Bamford, Geoffrey Best, Ian Bradley, W.H. Brock, E.G. Dunning,
J.R. de S. Honey, J.A. Mangan, A.J. Meadows, Alicia C. Percival, Patrick
Scott, Malcolm Seaborne, Brian Simon, Normal Vance, 1975

7171 0740 X

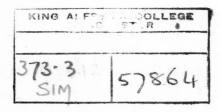

KING ALFRED'S COLLEGE

373·3
SIM

57864

Printed in England by
Bristol Typesetting Co. Ltd Barton Manor St Philips Bristol

Contents

Editorial Note

WITH the exception of Chapter 9, this book is based on papers delivered at a conference on the Victorian public school held at Digby Hall, Leicester, in September 1973 and organised by the University of Leicester Adult Education Department in conjunction with the Victorian Studies Centre and the Victorian Society. The conference was devised by Ian Bradley and Professor H.J. Dyos with the help of Mrs Jane Fawcett, Secretary of the Victorian Society, and was chaired by Professor Brian Simon. The organisers of the conference are particularly grateful to Brian Threlfall, Assistant to the Director of the Department of Adult Education at the University of Leicester, for his help in running the event.

Grateful acknowledgment is made to the following for their help with illustrations: Birmingham Public Libraries (Local Studies Department); Bodleian Library, Oxford; Dulwich College; Greater London Council; Mr A.F. Kersting; National Library of Ireland; National Monuments Record; Mr Malcolm Seaborne; Uppingham College.

As might be expected from material originally presented at a symposium, the intention is not to provide a definitive and comprehensive examination of the Victorian Public School, but to focus on certain features of particular interest. This accounts for occasional differences in interpretation, and for the fact that similar topics are dealt with to some extent from different angles.

List of Illustrations

Introduction

Brian Simon

I⟈ ɪꜱ no simple matter to define 'the Victorian age' except in terms of the length of a royal reign. It is even more difficult to give a succinct definition of 'the public school system', as will appear in this volume. But certainly the two matured together in the nineteenth century, in particular from about 1850 to its close. When Victoria came to the throne in 1837 there were some five years of Thomas Arnold's reign at Rugby to run. Barely two years after her death in 1901 there was appointed to the headmastership of one of the newer boarding schools, founded in 1843 with the primary objective of educating the sons of clergy at reasonable cost, a layman—in the phrase of *The Times* the single 'lay apple in the clerical dumpling', at any rate so far as the most prominent schools were concerned. This step, not long to remain an isolated one, might well be taken to mark the close of an epoch, though, as will emerge in this book, there are several good reasons for taking the story as far as the cataclysm of 1914–18.

The Victorian age is of interest from many points of view. It claims attention from the historian of education and of science; it is a main concern of the student of English literature, especially of the development of the novel, and an area of intensive activity by sociologists investigating the working of the first of the advanced industrial societies. It is not surprising, therefore, that one of the key developments of the period—the rise of an organised (and, indeed, unique) system of 'public' schools with a clearly defined ethos, serving a particular social class, and claiming both independence from and the highest services to society—should have attracted growing attention from the numerous points of view represented in this book. Since, however, the authors take up specific aspects, rather than attempting to cover every facet, and are more concerned with the changing ethos of these schools than with their organisation, it may be helpful, by way of introduction, to provide an outline of development in this sense.

Frederic Harrison, who had his own comments to make on the public school system, provides a broad outline of some of the changes that occurred in England during the seventy or more years of his life. This opened on the eve of the Reform Act of 1832, so that he was able to recall the Queen's coronation, the 'hungry forties', the Irish Famine, and the great struggle over Protection and Free Trade. Significantly, he next records how deeply stirred he was at school and college 'by the religious excitement of the Oxford Movement, the secessions to Rome, the wave of Evangelical Protestantism, and the revival of Catholic activity'. Subsequently he was 'in the thick of the agitation over the Neo-Christian development in the Churches, and the scientific triumph of the doctrine of evolution'. In later life he was much concerned with the course of labour legislation 'and the political emancipation of the working class'. A witness of the urban development associated with a near doubling of the population during his lifetime, he experienced the parallel growth in the area of the Empire which 'expanded to incredible volume', and this, in turn, brought a stirring of the heart 'by the long succession of our wars in India, in China, in Japan, in Africa, and in Australasia; by the Crimean War and the Indian mutiny'. The Harrisons were an unpolitical family, Frederic's father an architect living in a London suburb, but, royal occasions apart, wars were the public events which roused them, beginning with the first China War of 1839–41, the first Afghan War of 1839, the Scinde and the Sikh Wars of 1843 and 1845. While his infant mind failed to register the death of Scott, Goethe or Coleridge, the abolition of slavery in 1833 or the reform of municipal corporations two years later, Harrison records the impression made by the introduction of the penny post in 1840, attempts on the life of the Queen at about that time, and the reintroduction of income tax by Peel in 1842. For him 1848 was 'a wonderful time : every few days came news of another revolution, another capital in the hands of the people, covered with barricades—Paris, Vienna, Berlin, Rome—then the toppling of dynasties, and the popular assemblies and finally the 10th of April and the Chartist excitements'. By this time he was at

school—the new day school run by King's College, London—
and that day he recalls as 'a holiday and a day of fun'; no anxiety
is recalled, nor any recognition of the serious issues raised.[1]

The memoirs so introduced are compiled from contemporary
diaries, and it is from 1882 that some comments on 'Education
and the Public Schools' date.

Eton, Harrow, Winchester, and a half dozen more public
schools are really the nidus out of which is bred our present
aristocratic conservatism in Church and State. The entire
prelacy, civil and military service, governments, army and
navy, and even literary potentates issue out of these seminaries,
which are the true keystone of British society. And as I cannot
attribute either divine origin or celestial inspiration to that
society, I do not regard the public school system as an infallible
nursery of morals and an indispensable academy of enlighten-
ment.

Literally 'nidus' conveys 'nest', metaphorically the place of incu-
bation of a disease, and a further observation suggests that the
latter meaning was indeed specifically in mind. For Harrison
voices one of his main complaints as follows : 'The extravagant
value set on games today is a national disease. It degrades our
whole standard of manly excellence. It has brutalised our manners and ruined our tastes and habits.' That respectable news-
papers should devote whole columns to reporting the feats of
schoolchildren on sports fields seemed to indicate that 'the nation
is rapidly descending to be a race of drivelling vulgarians'.[2]

Such comments indicate how great was the departure from
the ideals associated with the name of Thomas Arnold—a matter
which is here dealt with specifically in Chapter 4 and which is
frequently alluded to in other parts of this book. An informed
and cultivated man, Harrison evidently felt that the public
schools in the 1880s constituted a powerful system with a common code, deriving from and contributing to an aristocratic
conservatism albeit with philistine characteristics. It is interesting
to look back from the standpoint here taken to a view, expressed
in 1865, one year after the report of the Public Schools Commission (the Clarendon Commission), which throws some light
on Harrison's impatient reference to the idea that the existence
of the public schools system is, somehow, its own justification.

This is the exposition by Howard Staunton in his grandly titled *The Great Schools of England: an Account of the Foundation, Endowments, and Discipline of the Chief Seminaries of Learning in England; including Eton, Winchester, Westminster, St Paul's, Charterhouse, Merchant Taylors', Harrow, Rugby, Shrewsbury, etc. etc.*

The significance of 'etc. etc.' is that it enables the addition, to the nine endowed 'great schools' originally selected for examination by the Clarendon Commission, of 'the four Chief Modern Proprietary Schools', which had duly made their mark by the early 1860s and attracted the attention of the commission. These were Cheltenham (1841), Marlborough (1843), Rossall (1844) and Wellington (1853). A further category that was to become even more energetic in thrusting upwards into the 'great school' sphere comprised certain local grammar schools endowed in the sixteenth or early seventeenth centuries (as were Rugby and Harrow). The particular example chosen by Staunton, though various others might have been (for instance, Sherborne and Uppingham), is Dulwich College, reconstituted by act of parliament in 1858 in the light of a great increase in the value of its endowment. Each of these three categories contributed a share to what emerged as the proper pattern of a Victorian public school, and in due course to the consolidation of an organised system of public schools.

'The great Endowed Schools', declared Staunton, 'are less to be considered as educational agencies, in the intellectual sense, than as social agencies.' Though in many respects defective—particularly in terms of mental or intellectual development—'they are the theatres of athletic manners, and the training places of a gallant, generous spirit for the English gentleman'. While 'England will, doubtless, in due time succeed in creating institutions aiming mainly at stimulating and storing the mind', by 'no process of transfiguration are the great Endowed Schools likely to be rendered institutions of this stamp'. Their function was different.

The aristocratical element has immense force in England [wrote Staunton]. The English aristocracy is the only aristocracy in Europe which is still powerful, and even the progress of democracy adds seemingly to its strength. The aspiration of the English aristocracy is to be, not the best educated, but for practical purposes the most cultivated. This class, however, does not exist for its own sake; does not exist merely to monopolise certain privileges; it exists that it may be the national ornament and bulwark; it exists that it may crown that social hierarchy which should symbolise the hierarchy of nature.

Since it was in the 'interests of the social hierarchy' that the English aristocracy be upheld—and preserved from the 'doom' that 'befell the aristocracies of Venice and of Poland'—not only schools but universities, church, army, navy 'should be aristocratic also', though still in entire subserviency 'to the most glorious of the national destinies'. From this it followed that the future of aristocratic schools must be decided not by radical or utilitarian reformers, nor mere theorists, but by 'the heart, and conscience, and reverence of the nation'. It was of this vital force that Staunton saw himself as representative, and it was on its behalf that he advocated the removal of particular abuses, the ending of 'absolute obscurantism' and the introduction of such improvements 'as commend themselves, not to superficial progress, but to the most exalted wisdom'.[3]

Staunton saw the social function of the public schools as the means by which the aristocracy may preserve its dominance; reform was considered necessary only so far as it perfected them in this function. In his illuminating study, *Godliness and Good Learning* (1961), David Newsome advances a rather different thesis to explain the popularity and rise of the public schools in the middle years of the century. In his view this was essentially a middle-class phenomenon. Schools and universities had come through a bad period in the late eighteenth and early ninetenth centuries. The main reason lies in the fact that these institutions did not then reflect any ideals of their own age. 'There was wanting an ideal; and, to save the public schools from the wholesale desertion of the middle class, this ideal had exactly to express the wishes and sentiments of the parents whose sons the schools needed to retain and attract.' At a time when the Evangelical revival was sweeping the country 'the way of salvation for the public schools was plain. The headmasters and assistant masters who came to the schools in the 1820s and 1830s were drawn from the class whose patronage they sought'; they 'knew exactly what they intended to achieve and the methods they were going to employ' even before appointment. It was men like Thomas Arnold and Charles Wordsworth who brought these ideals into the schools and transformed them in their image. As the middle class grew in power and influence, 'gradually displacing the aristocracy as arbiters of taste', they brought with them a re-awakening of religious spirit, appreciation of educational needs, high regard for learning, competition for honours. 'One of the most important manifestations of this rising influence of the middle class', concludes Newsome, 'was the emergence of the public schools as important national institutions.' It was pressure from middle-class opinion that led to reforms of the older public schools and grammar schools. It was the popularity of the reformed schools that led to the creation of many new public schools in the 1840s and 1850s 'largely fashioned on the Rugby model'. Their ideal was that of 'godliness and good learning'— the assumption that education and religion were essentially allied. At this stage they were characterised by 'intellectual toughness, moral earnestness and deep spiritual conviction'.[4]

But the term 'middle class' presents difficulties. It could be argued that the outlook of the industrial and commercial middle class was more precisely represented by the radical philosophers, led by Jeremy Bentham and James Mill, who devoted great attention to education and whose ideal institution was typified in the Hills' school at Hazelwood, Birmingham, or University College, London (the latter, incidentally, including an important innovatory school, University College School). The middle class, in this sense, fought hard and long for a 'modern' education, enshrining utilitarian values and involving the ending of the dominance of the classics (the central focus of public school education) in favour of science, technology, modern languages and the like. It was here that this section of the middle class exerted its influence—even if some of its members, gaining wealth and status, began, as the century progressed, to aspire to aristo-cratic pretensions and status, and therefore to accept aristocratic leadership and mores in education. As T.W. Bamford points out in *The Rise of the Public Schools* (1967), the demand for an education on the public school model came from that section of the middle class that was linked traditionally, through a complex web of connections, with the gentry and aristocracy.

It was for clergymen's sons that Marlborough was primarily founded in the early 1840s; and these also provided more than a quarter of the pupils at Rugby at the time of its reform and expansion. Cheltenham (1841) appealed particularly to the military and derived many of its early pupils from retired military families in the neighbourhood.[5] This points to the need for further research into the growth of the professions in the nineteenth century, and into the type of education thought appropriate in each case. Staunton himself had anticipated this difficulty. 'We speak, in England, somewhat vaguely', he wrote, 'of the *Middle Classes*, but the expression comprises a multitude so vast and various as to include persons exceedingly opulent and exceedingly poor.' The education of their children 'is an easy affair' for the wealthiest section; but for the poorest it is 'a burden and a perplexity of the most serious kind'. For them 'Gymnasia and Higher Elementary Schools are needed, and a National University'. But to these 'the aristocracy, the country gentry, and the more wealthy of the commercial class, would not, for obvious reasons, send their sons. They will continue to prefer Eton and Harrow, Oxford and Cambridge.'[6]

However, the point at which Staunton was writing, 1865, coincided with a period of change, not only in the public schools but in education generally. In a notable attempt to assess the development of the public school system and the various judgments of it, largely from within the system, E.C. Mack's two-volume study, *Public Schools and British Opinion* (1938–41) takes as a dividing point the year 1860, just before the appointment of the Clarendon Commission. After Arnold's initiative at Rugby, which did something to strengthen the resuscitation of other institutions, the history of the decades 1840–60, it is suggested, is one of conflict between liberalism and religious revivalism on the one hand, conservatism and the forces of advanced industrialism on the other. Up to the mid-1850s 'the more positive and important' influence was the former, and in yielding to a measure of reform both of the internal and social aspects of school life, schools retained the allegiance of the upper class while winning new support. Harrow was the only endowed foundation to be directly influenced by a pupil of Arnold (who also served under him as an assistant master), otherwise it was the new proprietary schools that took a fresh line. Those which did not respond in due form—Westminster, Shrewsbury, Charterhouse—fell behind, except for Eton, which was *sui generis*, and Winchester, which, if it moved somewhat, did so on its own lines. Then came the counter-influence of 'an imperialist and materialist industrialism' whose most concrete expression 'was the rise of organised athletics and its development into athleticism'—providing 'a beautiful illustration of the nature of the complex forces that were moulding the schools and of the characteristic outcome of the mingling of those forces'.[7]

Athleticism rapidly became established as 'the essence of school life' with an all-pervasive influence which tended to undermine all the key professed aims. It tended to stress the prevalent anti-intellectual bias, sound the death-knell of individuality in favour of conformity to a stereotype, substitute narrow moral aims by drying up a broad conception of human worth in favour of a philistine one, to sacrifice the professed moral end to the means in so far as glorification was accorded to the game. The expressed objective of the team game was subordination of selfish interest to the general good, but worship of 'physical prowess and competitiveness' produced something directly opposite. As 'the religion of athletics' achieves its full development in the closing decades of the Victorian period, it seems 'the perfect expression of a philistine age'.[8]

This aspect of public school life is examined from various points of view in the present book. Chapters 9 and 10 are directly concerned with it, while Chapter 7 deals with it in relation to the concept of 'manliness' and Chapter 8 takes the matter on from the games-field to the field of battle. Indeed, the transition in the late Victorian era from the form of religious and moral influence exercised by Arnold, to the form of control exercised by way of encouraging the religion of athletics must be of central concern to any examination of public school purposes and achievements. It, therefore, naturally enters into the discussion of the nature and extent of Arnoldian influence in Chapter 4, while the analysis and identification of grades of school in Chapter 2 makes use of games fixtures as a key indicator in defining status and interaction at different levels.

The development of the public schools into a system having common characteristics appears, then, as a product of a complex

set of circumstances. Three groups of institutions—the Clarendon schools, the new proprietary schools and some endowed
grammar schools—became fused into a single system and im-
pelled to take the same route as a solution to similar problems
or as a response to similar circumstances. The Clarendon 'nine'
themselves comprised very different institutions. Two (Rugby and
Harrow) served as examples of what could be done; two (Eton
and Winchester) were medieval foundations, inadequately reconstituted at the Reformation, which it was requisite to bring up to
date in mid-Victorian terms. The rest were of no great signifi-
ance. The proprietary schools, two of which (Marlborough and
Cheltenham) after initial difficulties very rapidly made their
mark, had to carve out by bitter experience quite new traditions
and approaches, and, partly to solve the crucial problem of
control, proved fertile ground for implementation of the post-
Arnoldian approach involving organised games, devolvement of
authority on prefects, and employment of young masters who
directly concerned themselves with their pastoral role, as well as
religious objectives and the exploitation of the chapel. The third
group, those endowed grammar schools aspiring to public school
status and benefiting from the diffusion of the desire for a public
school education by the middle class (however defined), were
themselves taking the direction pioneered by Rugby and Harrow
of breaking their links with the locality in order to establish
schools appealing directly to the middle class. Already by the
mid-1860s the Schools Inquiry Commission (the Taunton Commission) could note of Sherborne: 'Whatever may have been
the class of boy for whom the founder intended to provide
education, there can be no doubt as to the class who now actually
use it, and what might have been a mere provincial grammar
school at present bids fair to rank among our great public
schools.'[9]

When the Headmasters' Conference was established in 1869,
one of its chief instigators, significantly, was Edward Thring who,
as headmaster of Uppingham and representative of the thrusting
grammar school element, was determined to preserve his school's
independence from what he felt then to be a real danger of state
control arising from the legislation proposed as a result of the
Taunton Commission's report (1868). That 'danger' was averted;
indeed, the Endowed Schools Act (1869) was turned, by a

B

process of political lobbying not yet fully researched, into a key measure assisting the development of endowed grammar schools to public school status.[10] Following this legislation, those schools which caught the middle-class market were able to separate themselves more clearly from the ruck of grammar schools, and, even more, from the system of elementary schools for the working class consolidated in 1870. The nature of this task, in a democratic setting, necessarily gave rise to the evasions and contradictions which are characteristic of all expositions of the public school role and ethos and which provide so fascinating a field for the historian of ideas.

The decisive years, then, appear to be between 1850 and 1870. It may be noted that two more proprietary schools (Clifton and Haileybury) were launched in 1862, the year after the appointment of the Clarendon Commission but two years before it reported. It is symptomatic that, in that same year, the chief of the hierarchy of the Woodard Church of England schools for the different levels of the middle class, Lancing, acquired a new headmaster who determined, while retaining its special religious character, 'to make it a public school, whole, individual and complete'.[11]

From the 1850s, then, all the elements were present for what was to be a relatively uniform line of development during the remainder of the century, though it was first initiated only in a nucleus of schools and took a considerable time to spread more generally in dependence on social developments and the particular circumstances encouraging or preventing additional schools from entering on the social climb. It would, therefore, seem mistaken to make too much of the 1860s as a turning-point. Rather the decisive stage in the establishment of the public school system opened in the 1850s and, by 1870, this had become a largely interdependent and organised system with its own headquarters.

Broadly speaking, it may be suggested that there were three main stages in the development of the system. The first was the era initiated in the age of reform by the Arnoldian programme which, whatever judgment there may be of its achievements or limitations, was subsequently held up as a major and relevant step—whether by Arnold's biographer, by the author of *Tom Brown's Schooldays* (the first school novel, examined in Chapter

3), by the Clarendon Commission, which constantly held Rugby and Arnold up as models, or by later enthusiasts.

The second phase dates from the 1850s, when economic pressures lifted and industry and commerce gained a new buoyancy; not only did the new proprietary schools emerge with astonishing force into the forefront, but there was also a rapid development of a group of aspiring grammar schools, and—after the appointment of the Clarendon Commission had charted possible future pressures—concerted efforts by the oldest established schools to remedy the worst sub-standard conditions or disorders. The outcome, by 1870, was a system of schools sharing a common code or ethos, and determined to maintain this as a heritage independent of democratic control. To this end there had been established the Headmasters' Conference (HMC) with its specific task, in the words of its founder, to defend the schools 'in the hour of danger'.[12]

The third stage is that of efflorescence of the ethos, in the age of high imperialism up to 1914, to an extent which makes it difficult to discern the lineaments of separate origins beneath the stereotype—even if the system now extends to include both Roman Catholic (Ampleforth, Downside) and even Nonconformist schools (Mill Hill, The Leys). In the process various evils emerged as a key feature of the public school system. These included an overpowering philathleticism stemming both from the needs of the schools and from the all-pervading ideology of 'muscular Christianity' derived from the writings of Hughes and Kingsley. This ideology, it is argued below, had little in common with the specific ideals of the early reformers, but was appropriate to a nation now engaged on imperialist expansion.

Evolution of the schools as a system apart was accompanied by much greater interdependence. Masters moved from one leading school to another, and assistants were sent out to head schools aspiring to public school status. And here the role played by the universities should not be underestimated, for it was at the universities that the products of the various schools were compared and contrasted, and a few years in a college fellowship at Oxford or Cambridge often preceded appointment as an assistant master. In the middle and later years of the century there was a veritable network of personal contacts within the public schools community, and this was often a factor in determining staff appointments and transfers. Thus T.W. Jex-Blake, beginning as an assistant at Marlborough—under headmasters who came from Rugby and Harrow—became head first of Cheltenham then of Rugby. Also beginning as an assistant at Marlborough was H.A. James, who headed first Rossall, then Cheltenham, finally Rugby, where he succeeded Percival, who, as is shown in Chapter 5, had previously inaugurated the new proprietary school at Clifton before handing it over to J.M. Wilson, the pioneer science teacher whose work at Rugby figures prominently in Chapter 6. Haileybury, it might be added, began its career as a public school under A.G. Butler, elder brother of Montague Butler who had headed Harrow from 1859 but who was himself a product of Frederick Temple's Rugby, having served there as assistant master for a number of years. Temple's favourite pupil, Henry Hart, was obtained as an assistant at Haileybury on leaving Cambridge, then moved to Harrow when marriage required a larger income, before taking up the headship of Sedbergh in 1879, despite the warnings of colleagues. 'I have a fair knowledge of geography,' wrote one accounted the most brilliant of Harrow assistant masters, 'but I do not even know where Sedbergh is.'[13] Certainly it was an obscure endowed grammar school, characterised by an assistant commissioner to the Taunton Commission as merely 'cumbering the ground'—but Hart soon raised it to minor public school rank and the numbers from 88 to 202 by 1892. It was a recapitulation of the rise in the 1850s of Repton, of Giggleswick across the Pennines, of Uppingham, and other schools of this type.

Headmasters were, of course, of primary importance; their complete control over the school had been established once and for all by the Public Schools Act (1868), and, for the grammar schools, by the Endowed Schools Act (1869).[14] The formation of the Headmasters' Conference is, therefore, symptomatic: it brought together the 'very superior men' (in Thring's words) who embodied the public school ethos and who were responsible for every facet of school life. This was, in due course, to bring its own problems and necessitate the formation of a Governing Bodies Association as makeweight to curb the unduly conservative heads of a later age. The supremacy of the headmaster at this time is also borne out by the veritable hagiography of biographies of Victorian public school headmasters, in the tradition initiated by Dean Stanley. But the quality of assistants was also a key question, and at this period the public schools attracted young men whose brilliant academic results would earlier have indicated the Church. For the schools could offer better prospects, particularly the opportunity of a housemastership from which considerable profits could accrue; and success here could also be the shortest cut to high office in the Church. It took several headmasters, including Temple, to the archbishopric of Canterbury, more to bishoprics and wealthy deaneries, others to headships of Oxford and Cambridge colleges.

This highlights the relation between education and religion central to Arnold's thinking. It was only in 1841, one year before his death, that Arnold managed to combine the duties of both headmaster and chaplain in his own person. 'It seems to me the natural and fitting thing', he then wrote '. . . that the master of the boys should be officially as well as really their pastor, and that he should not devolve on another, however well qualified, one of his own most peculiar and solemn duties.'[15] Here lay the chief reason for the provision of school chapels and the gradual removal of boys from the parish church. Sometimes the step was excused on the grounds that the school had become too numerous and was crowding the parish out; in other instances it was simply taken for granted. The acquisition of a chapel marks an important moment in the development of what was eventually to be an integrated system of social and ideological control. Writing in 1898, J.E.C. Welldon, headmaster of Harrow, provided a typical example of the contemporary attitude on the place of religion in the schools.

> The religious tone of public schools is essential to them. A school in which religion does not play the highest part would not be in the present sense a public school; a school in which the religious teaching was not given principally by the headmaster would not be in that sense a public school. In every great public boarding-school the chapel is the centre of the school life. The holiest and most enduring associations of the school life belong to the chapel.[16]

But by the time Welldon—a future bishop—made this statement, only twenty per cent of public school masters were in holy orders. Although the headmasters might still be ordained, even this situation was not to last long into the twentieth century, when the inevitable change of power was finally achieved and lay headmasters confidently declaimed from pulpits commandeered from a national church which had ceased to occupy the predominant position it once held. Thereby, if to some extent lost to the Established Church, the bulk of the public schools were preserved as Anglican seminaries, for those preparing to enter posts in the establishment must properly conform to the state religion.

In *The Prefects: British Leadership and the Public School Tradition* (1964) Rupert Wilkinson stresses the similarity between the nature of the British constitution—or form of constitutional government—and that which developed within the public schools, as a key factor in the induction or preparation of a new social class to share political responsibilities under the aegis of the traditional governing élite—the gentry and aristocracy. It was an essential position of the Arnoldian reformers that the right kind of public spirit should be fostered which should, none the less, leave room for the development of individuality, even autonomy; the system of self-government by the boys themselves was therefore implemented in order to encourage the responsibility necessary in institutions intended to produce leaders rather than mere followers of orders. 'It is, we think, a great point in Public School Education that boys should be attached by it . . . to the ideas of Law, Order, System, Organisation, as distinct from any individual through whom, as the executive power, these things are carried out', wrote E.M. Goulburn in *The Book of Rugby School: Its History and Daily Life* which he, as headmaster following Arnold and Tait, brought out in 1856. While private schoolmasters could legitimately direct their own institutions, 'Public Schools should claim a reverence and love as Institutions, independently of the men to whom their interests have been entrusted for a time. Their discipline should be the pupil's initiation into the high and ennobling idea of Law.' This implied a classical education, 'the discipline of mental powers', and cultivation of 'the spirit of man'—a higher order than mind or intellect; under this head must be classed 'that faculty by which men apprehend Law, recognise government and are held together in the social system'. This function, Goulburn argued, is admirably undertaken in public schools precisely by virtue of their form of government. For senior boys are 'associated with the masters in the executive of the School' and in the maintenance of discipline. True, the stronger would 'occasionally tyrannise' over the weaker and press them into their service. This is 'one of the conditions under which all schools must exist, unless indeed the Boys were curtailed of all liberty of action, and subjected to constant espionage—an un-English method of education, never likely to succeed, even if it were desirable in this country'. The 'wise method', this exposition of the Arnoldian approach concludes, is therefore, 'to recognise this condition, to take it up into our system—to place it in harness and make it work for good'.[17]

It was largely by putting this principle into practice that the new proprietary schools, for instance, were transformed to fulfil their social function. Indeed, the prefectorial system, as it developed, clearly became a potent means not only of shaping behaviour and outlook but of doing so to such an extent that the original concept of autonomy could only develop within the narrow terms defined in what might now be called a social contract. Ten years after Goulburn's analysis, Marlborough, under the dynamic influence of a Rugby master, had not only inaugurated a 'house' system, developed athletics and games, built and brought into use separate classrooms in place of the Great Hall where all lived crammed together, but had also brought the prefectorial system to perfection. 'Prefects' courts were greatly utilised all through this period,' wrote A.G. Bradley in 1893, 'and offences calculated to injure the tone of the School as well as outrages to the dignity of the privileged order were investigated and summarily punished with the cane in the presence of the sixth and in the seclusion of their own retreat . . . The general tone of the School, we may say without hesitation, was on the whole exceptionally high.'[18]

If this was one method of social control developed in the schools, others included rigid supervision over every aspect of the boys' life through organised games, a full timetable of lessons and preparation, confinement within bounds (which had taken a long struggle to win), and various other restrictions. The individuality which had been a major objective now found little scope for development. While it became 'good form' in the 1880s

onwards never to criticise one's old school, autobiographies have
since revealed something of the experience of those whose main
memories are of boredom and suffering. 'Boarding school,' wrote
Lowes Dickinson in his memoirs. 'What a flood of black memories. . . Charterhouse I daresay when I was there [1870s] was
more sunk in barbarism than other public schools, and I myself
was more incompetent for the life than most boys. I will not
try to apportion the blame. . . But there is no doubt about the
misery, the futility, the worse than waste of precious years'; later
he refers to 'the long eclipse of life at school'.[19] In the early
1880s Roger Fry went to Clifton. 'The terms seem to have
dragged along heavily, respectably, monotonously,' wrote his
biographer, Virginia Woolf. 'The weeks, the days, even the
seconds separating him from the holidays are minutely counted
and struck off.' It is strange, she adds, how little the presence of
some remarkable men on the staff 'penetrated his shell; how
helplessly he endured a routine which was breeding in him
nevertheless a "sullen revolt" against "the whole Public School
system . . . and all those Imperialistic and patriotic emotions
which it enshrined".'[20] Harold Nicholson, at Wellington
in the 1880s, endured the same utter boredom from the
narrowness of his highly organised and minutely controlled
existence.[21]

These are probably not typical experiences; one could set
against them Rupert Brooke's famous evocation of life in his last
term at Rugby. But they indicate the possible cost of the transformation of the public school in the closing years of the century.

The reorganisation and ethos of the public schools, as developed towards the end of the century, profoundly affected schools
outside their circumscribed circle. Several masters, after serving
as assistants in public schools, moved to headmasterships in local
grammar schools up and down the country. One example is, of
course, James Prince Lee, who was appointed head of King
Edward's, Birmingham, in 1838, after eight years at Rugby under
Arnold; sixty years later J.L.A. Paton, after ten years at Rugby,
moved first to the headmastership of University College School
in 1899 and then, in 1908, to Manchester Grammar School. Between these years, very many others took a similar route, and
through these the public school spirit and outlook was diffused
throughout the newly reformed grammar schools as these were

gradually resuscitated following the Taunton Commission in the late 1860s. This is an aspect that has been little researched. Closely linked is the direct influence of the public schools on the new secondary school section set up following the Board of Education Act (1899). Once more there was a fear that the independence of these schools might be threatened by the somewhat radical proposals of the Bryce Commission (1895), notwithstanding that every reference to the public (or 'non-local') schools was couched in terms of the deepest respect. Michael Sadler, as an official of the newly established Board of Education (largely staffed by those educated in public schools), undertook a tour of the 'great schools' in 1899 bearing a message seeking mutual understanding. 'I am learning much from each Headmaster in turn. They are splendid men,' he wrote to his wife. '. . . I find myself at least as anxious as they are to save our great schools from the "many-headed beast" and from bureaucratic impertinences.'[22] Particular attention was paid by the Headmasters' Conference to gaining control of the secondary education section. The effort was successful, with the result that the new state secondary schools, established under the terms of the Education Act (1902), developed a curriculum, outlook and forms of organisation in line more with the ideals of the education of the gentry than with modern—or democratic—requirements.[23]

As indicated earlier, many aspects of the public schools are not covered in this book. One of these, which may prove important, is the attitude to sex and sin—and here the recent revelations concerning C.J. Vaughan, the most famous and immensely successful headmaster of Harrow (1844–59) and one of Arnold's favourite pupils, may prove significant; they reveal for one brief moment the contradictions at the heart of the system.[24] Another is the curriculum; this topic is touched on in various chapters, while Chapter 6 is concerned specifically with science and mathematics. The development of 'modern sides', particularly in the new proprietary schools, the link between changing curricula and new examinations and reforms in the armed services and civil service—these are clearly important aspects. A related question which demands further investigation is the nature and effects of the consistent primacy of the classics throughout the period; on this phenomenon Rupert Wilkinson advances an interesting thesis as to the 'counter-cyclical' function of institutions, that is, their tendency to offset changing trends in social and political life.[25]

But the public schools—each of them—were subject to a very complex set of forces, and, as the leading educational institutions in the country, each with its own inner development and character, present the educational and social historian with a wide field for research and study. No single symposium could possibly cover all aspects of interest or significance. Such was certainly never the intention of this book, which seeks only to bring a fresh approach to the study of certain aspects of that essentially Victorian institution—the public school.

Tom Brown's Universe:
The Nature and Limits of
the Victorian Public Schools Community

J.R. de S. Honey

'School is a little world,' wrote one of Tom Brown's Rugby
school-fellows, A.P. Stanley, apparently much to the satisfaction
of Dr Arnold. This chapter deals not with that microcosm, the
immediate world of the Victorian public school boy, but with
the wider firmament of the public school system, and not specifically in the days of Tom and Arthur and Flashman, but later
in the century, in the period when the influence of Tom Brown
and a whole corpus of public school literature had helped to
fashion the popular conception of the Victorian public school.
The 'universe' was the *system* : the individual schools may have
furnished the archetype, but the attempt to define the archetypal
Victorian public school and to analyse its characteristic institutions cannot proceed without taking account of the effect exercised
on the character of the schools by the fact of being part of a
system. This analysis aims to help define that system and to
identify those schools which, by being part of it, can properly
be labelled Victorian public schools.

The obvious starting-point for any examination of this community is the life and work of Thomas Arnold (dealt with in
Chapter 4), though, as I have suggested elsewhere,[1] the beginnings of the expansion of the public school system by the creation of the first three new proprietary schools in the 1840s took
place without any connection whatever with Arnold or his ideas.
But whatever the reason for this expansion, we can say that by the
development of existing public schools, the establishment of new
ones, and the transformation of old endowed grammar schools,
the provision of public school education in the second half of the
nineteenth century expanded into a recognisable system—a community of schools served by an infrastructure of prepara-
tory schools[2] which together tended to become the common

educational experience of the sons of the upper middle classes.
The schools of this system created a powerful 'machinery' of institutions, including compulsory organised games, house systems and forms of ritual, all of which served not only to ensure disciplinary control (in a period which still remembered frequent rebellions in the larger schools) but also to create an intense communalism which exalted the values of the school-community itself, if necessary at the expense of those of the home. The school's power to create alternative values and loyalties to those of the home was not due to the conscious design of head-masters; its acceptance by parents reflects, at least partly, the price they were prepared to pay for the non-scholastic benefits of the public school education, such as social status. This general-ised 'transfer of function' from parents to public schools which became so widespread among the British upper middle classes—at the very time when such a process was being halted and reversed in France—was accompanied by the school's accep-tance of certain social roles previously associated with the land-owning extended family. It was all the more remarkable that this transfer should have taken place in view of the schools' pro-fessed failure to deal with three serious problems. Fatal epidemic diseases were at their most virulent and frequent in schools at the very time when the transfer was beginning to become general, yet parents persisted in institutionalising their sons, with all the risks that this entailed. Secondly, this was also the time when the schools were most vocal in their protestations of their inability to cope with the problem of 'immorality'—a problem which needs re-defining because of significant changes of mean-ing with which the term was used between the 1830s and 1900. A third deterrent which parents defied in sending their sons to these schools was the incidence of forms of cruelty and barbarism, which parents were aware of but preferred not to acknowledge.

Meanwhile, identification with school values was perpetuated by the development of the 'old boy' phenomenon. T.W. Bamford has found that fewer than five per cent of Arnold's 'old boys' sent their sons to Rugby;[3] and at Winchester, according to T.J.H. Bishop, it was not until the last decades of the nineteenth century that a good proportion of the boys came from Wykehamist homes.[4] An intense 'old boy' consciousness is essentially a pheno-menon of the years after 1870, especially of the decades before

and after 1890, which saw the real beginnings of 'old boy' organisations holding commemoration dinners, active in games,
publishing registers of members and devising old school ties. All
this facilitated the operation of an informal system of patronage
which came to be known as the 'old boy network'. This network
came to be widened and generalised, for the development of public
school education as a system in the later Victorian period led to
the emergence of the wider community of 'public school men'
who recognised each other by certain symbols, notably the form
of English pronunciation, for whose standardisation in the late
nineteenth century (at the expense of regional accents) the public
school system was largely responsible. With this, and with further refinements such as 'public school slang' and perhaps even
the 'public school manner', public school men possessed a device
facilitating various forms of interaction and patronage, notably
in respect of the entrée to jobs, to clubs, to commissions in the
army, and even to marriage. To be a 'public school man' was a
ticket of general social acceptability in a period when rapid social
change and much greater movement between social classes made
it important to have some ready means of identification between
men of similar values, outlook, and general background, both
in Britain and in the Empire.

It was indeed the coming into being of this new community,
identifiable by these kinds of criteria—neckwear and speech
patterns—which made possible around the end of the century
the transition from the *old* stereotype of the 'gentleman' identifiable by his classical education—by his appreciation of Greek
epigrams and his use of Latin tags—to the *new* 'gentleman' type
identifiable by the marks of public school attendance; and this
transition, in turn, made possible some relaxation of the grip of
the classics on the schools' curriculum. But we must recognise
that the concept of the 'gentleman', whether old-style or new-
style, coexisted with another powerful stereotype, at least in the
later Victorian period, and especially after 1880: the concept
of the 'manly man', which has been investigated by David
Newsome.[5]

This new value of *machismo* (manliness) provides a vital clue
to our understanding of the functions of the Victorian public
school system and of the process of transfer of function which it
entailed. The desire to attain gentlemanly status as newly speci-

fied by membership of the community of public school men may
help to explain why parents should defy the powerful deterrents
of disease, immorality and cruelty in the period well after the
1870s and 1880s when such a community has come into existence and the benefits of its membership have become obvious.
But what of the period of inception? What of the years, say,
between 1840 and 1870 when the new schools were being
created and older ones transformed according to the new pattern,
but when the privileges of the new caste were not yet apparent?
An additional explanation is clearly necessary.

One powerful factor can help explain why, despite the new,
potent and sentimental ideology of the Victorian family, parents
exposed their sons to sickness, vice, brutality, cold, starvation and
privation—whether systematic or haphazard—in the prep
schools and public schools of the Victorian educational
system. There are striking, almost uncanny, parallels between
the process I have been describing in schools and the initiation
rites which are a characteristic of pre-literate societies, whereby
the young are systematically inducted into full participation in
adult life. One scholar[6] has drawn parallels between such tribal
initiation rites and the school study of Latin in the Renaissance
period, accompanied as it was by certain 'hardening' procedures.
These parallels are interesting, but it is possible to extend the
analogy to cover not just the curriculum and methods but indeed
the whole process of education in the Victorian public school.
In a pioneering study of such tribal rituals of transition, the
anthropologist van Gennep identified three major phases—
separation, transition, and incorporation—in the ritual processes
endured by the tribal young at the time of their 'social puberty'.
The description by van Gennep and by later anthropologists of
the character of these three phases and the activities associated
with them show them to include the tearing-away of the initiate
from mother and home and his claustration in a special environ-
ment, and the infliction of pain and even mutilation, with the
object of 'hardening' and of emphasising entry into manly
status.

These and a whole host of other features from tribal initiation
rites all find eerie parallels in the experience of the Victorian
public school boy, and these parallels are the basis for my claim
that the function of the Victorian public school system by the

end of the century was to produce *manly gentlemen*, the concept
of 'gentleman' having changed from that of a blend of patrician
manners and classical education to that of a person who exhibits
all the hallmarks of having been through a certain rigorous educational process in common with certain other persons. That
the *process* or *style* was more important by the end of the century
than the actual content is vividly illustrated by a remark in a
speech to the Old Etonians in 1916 by Lord Plumer, who had
been at Eton in the 1870s: 'We are often told that they taught us
nothing at Eton. It may be so, but I think they taught it very
well.'

If, as we know to be the case, to be a 'public school man' carried
such valuable social and occupational privileges by the end of
the Victorian period, which schools had the power to bestow this
precious label? Which schools, at about the turn of the century,
would in fact have counted as public schools?

Nowadays the fact of being represented on the Headmasters'
Conference gives a school, in a rough-and-ready sense, the right
to be regarded as a public school. Yet HMC membership is a
very blunt tool since it allows no distinction of status between
schools like Eton, Battersea Grammar School, Bloxham, Banbury
Comprehensive School and Manchester Grammar School, all of
which are, or have been, HMC schools in recent times. As
recently as 1967 a British sociologist claimed that 'the schools on
the Headmasters' Conference are not all public schools', and
that for him there were only 84 public schools. (The Headmasters' Conference in 1967 represented over 200 schools.)

In Tom Brown's day, and indeed up to about 1870, it was
relatively simple. Only the nine 'great schools' (the seven boarding schools and two day schools which featured in Howard
Staunton's account and which were selected for examination by
the Clarendon Commission (1861–64)) could, strictly speaking,
claim the title of public school, though several other schools,
founded from the 1840s onwards to give a similar education,
could have been classed with them. In its loose sense, the term
was widely and indiscriminately applied for much of the nineteenth century; the vagueness may be explained by the fact
that the public school system had not yet developed to a point
where definition was important. Furthermore, even the 'great

schools' were not all willing to recognise each other as being public schools—Shrewsbury, in particular, was not always so acknowledged. So wide a variety of schools, in fact, had some sort of claim—but with no certainty that it would be generally accepted—that we may conclude that the only essential common characteristic of the many categories of schools competing for the status of 'public school' by around 1900 was that they were all boys' schools having some pupils aged eighteen and over. (Victorian public schools for *girls* are also important, but should be regarded as a separate system with different functions.) There were 437 such schools in England alone in 1897, and probably at least 600 in the British Isles as a whole. The Victorians themselves had not decided, by the turn of the century, which of these 600 or more schools had the right to be considered public schools, though some attempt at definition could not be long delayed, because of the increasing importance to their products of provable credentials as 'public school men'.

One possible criterion of public school status was a school's academic results, for these were treated seriously by the Victorians, and the 'league tables' of schools gaining Oxford and Cambridge scholarships were given as much attention and analysis by the press in the 1880s and 1890s as they are nowadays, and perhaps even more. Furthermore, as we shall see, these results had an important bearing on a school's chances of representation on the Headmasters' Conference; though, as we shall also see, H M C membership was by no means coterminous with public school status in the Victorian period. By identifying the 77 schools—a very mixed bag of expensive boarding schools and humble day schools—who represent the top Oxford and Cambridge scholarship winners over the period 1885–92, it is possible to discover how far—and how little—this particular 'academic success' criterion can have helped a school's claim to be a public school : there are among them far too many humble day schools (like Boston Grammar School, Newcastle High School, St Olave's, and Carlisle Grammar School) whose pupils could by no stretch of the imagination have passed themselves off as 'public school men' in terms of the characteristics which were by now coming to be expected of that class. Similar lists of Oxford and Cambridge Higher Certificate results, army entrance and civil service entrance successes, also demonstrate the extent to which certain schools—again, both expensive and humble—obtained a certain kind of standing through well-publicised academic results. This standing, however, did not automatically imply public school status.

Can the Headmasters' Conference be used as a criterion? The Conference was founded in 1869 on the initiative of Edward Thring and others as a defensive strategy to protect the headmasters of endowed schools against imminent legislation which appeared to threaten their independence. The dozen who joined Thring at the first conference represented the lesser schools, though they were quick to associate themselves with the 'leading' schools by enlisting the headmasters of important public schools such as Eton and Winchester, and it was the heads of the larger, prestigious public schools who dominated the HMC's committee throughout the Victorian period. Membership of the HMC grew from 50 schools in 1871 to 79 in 1886 and just over a hundred in 1900; since 1937 it has hovered around the 200 mark.

Unfortunately, neither the *Public Schools Yearbook* (which appeared first in 1889) nor *Whitaker's Almanack* (whose editions from 1898 claimed to identify HMC schools) gave within the Victorian period a reliable list of which schools were actually on the Headmasters' Conference. The criteria for representation had in the Victorian period not yet been formalised, though contemporary practice tended to take into account the size of the school, the number of its alumni at Oxford and Cambridge, and the constitution of its governing body. This second criterion gave the HMC a heavy weighting of schools successful in the Oxford and Cambridge scholarship 'league tables' at the expense of other prestigious schools—an important example is Loretto—which were excluded on the third criterion of membership through the fact of being privately owned. So even if a reliable list of HMC schools had been readily available by 1901, its users would have had the difficulty of deciding whether all the schools on it dealt, in fact, with the kind of commodity in which they were interested: a commodity in which strictly academic successes were a very secondary consideration.

By the year 1902 (which may be taken as an appropriate date to mark the short period 1901–03 which saw the end of Victoria's reign, the passing of the Education Act which initiated a great expansion of English secondary education, and the HMC's

c

decision to establish a common entrance examination) the HMC list could not, therefore, be taken as an accurate index of those institutions which produced 'public school men'. Its approximately 104 establishments in 1902 still reflected a ranking of schools by scholastic success and omitted several which regarded both themselves and each other as among the top 50 schools (Groups I–III, page 28).

Moreover, the list was not readily available (no complete official list for 1902 seems to be extant), its published forms were not yet authoritative, and they showed some discrepancies. Nevertheless, since it contained *nearly* all the *leading* public schools, and above all because there was no other list, there is evidence that at the turn of the century the HMC list was beginning to be looked to as some kind of authority concerning the limits of a community of public schools which was becoming ever more self-conscious.[7]

Another source of evidence on the possible public school standing of schools by the end of the Victorian period is the *Public School Magazine*, which (with P.G. Wodehouse as its rugby correspondent) began publication in 1898 and ceased four and a half years later. Its title was a misnomer, for it early adopted an 'all-comers' policy and printed almost any kind of information about almost any kind of school having what would now be called a 'secondary' character. What is interesting is that when some of its readers filled its pages with letters complaining about the treatment of palpably non-public schools, one of them proposed that the term 'public school' should be limited to those establishments participating in the public schools rifle competitions at Bisley. This list is, in fact, an important element in the analysis which yields my suggested breakdown of schools in Table 1 (page 28).

Contemporary commentators have not been alone in their interest in discovering which institutions of the late Victorian period had the power to confer upon their products the label of 'public school men'. Since about 1928, when the process was begun by R.H. Tawney's famous essay on 'Equality' and Harold Laski's studies of the personnel of British cabinets between 1801 and 1924, the analysis of the relationship between education, privilege and the recruitment of social élites has become almost an industry in its own right. Sociologists and political scientists, as well as specialists in the history of the Victorian public school, have published numerous surveys based on widely differing types of sample.

Unfortunately, in their identification of public schools, nearly all these studies are founded on false premises. Firstly, they classify the school education of their subjects according to information contained in the HMC lists, which we have already seen to be fallible and misrepresentative. Secondly, the list used for this classification is the one current at the time of writing,[8] regardless of the fact that a proportion of the sample have been undergoing secondary education at a much earlier period;[9] in some studies, every subject in the sample had completed his schooling before 1902. When these techniques are further extended in attempting to measure the predominance of 'leading' over 'lesser' Victorian public schools, the results are likely to be equally dubious.[10]

If the HMC lists and the anachronistic methodology of recent analysts are thus proved to be of questionable value in arriving at a definition of public school status, it will be necessary to establish a new set of criteria for discovering those schools whose products would have been likely to regard each other as 'public school men' because they had some guarantee of having undergone the same kinds of experience at school.

It is highly feasible that the most useful criteron for the classification of schools whose pupils would have accepted each other as members of the 'public schools community' before the year 1902 (which I have selected as conveniently representing the end of the Victorian era in British education) is a consideration of which schools interacted with each other. Competition in various forms of examination (university scholarships, Higher Certificate, army and civil service entrance) provided one type of interaction which would tend to make the competing schools aware of one another. Of much greater significance was the fact that certain schools played games with each other, and that specifically 'public school' competitions were instituted which provided opportunities for much larger numbers of schools to compete, so that corps-camps and field days brought representatives of public schools together in a competitive atmosphere. This criterion of public school status—who played whom—parallels

Table 1
50–64 leading public schools by interaction, *c.* 1880–1902

GROUP I (22 schools)

Bedford (Grammar)	Glenalmond	St Paul's
Bradfield	Haileybury	Sherborne
Charterhouse	Harrow	Tonbridge
Cheltenham	Malvern	Uppingham
Clifton	Marlborough	Wellington
Dulwich	Repton	Westminster
Eton	Rossall	Winchester
	Rugby	

GROUP II (8 schools)

Blair Lodge	Highgate	Lancing
Eastbourne	Hurstpierpoint	Merchant Taylors'
Felsted		Radley

GROUP III (20 schools)

Bath College	Cranleigh	Loretto
Bedford Modern	Edinburgh Academy	Merchiston
Berkhamsted	Epsom	Reading
Blundell's	Fettes	Shrewsbury
Brighton	Forest	University Coll. Sch.
Cambridge (The Leys)	Leatherhead (St John's)	Weymouth
Canterbury (King's Sch.)		Whitgift

GROUP IV (14 schools)

Aldenham	Framlingham	South Eastern Coll. (St Lawrence),
Ardingly	Isle of Man (King William's)	
Chigwell		Ramsgate
City of London	King's Coll. Sch.	United Services Coll. (Westward Ho)
Derby	Oundle	
Dover	St Edward's, Oxford	Warwick

the now very dated 'Ivy League' classification of American universities, originally a group of east coast colleges who played each other at football.

I have therefore analysed the representation of various public schools in a number of activities in the 1880s and 1890s, with an emphasis on the decade leading up to the representative year

Table 2

40 lesser public schools by interaction, *c.* 1880–1902

Abingdon	Hereford Cathedral	Plymouth
Bedford County	Sch.	Pocklington
Birmingham (King	Ipswich	Portsmouth Grammar
Edward's)	Jersey (Victoria Coll.)	St Olave's
Blackheath	Leamington	Sedbergh
Brecon (Christ Coll.)	Leeds Grammar	Stonyhurst
Bromsgrove	Liverpool Coll.	Sutton Valence
Bury St Edmunds	Llandovery Coll.	Wakefield (Queen
Cambridge (Perse)	Manchester Grammar	Elizabeth's
Carlisle Grammar	Merchant Taylors',	Grammar)
Christ's Hospital	Crosby	Wellingborough
Cranbrook	Mill Hill	Grammar
Denstone	Monmouth	Windsor (St Mark's)
Durham	Newton (Abbot) Coll.	Worcester (King's
Giggleswick	Magdalen Coll. Sch.,	Sch.)
Guernsey (Elizabeth	Oxford	York (St Peter's)
Coll.)		

1902. These included public schools rowing events, gymnastics competitions at Aldershot, athletics championships, the Ashburton Shield (for rifle-shooting at Bisley), various cadet corps activities, and exchanges between individual schools at cricket, rugby and association football, fencing and racquets.

The scope of this essay does not allow full presentation of the great number of charts and tables mapping schools' interaction in all these activities which led to my conclusions about the community of public schools by 1902, nor of the methods of the research or the weighting which was given to some activities as opposed to others; a detailed account of the evidence and how it was handled is in the course of publication elsewhere.[11]

It is sufficient merely to state here that this analysis suggests the existence by the close of the Victorian period of a main community of some 64 schools who interacted with each other in two or more of a wide range of activities which by then had come to be regarded as characteristic of public schools. Because some of these activities were more prestigious than others, and because account has been taken of groupings of schools which had long-standing fixtures at, for instance, cricket or football with each other, it has been possible to break the total of 64 down into four groups consisting of 22, 8, 20 and 14 schools.

Mention (which, as we have seen, may mean very little) in the pages of the *Public School Magazine*, whether individually or allied with evidence of minor interaction with the 64 schools of Table 1, or with some other 'academic' criterion such as Higher Certificate entries, enables a further 40 schools to be treated as lesser public schools (Table 2). It has even been possible to take note of a further 60 schools which either receive a very brief mention in the *Public School Magazine* or which possibly qualify because of some slender 'academic' attainment.

By this analysis, the main public schools community by 1902 is seen as consisting of 64 schools which interacted with or recognised each other in varying degrees (represented by the four groupings). The last of these groups shaded into a further list of 40 schools, some of them of doubtful standing. There was an additional 'outside' category of 60 schools whose claims to public school status were highly questionable and whose inclusion in many cases merely represents the *Public School Magazine*'s attempt to extend the bounds of the public schools community. The figure of 104 (extending to 164) schools must therefore represent the most generous estimate that can be given of schools which had any sort of claim whatever to public school status before 1902, and at its outer limits—i.e. beyond 104 schools—the value of the list is less for the identities of the schools it includes than of those it omits. Any twentieth-century classification which goes beyond those limits is liable to be wrong.

I would contend that the 50 schools of Groups I to III had an indisputable status as public schools by 1902. The 14 schools of Group IV would certainly have claimed public school status, as they implicitly did by participation in 'public school' activities, though the 40 of Table 2 would not all have expected to be so regarded. We can be reasonably certain that the additional untabulated 60 schools could have counted on no such recognition. Interestingly enough, the author of an educational guide for parents in 1908, who leaned heavily on official statistics for numbers of secondary schools in 1897, contended that there were 20 or 21 'great public schools of the Eton and Harrow type', with 30 other public schools 'on the fringe' of that 'select circle'.[12] If, as between 50 or 64 schools on the one hand and

104 or 164 schools on the other, all would not necessarily agree where to apply the cut-off line to close the list of those schools which *were* regarded as public schools by 1902, at any rate we have the means of knowing which schools were *not*, and could not have been, so regarded. This knowledge will, as we shall see, be important in another context.

What does this suggested identification of the membership of the late Victorian public schools community enable us to say about the main characteristics of the schools of that community? To facilitate an answer to this question the 104 schools of Tables 1 and 2 may arbitrarily be divided into two, lumping together the schools of Groups I, II and III and calling them Class A, thereby distinguishing 50 schools which (apart from the 14 perhaps lesser schools of Group IV) could be claimed as the main community of public schools by 1902; and adding Group IV to the 40 schools of Table 2 and calling these 54 schools Class B. Again, we recall the writer who, in 1908, concluded that there were about 50 public schools, including 20 or 21 'great' ones.

Firstly, the main community of public schools (as represented by Class A) was overwhelmingly Anglican (Group I schools entirely so), and, as between the different emphases within Anglicanism, High Church rather than Evangelical. The sole Nonconformist school in Class A is The Leys (predominantly Methodist), and there were no Roman Catholic schools in it: Stonyhurst alone gets into Class B, though with Beaumont perhaps not far behind in 1902.

Secondly, the 50 leading schools were not all exclusively or even largely, boarding schools: some entirely or substantially day schools like Whitgift, Merchant Taylors', University College School, Bedford Grammar School, St Paul's, Dulwich and Bedford Modern are included. Moreover, several schools founded specifically for a lower-middle-class clientèle in the Victorian period had arived at an established place in the public schools community by 1902, including Lancing (which had been trying to lose its lower-middle-class image), Hurstpierpoint, Bedford Modern and Cranleigh, all in Class A; Class B had Ardingly, Framlingham and Bedford County School.

This day school and lower-middle-class representation illustrates a third characteristic: the schools were by no means equally 'exclusive' in the sense of having high fees. Alongside certain schools which it cost many hundreds of pounds per annum to attend as a boarder—and a lot even as a day boy—there were others where a day boy education could be had for a few pounds. Even for boarders there were scholarships and foundationerships, while some schools offered reductions for specific groups such as sons of clergy, doctors, or soldiers. These did not alter the fact that the boarding schools were virtually closed to the sons of manual workers, and even the day schools of Classes A and B could only have contained a small representation of boys of that class; yet it remains true that the leading 50 schools were not, *as a group*, the exclusive preserve of the rich, while the schools of Class B were even less so.

Fourthly, the geographical distribution of schools in Class A shows that, apart from six in Scotland, they were all situated in England, with a high proportion in the south and especially the south-east. The few public schools in the British Isles outside England and Scotland were in Class B.

The main growth in the size of the public schools community after 1902 was by the absorption of schools which had already existed, though outside that community, before 1902 : only a handful of new public schools of the Stowe and Gordonstoun type were founded. By far the largest category of schools newly achieving public school status were the Nonconformist and Roman Catholic schools, so sparsely represented in Class A or B by 1902, yet by 1939 constituting among the most expensive of the schools on the Headmasters' Conference and completely accepted as public schools by all other twentieth-century criteria, including games interaction. The changes in the character and status of schools such as these between the Victorian period and our own are a significant commentary on the sociology of Roman Catholicism and of Protestant Nonconformity in Britain in the last hundred years.

This kind of expansion bedevils the task of analysis when mid-twentieth-century HMC lists are used to classify the status of Victorian schools whose pupils entered élites. What we are really talking about is the power which attaches to attendance at certain schools to confer a certain status and other privileges. One thing which few of these analyses attempt to sort out is how school attendance confers such a status independently of university attendance—especially at Oxford or Cambridge, which of course have their own special power to project their products into élites. Particularly for the substantial proportion of public school boys who did not go to university (but rather into business, commissions in the forces, etc.), it was in the years immediately after leaving school that the job-gaining advantages of 'public school' status would have been most crucial, which is why it becomes essential to measure the status of the school at a date which reflects the pupil's actual attendance rather than by some HMC list thirty, sixty or even a hundred years later. Scores of examples could be given as to how such flawed procedures as those referred to have led to quite false conclusions about the extent to which the Victorian products of schools which *later* became public schools owed their start upon successful careers to the supposed fact of being 'public school men', when in truth their school can have conferred no such status at all. Furthermore, these dubious methods and assumptions serve to obscure a facet of the Victorian public school which has been insufficiently explored : the extent to which, because of the degree of non-exclusiveness of the public schools community (which mitigated the general tendency towards exclusiveness involved in the consolidation of the public school system after 1870), the schools themselves acted as agencies for social mobility by assisting the recruitment of an element of the less privileged into élites.

The School and the Novel:
Tom Brown's Schooldays

Patrick Scott

BY THE late Victorian period the school story was a recognised form of boys' literature. The establishment of the form, as of juvenile literature in general, was connected with the enormous overall growth in publishing during the nineteenth century, which saw a fifteenfold expansion in the number of new titles published annually and an even greater expansion in the number of copies produced. The very availability and popularity of school novels mean that historians need to take account of the pictures of school life that they popularised. This type of fiction provides a lot of incidental detail about school life (for verisimilitude), and it is detail of a kind that does not come up in more formal source material. School novels differ from retrospective memoirs or educational tracts in being pictures of working schools, of functioning systems, largely from the boy's viewpoint. Because the authors were adult, the 'boy's viewpoint' can be that of ten, twenty or thirty years before the publication of the novel, but most professional authors prided themselves on keeping the incidental details of their stories up to date. The school stories introduced boys to a picture of school life before they first left home, and they therefore served as an early element in the socialisation of the pupil to the community. They spread nationwide a stereotype of school life and schoolboy behaviour, far beyond the classes who attended public or even private boarding schools. They are a social phenomenon as well as potential source material. If any of these aspects is adequately to be investigated, however, individual school novels must be subjected to careful scrutiny, and some basic questions about the relation between the school novel, the school reality, and the novelist's idea of schooling, brought out into open discussion.

The prototype of the school novel, *Tom Brown's Schooldays*, raises such basic questions. It is both an 'historical' novel about Arnold's Rugby and a 'myth-making' novel, appearing to incorporate a morality, an idea of school life, which was to be dominant in late Victorian England in school novels and in schools. But ideas about the 'morality' of the novel have to a great extent obscured discussion of its historicity. Much criticism of *Tom Brown's Schooldays*, its author's only famous work, has from the very beginning been based on objections to the ideas that it is alleged to propagate, although recently some attempts have been made to justify the novel's 'muscular Christianity' as the practical expression of the sophisticated but rarified Christian Socialism of F.D. Maurice.[1] In the following discussion I shall attempt substantially to alter this view of the morality of the novel by challenging the conventional claims that have been made for its realism. The evidence is available to re-examine the autobiographical background to the story, and to look also at the process by which Hughes created the book. Except for a few early reviewers, it seems to me, both those who have praised the novel's realism and those who have defended or attacked its morality have read it in far too simple-minded a way because they have not recognised the connection between these two elements. There are problems in the tone and structure of the novel which must be tackled if the historical significance of the book is to be rightly assessed.

Tom Brown's Schooldays was published pseudonymously ('by an Old Boy') on 24 April 1857 and was an immediate success, going into a fifth edition by November of the same year—that is, a sale of 11,000 copies—and selling 28,000 copies by the end of 1862. At half a guinea a time for the one-volume novel, that was not a bad sale—about half what a Dickens novel would expect in its first five years. Fifty-two editions were published by Macmillan, the original publishers, before other firms began to publish as well after 1892.[2] It was Hughes's first book: 'What an easy fool the public is!' Hughes wrote to Macmillan three months after publication. 'Had I known it sooner I would certainly have plucked the old goose to some tune before this.'[3] He received £1,250 in the first seven months after publication, as Macmillan was kind enough to redraw the contract once the book became a success.

As so often when a book combines élite origins, mildly radical opinions, and publishing success, the reviews were fulsome. They all without exception paid tribute to the realism of Hughes's novel. The *British Quarterly Review* struck the common note : it was, it claimed, 'a capital book, brimful of the blithesomeness, fun, and frolic of boyhood, tempered with excellent sense and wisdom. . . It is a spirited record of genuine schoolboy life.'[4] On the appearance of the third edition, in October, *The Times* itself was moved to superlatives in acclamation : 'We hail this little work as the truest, liveliest, and most sympathising description of a unique phase of English life that has yet been given to the public.'[5] The *Quarterly Review* wrote that Tom Brown 'sets before us a real picture of the schooldays at Rugby of a boy of his class, and at the moment when Dr Arnold was working out his great educational experiment'.[6] The *Edinburgh Review* admitted much the same praise : '*Tom Brown* . . . is the exact picture of the bright side of a Rugby boy's experiences told with a life, a spirit, and fond minuteness of detail and recollection which is infinitely honourable to the author.'[7] Reviewers, rightly, saw it as the beginning of a new genre of school fiction : it would, feared the *Christian Observer*, 'set a fashion . . . inaugurate a taste'.[8] The *Dublin University Magazine* claimed that it was 'the first contribution in English literature to this branch'.[9]

Early reviewers, like their successors, tended to pick on much the same bits of the book to talk about. The *Dublin University Magazine* review may be taken as typical of much high-flown paraphrase when it declared :

Cut [*Tom Brown*'s] words, and they bleed good red school-boy blood. It glows with hot runs at hare and hounds. It is 'swinky' with glorious innings, leg-hits for six, drives for four, sweet chisels to cover-point for three. It shakes with cheers for two school-house matches at football, won running— better than the Balliol Scholarship any day! It is cool with pleasant baths under the alders in the steaming summer. It luxuriates in that righteous licking of the bully Flashman. It smacks its lips over that 'clipping set-to' between Slogger Williams and Tom Brown, and is full of a nomenclature more generally agonistic than the present age is apt to admire. It has a jolly smell of frying sausages, and altogether is the sort of book that elderly maiden ladies might not like unless they happened to light on the right passages.

Those are the incidents that writers about *Tom Brown's Schooldays* have continued to pick on—the School-house match, the 'war of independence' against Flashman who tortured small boys, the brave fight behind the chapel against Slogger Williams, the cricket match of the penultimate chapter. It is true that the set-piece of Arnold preaching in Rugby chapel on Sunday afternoon is cited, but the first sermon Tom Brown hears from his headmaster is itself more generally agonistic than sermons are nowadays apt to be. Arnold's voice was 'clear and stirring as the call of the light infantry bugle', and he 'brought home to the young boy, for the first time, the meaning of his life : that it was no fool's or sluggard's paradise into which he had wandered by chance, but a battle-field ordained from of old, where there are no spectators, but the youngest must take his side, and the stakes are life and death'. Arnold was 'the true sort of Captain, too, for a boys' army, one who had no misgivings, and gave no uncertain word of command, and, let who would yield or make truce, would fight the fight out (so every boy felt) to the last gasp and the last drop of blood' (Pt I, Ch. VII).

The other classic and frequently quoted speech in the book comes from the immediately preceding chapter, where old Brooke addresses the School-house after their football victory.

Why did we beat 'em? . . . It's because we've got more reliance on one another, more of a house-feeling, more fellowship than the school can have. Each of us knows and can depend on his next-hand man better—that's why we beat 'em today. We've union, they've division—there's the secret—(cheers). But how's this to be kept up? How's it to be improved? That's the question. For I take it we are all in earnest about beating the School, whatever else we care about. I know I'd sooner win two School-house matches running than get the Balliol Scholarship any day—(frantic cheers). (Pt I, Ch. VI.)

Brooke enrols Arnold as a supporter of athletics :

You all know I'm not the fellow to back a master through thick and thin. If I saw him stopping foot-ball, or cricket, or bathing, or sparring, I'd be as ready as any fellow to stand up about it. But he don't—he encourages them; didn't you see him out to-day for half-an-hour watching us? (loud cheers for the Doctor) (Pt I, Ch.VI)

The picture Brooke leaves us of the 'brave bright days of his boyhood' and 'the best house in the best school in England', modified as it is to be by struggle and by violence, provides what we may call the standard interpretation of *Tom Brown's Schooldays*, that in which 'the atmosphere of reality' which, it is claimed, pervades the novel is equated with what Ian Hay called 'the robust philistinism of the eternal schoolboy'. The morality of the book, then, becomes that of the late nineteenth-century school, of playing the game and being the good sportsman. Indeed, some critics have gone so far as to suggest that Hughes's novel created the ideal of manliness rather than simply representing it.[10] But more sober historians have attempted to show the games ideology of *Tom Brown's Schooldays* as representative of a non-Arnoldian late Victorian tradition of moral philistinism, opposed to the pure high-minded intellectual morality of Arnold and the early Victorian reformers; David Newsome has suggested a perversion of the Arnoldian ideal of 'godliness and good learning' into an anti-intellectual late Victorian ideal of 'manliness' typified by Hughes's novel. E.C. Mack sees *Tom Brown's Schooldays* as a selective portrait by 'the ordinary boy' of Arnold (rather than the sixth-former's picture given by Stanley in the *Life*) and claims that the novel 'adumbrated a relatively new Public School ideal. . . In no other aspect of his book do we feel so strongly the cheapening of Arnold's conception of a public school as in Hughes's insistence on the almost exclusive value of athletics.' Whether the critics see old Brooke's exaltation of house-spirit as an analogue of Christian Socialist interest in co-operative workshops or as a regrettable plea for social conformity, the picture given of *Tom Brown's Schooldays* is largely a static one, and one highly coloured by knowledge of public school education in the golden years 1870 to 1940. When Newsome or Mack claim to give an historical account of Hughes's ideal of 'muscular Christianity';

when A.J. Hartley praises it as 'a social document depicting a policy in miniature as a model for national society';[11] when Kenneth Allsop attacks it in *Encounter* as a 'fusty little idyll of golden philistine youth, locked up in a Victorian conditioning ritual and an arrested adolescence';[12] all these critics are identifying the morality of Chapters VI and VII as the 'message' of the book and reading the rest of the novel in their light, as an ostentatiously simple-minded work, belligerent in message as in tone.

This interpretation was well made on the novel's first appearance, by the *Christian Observer*'s review: 'What will be the fruits of . . . imitation of at least the earlier years of Tom Brown? Perhaps a body of first-rate pugilists, cricketers, sportsmen, and, it may be, soldiers; but a body also of sensual, careless, book-hating men.' If it is true, we must agree with the *Christian Observer* that 'this book is better out of a boy's hands than in it', rather than with *The Times*, which claimed that this is a book 'which an English father might well wish to see in the hands of his son'.

A modern reader of the book will find, however, much that seems to fit with this stereotype of 'muscular Christianity' somewhat uneasily. W.R. Hicks notes that 'the book contains a good deal of moralising, in keeping with the times', as if muscular Christianity had since happily become less moralistic. Alasdair Campbell suggests that the 'occasional sentimentality and long passages of moralising would probably discourage the casual reader'.[13] The recent television series and the film version of 1952 were alike in confining their borrowing from the novel to the events of Part One, rather than venturing into Part Two.

Desmond Coke, in his school novel of 1906, *The Bending of a Twig*, allowed his hero Lycidas Marsh to read *Tom Brown's Schooldays* before going away to school for the first time.

> From his father's remarks, as well as from his own small experience, [Lycidas] had always imagined that the talk of boys, who had not been so much with grown-ups as himself, was trivial in the extreme. . . He found Tom [Brown] and his friends talking soberly on many points. Indeed, there was one discussion on Naaman and Compromise, which, read as he might, he could not understand. This was upsetting; could

it be that the conversation of these boys would be above him? In order to be safe, Lycidas committed the whole argument to memory. They should at least not find him at a loss, if in the dormitories the talk should turn on Naaman and Compromise!

But for the rest he skimmed as quickly as he could through *Tom Brown*, that seemed so often to get strangely like the Vicar's sermons, or the books with SPCK upon their backs.

This is far from the 'philistine' novel the critics of Part One have led us to expect, yet it is an interpretation of *Tom Brown's Schooldays* which answers to much of Part Two, to the Arthur plot which is introduced by that ominously pregnant chapter heading 'How the Tide Turned'.

The problem of discordant tone, or broken structure, in *Tom Brown's Schooldays* was stated most sharply in an early essay of P.G. Wodehouse. Wodehouse pursues the problem on analogy with the discussions of Homeric authorship, under the title 'The Tom Brown Question'. He (or rather a fictional interlocutor in a railway carriage) argues that 'it is obvious that Part One and Part Two were written by different people'; that 'it was difficult to understand' that 'the same man created East and Arthur'; that the football match in Part One is probable, while the cricket match in Part Two is improbable because Tom, having won the toss, puts the MCC in to bat first on a plumb wicket, because he allows comic songs in the lunch interval, and because he has included Arthur in the first eleven not because he is a good cricketer but because 'he thought it would do him such a lot of good'. The Slogger Williams fight in Part Two is the only episode whose genuineness he allows, and then only before it is to be stopped. The rest of the second part of the book was written by the Secret Society for Putting Wholesome Literature Within the Reach of Every Boy and Seeing that He Gets It.[14] The Wodehouse arguments, in spite of their 'spoof' presentation, are by no means negligible as criticism. They point to a real change in the tone of the book.

Nor, indeed, was Wodehouse completely fantastic in discerning a didactic impulse in the work, the spirit of a Secret Society for Wholesome Literature. Before the novel was more than barely started, Hughes told his friend J.M. Ludlow that he 'thought

1 **Thomas Arnold,** headmaster of Rugby (1828–42).

2 Old Big School, Rugby, 1816. The schoolroom was virtually unaltered in Arnold's time, and the scene depicted here closely resembles its description in *Tom Brown's Schooldays*.

that good might be done by a real novel for boys'.[15] In the preface
to the sixth edition, Hughes went further :

> My whole object in writing at all was to get the chance of
> preaching : when a man comes to my time of life and has his
> bread to make, and very little time to spare, is it likely that
> he will spend almost the whole of his yearly vacation in writing
> a story just to amuse people? I think not. . . I can't see that
> a man has any business to write at all unless he has something
> which he thoroughly believes and wants to preach.

Mack and Armytage connect the strength of this didactic
impulse in the novel, with Hughes's preoccupation with the education of his son, then aged eight : 'Thinking over what I should
like to say to him before he went to school,' Hughes wrote in the
1890s, 'I took to writing a story, as the easiest way of bringing
out what I wanted.'

But to acknowledge the didactic impulse in the writing of the
novel is not to determine what it was Hughes believed or wanted
to preach : it does not answer Wodehouse's discernment of two
Thomas Hugheses, the muscular Christian, and the Dean-Farrar-
like pietist of the second part.

Tom Brown's Schooldays was written partly in the summer
law vacation of 1856 and partly during the succeeding six
months. J.M. Ludlow, followed by Mack and Armytage, has
connected the change of tone from Part One to Part Two with
the death of Hughes's daughter on 3 December 1856.

> The novel was not immediately completed [wrote Ludlow],
> for his first great domestic misfortune, the death of his eldest
> daughter from scarlet fever, interrupted it; and to those who
> can see below the surface, there is a somewhat different tone in
> most of the latter part of the book from that of the beginning.

Ludlow then adds a significant footnote :

> I say 'most of the latter part of the book' because it was not
> written consecutively. The story of the great fight, for instance,
> if I do not mistake, formed part of what he first gave me to
> read [i.e. in October 1856].

Wodehouse was right, it seems, after all. Here were two
authors, and the fight was a carry-over of work by the proto-

Hughes into the inferior work of the deutero-Hughes. It becomes too easy to see why the *North British Review* commented that the novel's 'vigorous and picturesque writing is to be set against a plan out of all proportion and [a] want of continuity, which severely tries a critic's good nature', or why *The Times* should remark that 'The later part of Tom's Rugby career does not occupy the space which it usually fills in the recollection of "old boys".' We see also why the religious-committed periodicals of the day set great store by the second part. The *Dublin University Magazine* commented : 'The second part may be said to contain the whole argument,' and the *Christian Observer* said of the Arthur plot that 'The history of this alliance is, to us, the most interesting part of the volume.'[16]

The question, however, begins to look different on closer inspection. The novel was begun in the long vacation, true enough, and there seems no reason to disbelieve Ludlow's report that he was given some sections to read early in September. These sections, as the Macmillan papers make clear, were first submitted to the publisher on 11 October 1856. Hughes invited criticism when he sent in the sections, and explained :

> I don't want to put in more [scrapes, bedevilments and bully-ing] : I only have a chapter of them at first for a plum, and to draw boys on to reading in the hopes of more, for as you may see, I get more serious towards the end.

This clearly indicates that the change of tone was part of Hughes's original plan. Macmillan wrote back to say that he thought the book would be successful, advising a single volume length, so that it could be sold as a present for boys, and asking for Tom Brown's confirmation to be inserted in the planning : 'Mr Maurice wd look at that chapter & wd give you a good hint or two.' On 20 October Hughes sent Macmillan a chapter outline (printed at the end of this chapter) which indicates the sections he had already completed. This again confirms that the general development of the book and the Arthur plot were part of the original planning of the book : it is in the October plan, not the April published text, that we find the ominous title 'Tom gets new ideas about the Bible'. Even Arthur's illness and recovery had already been written before the death of Hughes's daughter.

The planning of the novel, then, entirely refutes Ludlow's explanation of the change of tone from Part One to Part Two, though it vindicates his general account of the book's origins. If the tone of those portions last written were to be affected by the domestic tragedy, it would from the plan seem to be likely to affect chiefly the last two chapters (Arnold's death is not dealt with in the original outline). But the Macmillan papers also make clear that in January, February and March 1857, Hughes was having to write a new manuscript of the early chapters, because his first manuscript had got lost in transit. The 'rough' early chapters were finally written out *later* than the 'quiet' later ones. The situation got so complicated that Macmillan's printers produced the first proofs with the chapters of the early part of the second half in the wrong order. Any argument about the varying tone of the novel cannot draw on Hughes's family life as a causal explanation for variance, as the sections we have do not correspond to the order in which they were written or rewritten. As late as February 1857 Ludlow's 'sadder', 'quieter' Hughes was complaining bitterly to Macmillan about the way the harmless swear-words of the book were being pruned.

We must look for a second line of explanation for the shift of tone in the novel. Perhaps, as the admirers of Hughes's realism indicate by their preference for the first part, we may find that Part One embodies Hughes's autobiographical reminiscences, while Part Two, which contains the Arthur plot, is more formulaic, an expression of belief rather than a memory of actuality. Unfortunately, here too the burden of the evidence cuts against the explanation which would on the face of it seem the more reasonable. It is Part One which draws strongly on literary sources, while Part Two corresponds more closely to the incidents of Tom Hughes's schooldays.

The opening chapters, it is true, draw on Hughes's childhood as son of the Squire at Uffington in the Vale of the White Horse; it is true also that Hughes went to a private school at Twyford before being dispatched to Rugby in February 1834. Nothing of the stresses of his home-life emerge in *Tom Brown's Schooldays*, however. Squire Brown did not move from one village to another, as Squire Hughes had done in 1834, nor did he suffer, as Hughes's father suffered, from a 'morbid consciousness of sin'.[17] The family background of the first three chapters is simplified, stabilised, idealised, to provide a representative background for a representative hero. The tone, too, of the early chapters is derivative—from Carlyle, from Kingsley, and, surely, in the coaching chapter, from Dickens.

On Tom Brown's arrival at Rugby the sources become much more precise, especially the sources of the great School-house match. Self-conscious writing about Rugby School of the Hughes kind went back at least to 1835, the date when a group of sixth-formers and recently departed Old Rugbeians founded *The Rugby Magazine*. This had contained two semi-autobiographical school stories: Thomas Burbidge's rather sentimental account of the death of a pious consumptive called 'George Esling', and J.P. Gell's more interesting account of a Rugbeian who went mad through wilfully isolating himself from the society of his schoolfellows and working too hard.[18] In 1840 a successor to *The Rugby Magazine* was attempted, a paper called *The Rugbaean* which lasted only one number; this included a fictional account of a new boy's arrival at Rugby and of the rowdy exuberance he had to face. In 1848 C.H. Newmarch published a volume entitled *Recollections of Rugby by an Old Rugbaean*, which describes life under Arnold, with passages on island fagging, singing on Saturday night at the end of the half-year with solos from the new boys, an heroic football match, fags tearing up books for hare-and-hounds, and so on: Chapter XVII is devoted to picturing the new boy's arrival at Rugby, and his discovery of study comfort, and the delights of a long lie on Sunday morning. It concludes with a nostalgic account of travelling home in hired post-chaises in the days before the railways.

Three years later a still clearer forerunner of Part One of *Tom Brown's Schooldays* appeared in the form of a slim and anonymous pamphlet published by Crossley and Billington of Rugby. It was by William Delafield Arnold, the Doctor's son, then in the Indian army. (He was one of the three Rugbaeans who had drawn up the first rules of rugby football in 1845.) This gives an imaginary account of the first football match of the year, in lush language with Homeric echoes.[19] The epic comparison for football went back to 1840, to a set of Greek hexameters on the best known players in *The Rugbaean*. It had also been taken up in 1848 by Newmarch, who even included an invocation to the muses.[20] But Arnold made the football match an epic set-piece in which the smaller side won because of its greater discipline and *esprit de corps*, in which heroes emerged worth six of the other side, and which provided a happy and animated subject for self-congratulation during the Saturday evening that followed.

William Arnold's pamphlet acquired a certain classic status among Old Rugbeians. When George Melly wanted to write a football chapter in his *School Experiences of a Fag* three years later, he reprinted most of Arnold's pamphlet instead of writing the account himself, because, he said, it was 'dear to every Harbean'. And when the new headmaster of Rugby, Dr Goulburn, edited his nostalgic miscellany of school history and modern record in 1856, the year *Tom Brown's Schooldays* was begun, he too reprinted Arnold's pamphlet entire as the chapter on rugby football, as well as another Arnold account of cricket in the close, and the chapter from Melly's book on hare-and-hounds.[21] There is, then, before Hughes started writing in the summer of 1856, a strong tradition of Rugbeian semi-fictional reminiscence, and Hughes's account of Rugby in Chapters V, VI and VII of Part One follows the tradition closely. When the *Quarterly Review* refers to the 'mimic war' and 'Homeric conflicts' of the football chapter, it was drawing attention not to Hughes's originality but to the way his book fits into the tradition.

Similarly, the authorial harangue on the relative merits of private and public schools, and on the virtues of the prefect system, has its predecessors too: not merely in the general controversy stimulated by Dr Vaughan's expulsion of one of his Harrow prefects in 1854, but specifically in writing about Rugby School. It is found in Stanley's *Life of Arnold*, in Arnold's own 1835 essay 'On the Discipline of Public Schools',[22] in Chapter XVII of Newmarch's *Recollections* of 1848, and particularly in the preface and conclusion of Melly's *School Experiences* of 1854, which was written to vindicate the public schools against criticism following the Vaughan case. The interpretation of bullying at the school that Hughes gives is very similar to that of Melly three years earlier: that is, that there is bullying at public schools—and Melly also specifies tossing in blankets—but that the boys should overcome it by public opinion and prefectorial supervision, not the masters by closer control. The point in which Hughes has altered the traditional debate is in heightening the degree of bullying—no other witness to the late 1830s at Rugby agrees that boys were roasted at the hall fire— and the purpose of this incorporation of Rugby legend into the traditional picture of Rugby reality will need further discussion. In summary, then, Part One is a traditional and rather formulaic presentation of the Rugby world in the late 1830s : Tom Brown travels by the old coach and four.

On the other hand, when one looks for the sources behind Part Two, the unrealistic 'pious' half of the novel, one finds that they are of an entirely different character. Instead of being literary sources, previous nostalgic presentation of Rugby life, they are, substantially, incidents and personalities from Hughes's own experience at Rugby. Tom Brown travels on the railway. The only exception to this broad contrast is the quarrel with the keeper over fishing rights, in the very last chapter of Part One, which is based on a continuing battle between the Rugby boys and a local Conservative, and therefore anti-Arnoldian, landlord, Mr Boughton-Leigh of Brownsover Hall.[23] But in the second part, from the very beginning, the autobiographical substratum is much clearer. For example, on Arthur's first night in the School-house dormitory, he knelt down to pray and 'a big brutal fellow' threw a slipper at him, only to be pelted himself with Tom Brown's boot (Pt II, Ch. I). Writing of this incident, Hughes said that in 1834

> The private prayers question was still acute, especially in one large bedroom in [Arnold's] own house. This was dominated by two notorious bullies who set their face against boys kneeling by their bedsides. The late Lord Portsmouth (then Mr Fellowes) was put into this room as a new boy, and on the first night knelt down to say his prayers; on which the brutes I have alluded to held him down on his knees, and 'slippered' him. No other boy interfered, in fact the other 10 or 11 were quite small, and the praeposter of their room had not come up, as it was before 10 o'clock.[24]

If one feels Hughes himself to be a suspect source, there is also the evidence of William Gover, who in Prince Lee's house moved to a new dormitory in January 1836 and was pelted with shoes when he knelt down to pray.[25] Lieut.-Col. Selfe at the beginning of the twentieth century collected fairly well-authenticated memories of a number of Hughes's contemporaries suggesting originals for the naturalist schoolboy Martin, for the bird-fanciers chapter, and for the fight with Slogger Williams. The cricket match, much though Wodehouse despises the behaviour of Tom Brown as captain, turns out to be a more or less ball-for-ball account of Thomas Hughes's last match against the MCC at Rugby in June 1841, and Selfe prints the score-sheet to prove it.

Even the chapter which seems an obvious importation either from Victorian tract material or from Hughes's own tragic family circumstances (Ch. VI : 'Fever in the School') is faithful to an autobiographical basis. In Hughes's last half-year at Rugby alone, two boys died of fever, one in April and another in May.[26] The memorial inscriptions in Goulburn's *The Book of Rugby School*, transcribed from Rugby chapel, make the picture even clearer : one of the masters died that year, and was buried in the chapel, and so did and were Charles James Fox Snowden, aged fifteen, and John Walker, aged sixteen. E.E. Kellett was right when he wrote about *Tom Brown's Schooldays* :

> Over it, as over the Iliad, broods the tragedy of a coming death. But this was part of the truth of the tale. Few lustrums pass over any large school without seeing at least one fatal illness, and school tales which avoid this omit one essential feature of the scene.[27]

What was the effect of schoolboy deaths on early Victorian schools? George Melly, who was at Rugby in the years 1844 to 1848, recalled that in his house, 'one half-year, death laid his hand heavily upon us : one of the youngest, a child in years, and of infantine purity in his life, was snatched away from us'. The boy confessed on his deathbed to tearing a leaf from another boy's book, and when the story spread about 'serious thoughts filled all the household'.

Nor were serious thoughts and Arthur-like conversations confined to the terms or houses which saw a fatal illness. The reminiscences of those who were at Rugby under Arnold include not only the serious-minded A.H. Clough, but H.W. Fox, who in March 1835 found Legh Richmond's *The Dairyman's Daughter* 'an especial means of grace', and Spencer Thornton, who carried out district visiting among the poor of Rugby. It is true that Fox felt isolated at Rugby from anyone with whom he could talk about his beliefs.

> I have no one to converse with on religious subjects; if I begin to do so with any, they either show a complete reluctance, or a great coldness to it. I, however, feel that it is for the best, for it leads me to rest on God as my only friend, and to open my heart to him more.[28]

But both Arthur and Tom have the decency to feel difficulty in conversing on religious subjects. A more interesting, because more detailed, record is given in Gover's memories of his time at Rugby in the years 1835 to 1837. He notes that he moved into a new study for the winter half of 1835 : 'When I got into the quiet of my new study, I resolved to read a portion of the Scriptures daily, and by keeping strictly to this rule, I read through the Holy Scriptures at Rugby. Perhaps,' he adds, 'Arnold's Sermon XII, in *Christian Life*, preached 8 November 1835, led me to undertake this duty.' Gover was never one of Arnold's inner circle of trusted sixth-formers, so his testimony to Arnold's religious influence is especially interesting; he does, however, criticise Arnold for using attendance at communion service as evidence of loyalty or disloyalty to Arnoldian school ideals, something very relevant in considering Hughes's treatment of East's scruples about confirmation.[29]

The contemporary evidence, then, goes to show that the piety and high-mindedness of Part Two of *Tom Brown's Schooldays* was a true presentation of Arnold's Rugby as Hughes would have experienced it, while the gentlemanly philistinism of the first part, authentic enough in its outline, is much closer to previous literary simplification of life at Rugby School. The historian will find safer evidence of Arnold's Rugby in Part Two than in Part One, splendid though that is. Once more, as is also the case with Dean Farrar's school novels, the literary-critical test of 'realism' proves a poor aid for the historian attempting to discern the real.[30]

I hope now to go on to show that an intelligible relationship exists between the two parts of *Tom Brown's Schooldays*, so different in tone and discontinuous in narrative content. The key to that relationship lies in the gradually changing nature of the novel's approach to reality, until the final chapter, on

Arnold's death, records a purely historical event. The changing approach images the development in Tom Brown's personality as he grows older and attains maturity and individuality of character. We must not look for a static ideology in the statements of either part, but should instead see Hughes's ideas as expressed in the structure he has given to his novel and in the gradually developing picture of school life, and then of adult life, which is presented.

A simple guide to Hughes's intention is given by the epigraph from Tennyson's *In Memoriam* which divides Part One from Part Two :

> I [hold] it truth, with him who sings
> To one clear harp in divers tones,
> That men may rise on stepping-stones
> Of their dead selves to higher things.

The Times in 1858 confessed that it was an 'unsolved problem' how public school education was ever effective, how 'those fierce passions are tamed, how the licence of unbridled speech is softened into courtesy, how lawlessness becomes discipline, how false morality gives place to a sound and manly sense of right, and all this within two or three years, with little external assistance, and without any strong religious impressions'. 'Parents', it concluded 'may well abstain from looking too closely into the process, and content themselves with the result.' It was the supervision of this civilising process that Dr Arnold had seen as his great duty. In a justly famous letter, written before he took up the headmastership in 1828, he wrote :

> My object will be, if possible, to form Christian men, for Christian boys I can scarcely hope to make; I mean that, from the natural imperfect state of boyhood, they are not susceptible of Christian principles in their full development upon their practice, and I suspect that a low standard of morals in many respects must be tolerated amongst them, as it was on a larger scale in what I consider the boyhood of the human race. But I believe a great deal may be done.[31]

He was to reiterate this belief seven years later, when he wrote :

A boarding school is a society wholly composed of persons whose state, morally and intellectually, is by reason of their age, exceedingly imperfect. . . While on the one hand the boys stand to their masters in the relation of pupils to a teacher, they form, on the other hand, a complete society amongst themselves; and the individual boys, while influenced by him in the one relation, are unhappily in the other more influenced by that whole of which they are members, and which affects them in a much larger portion of their lives.[32]

When Arnold came to consider sending his own boys away to school in 1831, he harped on a similar theme:

I am a coward about schools. . . I am inclined to think that the trials of a school are useful to a boy's after character, and thus I dread not to expose my boys to it; while on the other hand, the immediate effect of it is so ugly, that, like washing one's hands with earth, one shrinks from dirtying them so grievously in the first stage of the process.[33]

There is a tension, of course, between the two ideas in Arnold's writing—between the idea of a barbarian, primitive school society complete in itself and the idea of the process by which individuals evolve from their barbaric state. Quite clearly, any individual boy could be perfectly socialised in the barbaric society without making appreciable progress towards becoming a Christian man. The strength of Arnold's ideas, however, can be seen in an article written by his pupil Stanley for the second number of *The Rugby Magazine* in 1835, with the significant title 'School a Little World'.

We form a complete social body [Stanley wrote]—a society not only of scholars, but of human beings—not only of individuals, but of citizens—a society in which, by the nature of the case, we must not only learn, but act and live; and act and live not only as boys, but as boys who will be men.[34]

The analysis made by Arnold of the institutional life of a school has been taken much further by modern sociological study of such relatively self-contained institutions as schools, asylums, or prison-camps, and the process which *The Times* considered an 'unsolved problem' has recently been systematically analysed. John Wakeford, in his book *The Cloistered Élite* has suggested that the ordinary pattern of adaptation to the school institution can be divided into three stages. In a boy's early years at the school he will most frequently show an ambivalence about the formal rules and regulations of the school, and near total indifference to the school's ultimate goals—in the case of Arnold's Rugby, to the ideal of Christian man. In his middle years at the school, he is likely to develop from this attitude to either a retreat from the official world of school, as far as possible, or to an intransigence which rejects, again as far as possible, both the school's formal behaviour patterns and its declared goals. In his last years at school, he will probably develop further, either by finding new goals of his own, or by embracing the school's goals and educational aims, or by returning to the ambivalence of his early years.[35] The sociologists have spelt out the truth that Dr Arnold so much disliked : that certain kinds of social structure generate circumstances in which infringement of social codes or institutional rules constitutes a 'normal' response rather than a sinful deviance.[36]

Tom Brown is shown in the novel as going through these three stages. First of all, before he goes to Rugby, we are shown, not his individual character, but the culture in which he has been brought up and with which he must face the closed world of school. Chapters VI and VII of Part One introduce us to the institution in which he will now live; and his changing of his cap for a catskin on East's orders, his first efforts at football, singing, being tossed in a blanket, and fagging for old Brooke show his desire to adapt to the new world of school. Of the larger aims of the school he is ignorant, as of the higher morality, and his willingness to follow School-house rules is soon substantially modified. As East says, looking back on this section of the book from the second part : 'When you and I came to school there were none of these sort of notions. . . What one has always felt about the masters is that it's a fair trial of skill and last between us and them—like a match at foot-ball, or a battle'. (Pt II, Ch. VII) Tom and East are not wholly at odds with the school world, for they try, albeit unsuccessfully, to take part in the famous Barby run at at hare-and-hounds.

In the next stage of school life, though, they develop from ambivalence into intransigence : 'So East and Tom, the Tadpole, and one or two more, became a sort of young Ishmaelites, their hands against everyone, and everyone's hand against them. . . They . . . rendered no willing obedience.' (Pt I, Ch. IX) 'They don't feel that they have any duty or work to do in the School,' sighs Dr Arnold (*ibid.*). Their intransigence is in contrast to the retreatism of the mad naturalist Martin, whose door was 'barricaded by a set of ingenious bolts of his own invention' (Pt II, Ch. III).

In the third stage Tom takes up gradually the acceptance of institutional rules (though this happens incidentally), and by accepting responsibility for Arthur he comes step by step to an understanding of the institution's long-term goals. This enables him to criticise and modify the social codes of the institution (in Bible-reading, prayer in the dormitory and rejecting aids to translation), so that his behaviour more accurately reflects the Arnoldian goal of moral improvement and service he has taken as his own. The final scene in Rugby chapel shows that he has outgrown the institution in which he was educated, and has ideals of his own independent of the little world of school and of its law-giver. The final sentence of the novel confirms the central message that even the highest religious truths are learned through social relationships, and not in isolation.

This developmental pattern in the novel, the process of an individual's education within the relatively static society of the school, is reinforced by the gradual changes which the author's chosen style undergoes in the course of the book; the sequence of literary styles can be roughly listed as explanatory, epic, narrative, confessional, and elegiac. The relatively impersonal first stage in Tom Brown's education and adaptation to the school are replaced by the more personal, almost sentimental, styles of the confessional monologue and the elegy for focusing down on his internal moral development. One may note also that in terms of fully extended set-piece descriptions, Hughes plays the trick of superimposing a single seasonal games pattern upon the eight years of Tom Brown's Rugby career. These eight years constitute a single natural process. Tom arrives at Rugby in the late autumn for football, followed by the winter sport of hare-and-hounds through the mud. The swimming and birds-nesting of summer do not give way to cricket until the 'Fever in the School' chapter, which is almost immediately followed by 'Tom Brown's Last

Match'. The book concludes with a summer vacation holiday in the highlands, on a 'fishing ramble'.

But the games are introduced not merely to emphasise the sense of process that we get from the novel, but also to represent the different kinds of social relationships maintained by the hero at different stages of the story. In a very significant passage near the end of the novel, Tom and George Arthur are talking to the young master about cricket :

'What a noble game it is, too.'

'Isn't it? But it's more than a game. It's an institution,' said Tom.

'Yes,' said Arthur, 'the birthright of British boys old and young, as *habeas corpus* and trial by jury are of British men.'

'The discipline and reliance on one another which it teaches is so valuable, I think,' went on the master, 'it ought to be such an unselfish game. It merges the individual in the eleven; he doesn't play that he may win, but that his side may.'

'That's very true,' said Tom, 'and that's why football and cricket, now one comes to think of it, are so much better games than fives or hare-and-hounds, or any others where the object is to come in first, or to win for oneself, and not that one's side may win.'

'And then the Captain of the eleven!' said the master. 'What a post is his in our School-world! Almost as hard as the Doctor's : requiring skill and gentleness and firmness. . .'

(Pt II, Ch. VIII)

Each of the sports and pastimes in the novel is representative of a particular kind of social participation. At the 'veast' Tom is introduced to traditional sports and traditional social relationships : at the beginning and end of his school life he participates in the two team sports of rugby football and cricket, for at these points in his school career he is participating, at the start ignorantly, at the end knowledgeably, in the social life of the school. In hare-and-hounds he and East work together in a desperate imitation of their elders, and the Doctor happily forgives their late return, although they should not have been taking part in the run. The fishing and climbing is clearly individualist and exciting, but thoughtless and antisocial, as Tom's behaviour generally is during the second section of his school career. His assumption of responsibility for Arthur, and the relative isolation of his moral stance, is aptly symbolised by the fight behind the chapel—Hughes makes it clear in the most misquoted passage in the book that he thinks the morality of conflict and fighting a lower moral code than that of peace; none the less, fighting represents at this stage Tom Brown's attitude to his own beliefs and to other people. Cricket can be the background to the unfortunate Thompson's deathbed because it represents ordered traditional (and also moral and gentlemanly) social relationships. As the Rev. Thomas Waugh wrote in his book *The Cricket Field of the Christian Life* (1910):

> It is a clean, gentlemanly enjoyable game, and does not lead the players or spectators into such a frenzy of excitement or brutality as is too often the case on the football field.

Tom Brown sees himself as a more important person in the running of the school than the Doctor himself, but as captain of the eleven he is really the maintainer of an existing social system, rather than the developer of a higher one. Finally, is it too fanciful to see the 'fishing ramble' as a symbol of the moral and intellectual world of the undergraduate?

Now if Tom Brown himself develops so markedly in the course of the novel, and if the development is as firmly mirrored in developments of style and in constant symbolism as I claim it to be, then we may also read the morality or ideology of the novel as developing rather than static, even when it proceeds from the jolly-avuncular voice of the narrator himself. The advice proffered and the speeches made at each stage of the novel are in some sense modified, and at first simplified, by the events they spring from. Squire Brown's advice to his son when he first goes to Rugby is not Thomas Hughes's adult creed, but the highest moral factor appropriate to the boyhood of the human race; when Tom Brown puts forward much the same idea of morality at the age of sixteen, however, it is shown by Arthur to be inadequate (Pt I, Ch. IV; Pt II, Ch. VI). When Brown and East are praised by Hughes in Part One for heading a successful rise against the most abominable and unrighteous vested interest of fifth form fagging, and Flashman's bullying, an Ishmaelitish separation from respectable majority parties is without qualification enjoined as brave and gallant. When East tries to maintain the same position about the false respectability of confirmation in Part Two, he is shown now to be refusing the offer of an alliance in his moral warfare and wilfully isolating himself (Pt I, Ch. XI; Pt II, Ch. VII). Against old Brooke's speech to School-house can be set Hughes's own attack on athleticism in *The Manliness of Christ.* While there are not neat parallel passages modifying or developing all Hughes's authorial sermons in the novel, each of them is most fairly read in this way, as the expression of the morality of each single incident recounted or each stage of Tom Brown's development recorded, rather than as the timeless expression of the author's own muscular Christian philosophy for which he claims universal relevance. As Arnold said, the schoolboys of the 1830s were 'not susceptible of Christian principles in their full development upon their practice'.

A developmental reading of *Tom Brown's Schooldays* disposes to some extent of the two further charges that can be brought against the novel : cruelty and sentimentality. The violence of the novel is almost entirely confined to the first half of the book as is most of the roughest interpersonal or intercultural conflict. As to the sentimentality or priggishness of Part Two, it could be claimed that this is a realistic expression of one phase of adolescence : in the fever chapter Tom Brown is sixteen. Thomas Hughes himself admitted that Arnoldian morality turned some boys into prigs, but claimed that this was only a stage in their moral development : a boy with a humble, true and childlike faith, Hughes claimed in the preface to the sixth edition, may appear a prig and a pharisee, but in a few years 'the "thoughtful life" has become habitual to him, and fits him as easily as a skin'.

Tom Brown's Schooldays is not, of course, a perfectly written novel, any more than Thomas Hughes was a perfectly consistent thinker or moralist. Nevertheless, I would claim that a reading of the novel in terms of that moral evolution which Arnold discerned in the history of individuals as well as in the history of the human race makes it a lot less imperfect a novel than do readings in terms simply of Kingsleyan Christian Socialism or the late Victorian public school spirit. The moral evolution reading explains the apparent inconsistencies of tone, and even the differences in the treatment of the football match and the cricket match, at which Wodehouse pointed so scornful a finger. The almost universal condemnation of the second half of the novel as unrealistic is shown up for the culturally limited criticism that it is, betraying the reluctance of many readers to submit themselves, even in imagination, to the ideological development the novel demands. Among the early reviewers, it was Kingsley who hit on what Hughes was attempting to do. *Tom Brown's Schooldays*, Kingsley wrote, was about a schoolboy's discovery of the 'unseen world above' him. 'It is because Tom Brown does make this discovery—naturally, gradually, blunderingly, as a living boy would make it—that the book is valuable in our eyes.'[37]

The case of *Tom Brown's Schooldays* enables us to recognise two general principles for the historical consideration of school novels. First, the ideas of a novelist must be considered in relation to the structure of his novel, not simply read off from authorial asides, related or unrelated to an immediate context. Secondly, historians cannot afford to limit their attention simply to works they find realistic : the realism test is artificial and far too dependent on the cultural background or imaginative flexibility of the critic. Often literary sources, like other sources, are 'truest' to their time, and most useful historically, at precisely that point where a modern reader's disbelief is least willingly suspended. Perhaps it is only now, as the late Victorian public school spirit becomes, like the Arnoldian spirit before it, not merely repugnant but almost unimaginable, that it is becoming possible to read *Tom Brown's Schooldays* as Hughes meant it to be read, and not simply as it has been misread by the affectionate or hostile generations who come between us and him.

THE CHAPTER PLANS OF
TOM BROWN'S SCHOOLDAYS

The first column gives the projected chapter plan from a letter of Hughes to Macmillan, 20 October 1856 : in the Macmillan papers, Vol. CXXXIII, B.M.Add.MS.54918, f.4. Chapters already completed are italicised; those partly written are asterisked. The second column gives the final plan in the published text.

3 Rugby masters, 1860. Fourteen of the eighteen members of staff were clergymen. They include Frederick Temple, headmaster 1857–69 (standing, centre), T. W. Jex-Blake, headmaster 1874–87 (standing, third from right), John Percival, headmaster 1887–95 (seated, third from left), and J. M. Wilson, later headmaster of Clifton 1879–90 (seated, sixth from left).

4 Rugby masters, 1903. The staff now numbered thirty-eight, of whom only the headmaster (H. A. James), the chaplain and two others were clergymen.

5 The School Prefects, Malvern College, 1868. Although Malvern was only founded in 1862, by 1868, as this early photograph shows, the prefectorial system was fully established.

Part I

* I	The Brown family, Vale of White Horse.
II	Boyhood of Tom Brown, village stories, first school.
III	*Tom goes to Rugby, Coach, etc.*
IV	*Tom's Reception and first friend.*
V	*School-house match.*
VI	*Singing, first night.*
* VII	2nd half year, island fagging, state of school.
* VIII	Bullying as it used to be.
* IX	All manner of trouble into which Tom tumbles.

I   The Brown Family.

II   The 'Veast'.

III   Sundry Wars and Alliances.

IV   The Stage Coach.

V   Rugby and Football.
VI   After the Match.
VII   Settling to the Collar.

VIII   The War of Independence.

IX   A Chapter of Accidents.

Part II

X	*Arthur comes, prayers in the bedrooms.*
XI	*Tom gets new ideas about the Bible.*
XII	*Arthur makes his first friend.*
* XIII	First results of Arthur's friendship.
* XIV	Tom Brown's first and last school fight.
XV	Fever in the School, *Arthur's illness and recovery.*
XVI	*East and Tom open their minds.*
XVII	The Sixth, Arthur's Successes.
* XVIII	Arthur is lifted up and taken down. Correspondence with Tom.
XIX	Last half-year. Cricket matches, speeches, etc.
XX	Conversations before leaving.

I   How the Tide Turned.

II   The New Boy.

III   Arthur makes a Friend.
IV   The Bird-fanciers.

V   The Fight.

VI   Fever in the School.

VII   Harry East's Dilemmas and Deliverances. [Includes the passage on confirmation]

VIII   Tom Brown's Last Match.
IX   Finis. [Arnold's death]

E

Thomas Arnold and the Victorian Idea of a Public School

T. W. Bamford

THOMAS ARNOLD was at Rugby from August 1828 until he died in 1842. His experience as headmaster was spread over two years of George IV, seven years of William IV and five of Victoria, so that his tenure under the Queen, was, as it were, a minority one: at the time of his death Victoria had almost another sixty years to reign. Arnold had, therefore, no effect on the main Victorian scene as a participant in affairs, and his influence was restricted to his reputation. Sixty years is a considerable span of time and significant changes are to be expected in public schools just as in any other phase of human activity. Arnold himself would have expected such a process of change, welcomed it, and even helped it along, for he had once declared: 'My love for any place or person, or institution, is exactly the measure of my desire to reform them.'[1]

In the year before Arnold died Cheltenham was founded. This was the first of the new foundations that were such an important feature of Victorian development. Six others followed before the end of the decade,[2] and by the end of the century the total number of new foundations was between forty and sixty. It is a formidable list without any precedent. It follows that when Arnold left the scene the system was about to explode with a rapidly developing crop of new ventures. Each school was set up by enthusiasts who saw it responding to a special need. The resultant variety was bewildering and quite outside the experience or even the vision of Arnold himself. Indeed, for any estimate of his influence upon the Victorian scene it is necessary to compare the situation Arnold left with that sixty years later.

In 1900 headmasters and others were inclined to stress the elements of character formation which were said to contribute to the public school ideal—religion, discipline, culture, the true spirit of athletics, the spirit of service[3]—and to ignore the more obvious advantages of vocationalism or examinations. Although one cannot ignore the character aspect, there were several other more tangible factors.

The first was the public schools' intimacy with Oxford and Cambridge at all levels from the background of staff to the placement of pupils. The second was the confidence in scholarship as the means of producing clarity of thought. To some extent this was connected with examinations, and although there was severe criticism of examinations at all periods,[4] yet the real test of scholarship was the 'open' to one of the older universities. It is true that the scholarship system at all levels increased rapidly between 1860 and 1900, but the work of Samuel Butler illustrates the power of competition at an earlier period, and the same attitude may be seen in Arnold himself in his public commendation of Stanley.

A third element was leadership. One might argue about the meaning of leadership, but it would be impossible to dispute that the growth and reputation of the public schools in the nineteenth century was connected with the preparation of boys for the new professions of the home and overseas civil services, the officer ranks of the armies of Britain and the Empire, the Church, and other exalted and prestigious areas of the British establishment.

A fourth element was the idea of a public school as a place of excellence. It seems natural that the assumed superiority of the education provided at the schools should be matched at least by the magnificence of the site, buildings and estate. Many have argued that this search for the 'gentry image' became such an obsession that it degenerated into a mania sacrificing the energies and resources of the schools for the sake of mere ostentation and display. This ruthless pursuit of the external image represents the greatest single indictment against almost all Victorian headmasters, applying even to Arnold and Rugby. He admitted his own feeling for grandeur,[5] but at least no one can claim that he was party to the grosser abuses current at the other schools, for he recognised them and withstood them at Rugby.

If we accept the five points of high principle mentioned earlier and add the others, we get a list which covers most of the values of the public schools before 1914: religion, discipline, culture, the true spirit of athletics, the spirit of service, Oxford and Cambridge links, the scholarly mind, leadership, gentry aspirations.

If we now look back to the early Victorian period, to Arnold's time, how much of all this was evident then? Arnold would have recognised the point in all these claims, although he would certainly have disputed the significance of some and would have put different interpretations on others. He would not have been impressed with the 'true spirit of athletics', although he was definitely in favour of spirit on the playing fields. The special uniqueness of Rugby in handling the ball had already been invented and had attracted considerable national, even royal, interest. But Arnold would not have agreed that the organised playing field was the laboratory of character building. Whether others at the time saw a wider vision is uncertain, but thoughts on the nature and influence of athletics and games were certainly changing. Inter-school rivalry was well established, and the fact that many masters in public schools were renowned athletes makes it likely that the origins of the 'true spirit of athletics' are to be found early in the century in spite of most modern opinion which would place it in the post-1850 period.

Again, Arnold's view of culture was almost entirely classical. He was interested in science and invention and held the view that industry was the great hope for the emancipation of the masses; but he saw culture as essentially embodying a spirit of the perfection of man as a thinking socialised being, and that meant Greece and Rome. This was to remain the predominant attitude of many public school men throughout Victoria's reign, although towards the end a new vision of culture had arisen, at least among the radicals, manifesting new standards of grandeur, wealth and prosperity, and embracing the Empire at one extreme and the social and industrial concepts of Sanderson of Oundle at the other.

The same change of emphasis between the early and late periods of Victoria's reign would apply to the important concept of leadership, which could perhaps be regarded as concerned with personality and organisation, with superiority in assessing a situation, giving orders and getting them accepted, preferably willingly. As far as the public schools are concerned, there are at least three ways of looking at this phenomenon. Firstly, there is the relationship with birth and wealth arising from the responsibility of managing family estates and the preservation of a particular standard and style of living. Those who came from this background were the gentry and aristocracy, whose privileged position made them natural recruits for national leadership. About half their sons went to the public schools in the early Victorian period,[6] particularly to the top three or four (e.g. Eton, Harrow, Rugby). In one sense training for leadership in these very few schools was a superfluous exercise. The future leaders just happened to be lodged there to spend their youth.

This aspect of leadership is particularly relevant to Arnold. Although he had reservations about their ultimate role, he saw the upper classes as naturally endowed to give guidance to the nation.

When an aristocracy is not thoroughly corrupted, its strength is incalculable. . . . The great amount of liberty and good government enjoyed in England is the security of the aristocracy; there are no such pressing and flagrant evils existing, as to force men's attentions from their own domestic concerns, and make them cast off their natural ties of respect or of fear for their richer and nobler neighbours.[7]

I say plainly—and I beg not to be cried down unheard— that those great means of blessing are the Aristocracy and the Christian Church.[8]

But throughout the writings and sermons in which he propounded his doctrine ran a warning note : privilege had its duties as well as its rights. He was often appalled by the upper classes' lack of a sense of duty.

There is no earthly thing more mean and despicable in my mind than an English gentleman destitute of all sense of his responsibilities and opportunities, and only revelling in the luxuries of our high civilisation and thinking himself a great person.[9]

He hoped that the Reform Bill would stir the upper classes to fulfil their proper role.

The world never yet saw a race of men better fitted to win it [influence] than the nobility and gentry of England, if once raised from the carelessness of an undisputed ascendancy.[10]

For Arnold, therefore, leadership came most naturally and

easily to those born in the upper classes, but the occupation of a social niche by itself was not enough : leadership could only be won by example. He also felt that this situation was only a temporary one destined to be replaced ultimately by more democratic procedures once education and dignity had suffused the nation.

This attitude is related to the second aspect of leadership, not necessarily linked with birth or wealth but with the concept that it can be worked for and deserved. In this sense it is a public relations exercise often coupled with membership of a structural élite such as the medical profession, the army or the administrative ranks of the civil service. Some historians have even seen the civil service's philosophy of 'cultured amateurism' as reflecting its growing tendency to employ old public school boys. If this was so, Arnold would undoubtedly have been shocked by it. It was his deeply held conviction that leadership was a moral concept involving commitment and example, acting in a moral manner, and working in a democratic way for the benefit of the administered. Respect for authority was essential provided that the authority was legitimate. But the problem was difficult since the schools were involved with leadership both in Britain and in the Empire. The situation in Britain and those colonies such as Canada and Australia which were populated by people of British origin was reasonably straightforward if complex. The cultures were the same—Christian, classical, democratic, European. The real difficulties were encountered in those countries which were particularly associated with the ex-public school administrators in the Victorian age—India, Africa, the 'coloured' empire generally. There was absolutely nothing in common in religion, philosophical background, language, race, and hence morality too. The colonial civil servants believed that they had a duty to educate and act in a missionary manner : but they also had to consider the legitimacy of the situation. English officials could hardly have been regarded as citizens of the countries they administered and hence could not claim to be acting primarily in the interests of those countries, unless perhaps they were regarded as agents of change. But as active agents of change they would have been directly opposed to the 'cultured amateur' concept and, by extension, to the entire spirit of British administration.[11] It is impossible to be certain as to what view Arnold would have taken of the problem, for whereas he wrote a great deal about colonisation, he was not usually concerned with colonies of an alien nature. He was referring to those colonies of the parent state which are generally known as 'outposts of the Empire'. One thing, however, is clear : he would have been more and more worried, as the century went on, about the nature of the situation and moral questions created by the Indian mutiny and by the growing mystique of Empire.

A third way of looking at leadership is not concerned specifically with birth nor with the concept of Empire but with social and educational aspects of a deeper and wider significance. It could be argued that the simplest and easiest way of creating leaders (other than confirming birthright) is to cut them off as a group from the rest of society. This would involve the creation of a social barrier or gulf. It cannot be doubted that such a gulf was created, whether by accident or design, by the public schools : they clearly conferred an élitist status on their middle-class pupils, while at the same time confirming the privileged position of the gentry and aristocracy. The role of the schools as agents of social discrimination became more and more pronounced as the century progressed and as England became an industrial, commercial country of large towns and cities. This is apparent in the care taken by the schools over their collective identity in every aspect from buildings to games. If we look at the list of distinctive points given earlier, we can see this expressed in culture (classics), curriculum, religion, Oxford and Cambridge, games, rural and gentry surroundings. It is, perhaps, not generally realised how effective social or hierarchical gulfs can be in promoting leadership and the acceptance of decisions.[12] The lower echelons assume that the leaders have important secrets and access to the major corridors of power in all professions and walks of life. It is a simple fact that a great many nineteenth-century leaders came from these schools, and it could therefore be argued that they comprised a reservoir of leadership potential. In this way they became the cradle, as it were, of power and influence geared to political ends. In this respect, Arnold stands on the threshold of change. After him came great expansions in industry, commerce, empire, invention, social welfare, professional growth, all needing increasing numbers of so-called leaders. Parallel with this went the explosive growth in the number and size of schools and a widening of their area of social catchment. The schools offered more and more the expectation to parents that they were concerned with leadership and its active promotion. This is the 'expectation role' which they fostered since the middle of the century and which reached its zenith shortly before the Education Act of 1902 reorganised the British system of secondary education and enabled the 'grammar' schools to begin the long process of competing for educational honours.

All this raises the highly important question of whether Arnold turned the schools into a political force. If politics is defined as having some influence on power, then he clearly did have an influence, and a major one at that. At the same time, in the narrower field of party politics, he vehemently denied the accusation that he influenced the boys himself. His influence on the political importance of the schools was not confined to the boys but also affected the status of headmasters, so that his concept of the headmaster as a person who should move on (to higher things) became a reality after his time. Although it is fair to say that he did not create this political force himself, there is no doubt that his reputation and example gave considerable impetus to the movement that had already been started in this direction.

Apart from the true spirit of athletics, culture and leadership, most of the other concerns of public schools had also altered somewhat by the end of Victoria's reign. (Religion, in particular, underwent several significant changes which will be considered separately.) But the properties outlined earlier as applicable to 1900 do not necessarily paint a complete picture. Were there in fact any ideas present in the 1830s and 1840s which had been abandoned or modified drastically by 1900?

There is at least one such major element—the method of school organisation and its link with the concept of freedom : the free man in a free society, or rather the free boy in a free school society. At first sight this might seem to be an abstract philosophical topic, but it is, in fact, a down-to-earth practical issue closely connected with the routine of everyday school life and the spirit of freedom in youth. The most noticeable single change experienced in the public school system during the post-Arnoldian period was in the prevailing attitude towards personal freedom. By the end of the century schools had become highly organised regulated societies with meticulous timetabling. The headmaster knew where any boy could be found at any moment of the day.[13] It was the opposite extreme to that of the early Victorian period. It seemed self-evident to the public school masters of the early nineteenth century that a man could only grow into a free man if he had experienced freedom in youth. It was the responsibility of the headmasters to provide such freedom. This they did in every way possible, reserving formal school discipline for the classroom sessions. There were certain checks, such as at meals or bedtime, while the prefects sometimes organised house and group games and similar activities, but on the whole the boy had ample opportunity every day—long hours usually—to exercise his freedom. He could go where he liked, with whom he liked, without hindrance. At a time when the boys were distributed among the private houses of 'dames' and other local worthies and were part of town life as much as of school life, nothing else was possible. The whole atmosphere is very evident in *Tom Brown's Schooldays*.

From the standpoint of later times, this system appears to lack any kind of order, and it seems to ignore the concept of the master as a responsible tutor with an overall eye. The situation is therefore apt to be misunderstood or interpreted variously as lack of organisation, callousness, laziness, lack of professional standards, inefficiency, ignorance of what was really happening, and so on. None of these implied criticisms is true. The headmasters and staff knew precisely what they were doing. Many members of staff were 'old boys' and had gone through the system in their turn. It even applied to Eton and Long Chamber. Somewhat later, C.J. Vaughan, headmaster of Harrow and one of Arnold's favourite pupils, spelt out this spirit in a way that cannot be misunderstood. A celebrated incident of schoolboy indiscipline had occurred, and Vaughan set out his case to Lord Palmerston in the clearest of terms, using the argument of Arnold that it was impossible to have enough assistant masters to cover discipline. 'There should be no greater number of school fellows living under one Master than of brothers commonly living under one parent,' and, in fact, the number should be even less than that since the bond of affection was missing. Hence the reason for fagging and prefects. In any case Vaughan disliked the business of appointing ushers 'whose business it shall be to follow boys into their hours of recreation and rest avowedly as spies, coercing freedom of speech and action, or repeating to their superior what such observation has gleaned'. This, he indicated, would be ruinous to what is the glory of the English public school—its liberty.[14]

In other words, the unattended, untimetabled, unescorted hours of a boy's day were as much part of his education as the classroom itself. In these private hours he came across pleasures or, to use Arnold's word, 'evil'. But education to the minds of these headmasters was not sheltering the boy from evil but encouraging him to come into contact with it, recognising it, standing up to it and conquering it. Arnold did not understand innocence. Evil was everywhere; it was impossible to avoid it, and the boy's face ought to show the struggle. The difference between Arnold and the other headmasters on this point was that for Arnold the struggle involved religion and morals; for the others it concerned the adaptability of boys and their attempt to find their own niche in their own society.

Too much has been inferred from the fact that Arnold 'trusted' the boys, as though this was a new phenomenon. Other headmasters exercised a similar 'trust' : indeed, it was absolutely necessary if the boys were to enjoy freedom of the total kind that was widespread across the schools from Keate to Arnold and handed down by them to later headmasters like Vaughan. Freedom, of course, had its risks. Occasionally it resulted in excesses that the boyish code of silence could not hide, and there was always the danger of such incidents being reported in the press. It affected all the headmasters of the major schools at one time or another, and they just had to ride out the bad publicity and hope that it did not affect next year's entry. In fact, there is even evidence to show that bad publicity was good for numbers, but our realisation of this is the result of some rather painstaking modern research and certainly none of the headmasters would have believed it.

There is a world of difference between the free (if abused) atmosphere in the early Victorian schools and the busy organised existence at the end of the century. It was so marked and affected the schools so much that it would have been obvious to any outsider entering the school in 1840 and again in 1900. The change was undoubtedly due in part to the growth of the supply of schools and increasing demands of parents in a competitive situation, coupled with the spread of housemasters and the growing isolation of the schools. David Newsome places the change in attitude of the schools to games in the 1860s and 1870s, and no doubt this was a parallel development, if somewhat later. The timing of such changes was, of course, liable to vary from school to school, but it is reasonable to regard the 1850s as the period which marked the beginning of the growing reaction to the traditional freedom of boys.

Finally, it is necessary to consider the field in which Arnold had the greatest reputation—religion. It is hardly necessary to point out that the schools were already heavily religious before his time. A worthwhile assessment of Arnold's influence on the role of religion in school life should instead be concerned with the relative intensity of religious orientation, with its moral force, and with the general attitude to Christianity.

For Arnold religion was an essential part of the total situation, and an obvious one. There was virtually nothing (except, perhaps, some of the games) that had not a religious, and therefore for him, a moral element. Cheating, lying, cruelty, idleness, etc. were all sins against God. Present-day psychologists might argue that lying may be the result of a social or psychological confrontation; Arnold would have said it was the devil at work. He saw human life in simple and literal terms as a struggle between good and evil. The spectacular confrontations with evil could be terrifying, and the measures taken by Arnold could naturally lead to the charge of sternness. Bertrand Russell even suggested that he created a generation of cruelty and sacrificed intelligence to virtue.[15] There is no doubt that he could be cruel and that he was almost obsessed with virtue, but his actions had a purpose not necessarily connected with his own self-satisfaction. At least one of his major acts of cruelty can be explained away (if not forgiven) as in the interests of the institution, and a similar explanation could apply to many of his expulsions. He himself made no secret of the fact that a teacher must be tough: 'The first, second and third duty of a schoolmaster is to get rid of unpromising subjects.' How much heartache lay in that honest but ruthless rule! But any practical reformer must be ruthless. Certainly he gave a lead that most headmasters of the nineteenth century followed, and many still do.

The second aspect of Arnold's religion lay in its role as a social cementer, as a factor in social cohesion. He saw Christianity as an essential ingredient in citizenship, and held that anyone who would not contribute to its essential tenets was lacking an essential basic morality and therefore could not be a citizen in the full sense. What was necessary at national level was equally necessary at school level and led to exclusiveness—an idea which is much out of fashion nowadays in our general comprehensive thinking on education. In addition, the common practice before Arnold's time of public school masters being clergymen was much praised by him, though this practice also was not to survive for long, and Arnold would have been saddened to see it in decline by 1900. But it is not without significance that when the chaplaincy of Rugby fell vacant in 1841 Arnold decided to assume the post himself in addition to his already onerous duties as headmaster.

A third aspect of public school religion (if not of Arnold) was manliness or 'muscular Christianity'. This is usually regarded as a post-Arnoldian development. It is, however, difficult to separate the headmasters of the early years of the century from those at the end of the Victorian period on simple religious grounds, although it is perhaps possible to separate attitudes to religion. The early headmasters had an eighteenth-century approach in which religion had a certain place in life; for Arnold religion was life itself, obvious at all times, a source of pride, a badge to be worn, intense, an emotion that should be obvious in the face. For those at the end of the century there was a concealment of the emotions, the 'stiff upper lip'. Those before 1830 also had the capacity of distinguishing manly virtues from morals, and in this sense Arnold represents an intense interlude.

Finally there was the deeper problem of the Tractarian movement. This attempt to rouse the conscience of the nation led to intense controversy, and Arnold was in the thick of it.[16] His intervention on behalf of the anti-Tractarians was violent and prevented his own advancement. It is difficult to avoid the conclusion that his influence on the schools must have been divisive at least, for some of the founders and headmasters, like Woodard, drew their basic philosophy from the thought of Newman. It is, however, a complex issue which calls for more research.[17]

Perhaps the greatest limitation on the influence of Arnold, or indeed of anyone else, comes from an analysis of the phrase 'the Victorian idea of a public school'. There is an implied assumption that the schools conformed to a single type throughout the period. In many ways this is indeed true, but it is difficult to generalise. Each school was different from the rest, and the changes in Rugby were not those of Harrow and certainly not those at Eton. As autocrats the headmasters were hardly open to influence from rival establishments. This applied particularly to the old high-ranking schools with their own traditions. There were even complications within a single school when headmasters of strong personality followed each other. Rugby had three such men after Arnold : Tait, Temple, Percival. It is difficult to see any of these accepting blindly the ideas of a predecessor, and, indeed, it is well known that Tait altered many of the arrangements and 'principles' that Arnold himself had established. Again, some of the differences between schools were deep-rooted and built into the foundation. Thus Rugby was Church of England and Arnold Low Church, while the empire of Nathaniel Woodard was strictly High Church. Such differences were even more striking with Roman Catholic or Quaker schools. Moreover, it has been shown that although each school retained its own social pattern of recruitment, the variations between the schools were considerable, ranging throughout the social classes. In addition, some schools were new, some old, a few large, and the rest small. It is tempting to generalise, and such rationalisations have their uses, but they should not obscure the essential individuality of each of the schools and the people contained in them.

It follows that the influence of any one person is unlikely to spread across the entire range. Matters which are more likely to have a universal impact are general economic factors and social trends.

It has already been noted that Arnold expected and encouraged change, and with a group of such highly independent institutions as public schools he would have expected divergence and differentation rather than a growing together. He would have expected the situation in 1900 to be markedly different from that in his own day. He would undoubtedly have accepted many of those changes that have been noted as being against the trend of his own thought. Even so, he would have been shocked by some of the developments. The first and probably the most important was the treatment of staff. Equally he would have disliked the elaborate timetabling and lack of freedom for the boys, for in such a system it was impossible to achieve a total religious involvement or to produce real moral fibre. He would have thought the organisation of schools a retrograde step, since it did not encourage self-government with corresponding responsibility. Also he would probably have been concerned at the aloofness of the schools and their non-involvement with the state. To some extent this last point is conjectural, but it would be in line with his thoughts on the social classes, his views on the development of middle-class education, and his hope that the upper classes would give a lead and join with the rest in mutual enterprises.

All this still does not answer the fundamental question : was the influence of Thomas Arnold of any significance in the later nineteenth century? There is some evidence that he influenced the schools as a political force, but, as has been shown, in the other aspects taken separately and examined in detail—religion, discipline, morals, freedom, athletics and the rest—his influence was minimal, if not disruptive.

One obvious conclusion would appear to be that his long-standing influence can be ignored. This may be a logical deduction, but it is quite erroneous. It is virtually impossible to open a book on public school education in the second half of the nineteenth century which does not mention the so-called Arnoldian principles, with their emphasis on moral character and religion, as bases for discipline and the guarantee of a good life and good behaviour. Some of these ideas (as stemming solely from Arnold) have been eroded by historical research, but the fact remains that they comprised a core of ideas that were subscribed to by numerous influential figures, including the founders and headmasters of many new schools. In this sense, there can be no doubt that in 1900 he was still metaphorically a living influence.

In his lifetime Arnold was a public figure. Thereafter his name was kept constantly before the educational world and the public by Hughes and *Tom Brown's Schooldays*, by Stanley, by his son Matthew Arnold, by his illustrious successors in office, and by the spread of rugby football. In addition something of the memory of his intellectual efforts outside education remained, in his work in history, classical scholarship and religion. Nowadays, with the resurrection of works long forgotten, he is also acquiring a new reputation as a student of society. By 1900 he was already generally considered the greatest headmaster of the nineteenth century. Beside him, his nearest rivals pale into insignificance. Thring was almost a nonentity in his narrowness, while Temple and Benson lacked intellectual scope and dynamism. His name was still in common currency at the end of the era. In the general need for new institutions to find authority from the past, he provided that authority.

Some Victorian Headmasters

Alicia C. Percival

THE HEADMASTERS who, from the midpoint of Victoria's reign, began to gather at the yearly meetings which later became known as the Headmasters' Conference (HMC) came from schools of very different types and origins. Yet within a few years of their first meeting, an image of a public school was emerging which it was generally accepted such a school did, and should, resemble. This image was far more broadly based than that of the nine 'great schools' which for half a century had claimed the title of 'public school', as it took in also old grammar schools, usually dating back to Tudor times and lately revived, 'charitable' foundations, expanded from their original function, and the new establishments recently set up in order to supply nineteenth century needs.

How deeply all, including these last, had been absorbed into the unified image can be made clear by considering some well-known lines of poetry relating to such schools :

> There's a breathless hush in the Close tonight—
> Ten to make and the match to win . . .
> His Captain's hand on his shoulder smote—
> 'Play up! play up! and play the game!'

> This is the Chapel; here, my son,
> Your father thought the thoughts of youth . . .

> He saw the School Close, sunny and green,
> The runner beside him, the stand by the parapet wall,
> The distant tape, the crowd roaring between . . .

Yet the close and the chapel here recalled, in words that were to become entirely representative of the idea of a public school, were not at Eton, Harrow, nor Rugby. They were not at any

ancient, traditional seat of learning surrounded by ivy-clad walls
and set among immemorial elms. The place so evocatively referred to was in fact Clifton, a school which had only been
founded about a generation before these words by Henry Newbolt
were written. But had it been five hundred years old, this Clifton
day boy could not have remembered the place more clearly nor
portrayed it more vividly.

Old, new, or renewed, the schools in their various ways were
almost consciously presenting the one image. This unity in
diversity was characteristic also of the headmasters of the period,
many of whom had effected enormous changes in the ethos,
traditions and even appearance of their schools. The Headmasters' Conference was always composed of individual headmasters (i.e. it was never the school as such that sent a representative but the man who was invited),—and plenty of individuality
they showed! In my *Very Superior Men* (a title which echoes
the memorable phrase of that supreme individualist, Edward
Thring) I have already attempted some portraits of the early headmasters; here I propose to deal with four who came after the
pioneers. I do not apologise for including one headmaster who
continued well into the twentieth century, especially as it was on
his arrival in the nineties that he set the pattern by which he
directed his school's development. Moreover the development of
public schools as a whole does not fall into periods divided by
reigns or centuries. The war of 1914–18, and the rethinking of
principles which followed it, shook every type of educational
tradition, perhaps especially those which had continued strong
and unaffected from Victorian times.

For my first example of a Victorian headmaster, however, I
go back to one who undertook his work some years before even
the inauguration of the HMC. It was under Dr John Percival
that the school founded at Clifton in 1862 early developed into
a public school of the recognised image, so effectively portrayed
in Newbolt's verse.

John Percival was a Northcountryman; he figures in Newbolt's
The Twymans, a novel descriptive of Clifton, as 'Dr Cumber-
land', although in fact he was born, in 1834, at Brough Sowerby
in Westmorland. He lost his mother when quite young and was
brought up by an uncle and aunt, going first to a local school

F

and then to Appleby Grammar School, to which he used to ride on a rough pony. A somewhat solitary life in the dales gave him a strength of character and an attitude quite Wordsworthian in its upliftedness and self-reliance. This, when he became a head-master, gave him the reputation of being aloof and austere. He took little interest in his own origins or in his father's second family, but one characteristic of his Northcountry upbringing remained with him : his speech. It is perhaps significant that a remembered phrase of his was 'a tooch o' the barch'.

His harsh exterior was softened by the influence of his wife, Louisa Holland, who made his life and work much easier as she brought out his gentler, more sympathetic side, which he had difficulty in expressing. That he had both affection and sym-pathy is made clear again and again, in the accounts of how he and his wife once spent their holiday abroad nursing a young master dying of consumption, or how a boy who had met with an accident and developed concussion was cared for in their house for several weeks, or his kindness to another boy whose 'delicate constitution' took the unfortunate form of making his brain sometimes brilliant and sometimes 'like cotton wool'. 'Percival', he said, 'saw my weakness and did not press me at those times; indeed, I have put my head on my arm in the Upper Bench and slept under his nose.' Even when he expelled a boy, which (like Arnold) he did not hestitate to do, he would show him kindness afterwards and help him to start off afresh. A good summing up of Percival seems to be :

> A great and famous scholar, a very strict disciplinarian, but a very kind man. I have never forgotten his kindness to me when I was confirmed. His influence was wonderful; it per-meated right through the School.[1]

Still, the reputation for sternness persisted, both at his own crea-tion of Clifton and even more at his re-creation of Rugby and perhaps serves to remind us of his tough northern origins.

However, when he got his scholarship to Oxford, Percival left the north behind him and never, unlike Arnold, settled there. At The Queen's College he had a brilliant career, taking a double first in classics and mathematics and studying also 'natural philo-sophy' (i.e. science). Perhaps because of this latter interest, he at once established at Clifton a 'modern side' and not only taught science himself but collected a fine staff of scientists, at least three of whom became Fellows of the Royal Society.

Naturally, however, it was as a classic that he was offered a post at Rugby as assistant master, where he remained only two years before getting his headship. There had been a short break after Oxford due to illness, probably from driving himself too hard. It was while he was recuperating that he met his future wife, who came of an East Anglian family.

At Rugby Percival was not, of course, under Arnold, who had been dead for nearly twenty years. But the school was still deeply influenced by that great headmaster and was setting hard in traditions and organisation—in ways which Arnold himself might very well not have approved. On the other hand, the influence of Frederick Temple, the future archbishop, has been underestimated. Like Percival, Temple was a countryman, born in humble circumstances, forthright in speech and uncompromising in procedure, and his influence may have enhanced Percival's own trend towards an outward hardness. Temple could not bear cant of any sort and was prone to sarcasm, possibly not realising the pain he sometimes caused; with Percival it was rather that he expected an exacting standard (of himself no less than of others) and while insisting on it, failed to praise or give credit to those who exerted themselves to reach it.

How Percival arrived at the headship of the new school, Clifton College, is rather curious. A group of far-seeing, courageous and public-spirited citizens of Bristol had met to inaugurate a scheme for establishing a school, to be financed as 'The Clifton College Company, Ltd'. Four hundred shares of £25 were soon subscribed, on which in fact no dividends were ever paid, and when the company was eventually reorganised to become a chartered company, only two of the shareholders demanded to be repaid. (The sole privilege remaining was that of nominating a boy to the school.) When the progress of the original idea seemed to warrant it, a headmaster was appointed, recommended by Temple from his Rugby staff. But the Rev. Charles Evans, having made arrangements for the opening of the school in September 1862, having appointed staff, and having even had his coat of arms affixed to the headmaster's house, suddenly in August applied for and secured the headship of his old school in Birmingham and withdrew from Clifton. The Clifton historian's comment, 'This retirement occasioned the council great anxiety'[2] sounds like the understatement of the century; it must have caused consternation. Temple was again appealed to and suggested Percival, who, against some competition, was chosen. To the two counts raised against him, that he was young (twenty-seven) and unmarried, he answered that one would be remedied in a few years and the other in a few weeks. He married in October and had two days' honeymoon at Clevedon, not far from Bristol.

The school was all to make, and, not surprisingly, the new headmaster tended to be guided in some ways by the Rugby tradition. By using the same terminology (e.g. 'Big School levée' for a meeting) and the same customs (e.g. having all the sixth form as prefects) the ethos of Arnold as interpreted by Temple was established—and later, when made articulate by a Clifton poet, inspired a group of schools far beyond Clifton and Rugby.

> This is the word that year by year
> While in her place the school is set
> Every one of her sons must hear . . .

But it was due largely to Percival that Clifton so quickly embodied this spirit.

It was never his intention to make Clifton a mere copy, and one way in which he set about giving the new place its identity was by recruiting a very remarkable and utterly diverse staff. Few of them, except the Manx poet T.E. Brown, have left names notable outside the school, but one has only to glance at its history to be struck by the impact each man made in his own way. This was possible only because Percival dominated them all, otherwise they might well have torn the school to pieces, but 'he seemed to stand head and shoulders above his assistants'—almost literally : Percival was a fine figure of a man with an imposing presence and clear-cut features. His forceful personality reigned supreme over every aspect of school life. Sometimes it was said he was too masterful and arbitrary, too much of a driving force. T.E. Brown had the right metaphor :

> Like an inspired demonic conductor of an orchestra; he has lashed us into Bacchic fury—wind and strings and voice—forte, *forte*, FORTISSIMO. . . He is divine but we want rest ![3]

Perhaps inevitably, he began with the boys on the intellectual side; he taught the sixth form himself, and his pupils soon began to achieve academic brilliance and important scholarships. He was not troubled with any idea of opposition between 'character' and 'intellect' (a definitely post-Arnoldian distinction), but he frankly took the Platonic view in its negative aspect : 'The second-rate in matters moral and intellectual always go together.'[4] But to a far greater extent than had been done at Rugby by Arnold or anyone else, he widened the curriculum. Science was taught throughout the school. He constantly complained that he himself had to devote too much of his time to teaching it instead of taking more forms in classics; but he was particularly anxious to establish a 'modern side' that should have self-respect. It was a great disappointment to him that, against every attempt of his, it did become 'the refuge for the less cultivated, the less capable . . . the unambitious'.[5] He introduced modern languages, German at least being taught by a German. In teaching history, he followed Arnold's practice of releasing it from its classical bondage : English was not yet taught as a subject in its own right, but he laid great stress on the library (built 1870). Divinity and scripture he taught as much through his sermons as in the class. There was no chapel when the school opened, but three years later the widow of Canon Guthrie, who had been one of the moving spirits both in founding the school and in appointing its headmaster, proposed to set in hand the building of this as a memorial; it was completed in 1867. Before that the services had been held in Big School, a room of sufficiently ecclesiastical appearance as to make it suitable for his addresses.

A note on Percival's puritanism is relevant here, especially regarding his famous edict that boys' knickers should cover the knee. This was at Rugby; at Clifton the reference to the length of knickerbockers is not till 1892; elastic bands are not mentioned. It rests on hearsay that Percival considered knees indecent and provocative; the story may have originated in the practice, followed at Rossall and elsewhere, of fastening knickerbockers below the knee for convenience when playing football. A protest was, however, made to Percival 'in the interest of the onlookers in the grandstand' when the Old Cliftonians proposed to run in the school sports without stockings. Certainly Percival was something of a puritan, like an Old Testament prophet—stern and lacking in humour, but, at his best, inspired. Games, incidentally, were started at once at Clifton but were not compulsory; indeed, Percival deprecated too much *talk* about games and too much of the boys' energy being spent on them—as on too many amusements.

The headmaster remained on good terms, not only with his governors (all local men) but with the neighbourhood in general, helped by the care and tact of his wife. He took a great interest, for instance, in the establishment of Bristol University and presided over the committee which worked for this objective. Again, when the Clifton High School for Girls was established, he was included on the board of governors. He opposed discrimination against women at a time when such a stand was not popular; in this and in similar matters he was a great deal more liberal than his boys, to judge from the record of the school debating society.

One excellent place of organisation which helped to build up the fund of goodwill among local parents (to which his correspondence bears witness) was his founding of a house for the 'town boys'. In many schools the tradition (though not always the reality) was of disparaging day boys and scattering them among the various houses without proper accommodation or arrangements for them, nor ensuring that they did or could participate in school life. Percival set his face against this from the first and appointed a Town House master, putting the house (for which there were quite severe regulations) on a level with the others in matters such as the playing of matches, etc. Later there were so many day boys that it was divided into North Town and South Town. Boys were expected to be in the Town House at all times when not at home, and to take part in all school activities and functions. It was a very successful idea and was taken up by other schools, such as Cheltenham, where the problem also arose of integrating local boys with the school. A Jewish house was also established; this too was in consonance with Percival's liberal outlook; he wanted boys to participate fully in school life but felt it wrong that they should strain their (or their parents') consciences by being unable to carry out their own religious practices. For such a profoundly religious Christian, this was a remarkably sympathetic attitude.

Percival's liberal (we should nowadays say 'democratic') turn of mind may be illustrated by a scheme he had, far in advance of his time, for extending the benefits of Clifton College education to 150 boys who would take the place of foundation scholars in the old endowed schools. They would pay little or nothing, the college contributing half the fees and the rest being provided by various funds or subscriptions. Such a scheme was not put into practice until the recommendations of the Fleming Committee were adopted in the 1940s, and even then it was on nothing like the scale envisaged by Percival. The governors of Percival's day would not agree, and although it is possible that by persistence (one of his most successful weapons—he took three years to get them to agree to the Jewish house) he might have brought it about, he had not done so when he left. In thanking the governors for their testimonial when he was leaving, he said :

> I should not be speaking with that frankness which you have a right to claim, if I were to keep back that, had the changes in the Constitution which I advocated some time ago, including the abolition of social distinction, been carried out, nothing would have induced me to leave Clifton . . . as that reform would have given me the one educational opportunity which I covet and the loss of which I can never entirely cease to regret.

Percival only twice tried to move, on each occasion to the headship of Rugby. (The Rugby governors, to their own detriment, twice appointed someone else; then, ironically, many years later, they actually asked Percival to become headmaster.) On the second occasion, in 1874, the sixth form passed this charmingly worded resolution :

> That the VIth wish to express to Mr Percival that, while they are far too proud of him not to regret deeply that he has suffered a disappointment, they have not words to tell their thankfulness that he is saved to Clifton and themselves individually, bound to him as they are by ties of respect and affection, the strength of which perhaps they never fully realised till they seemed about to lose him.[6]

After seventeen years of building up Clifton, however, Percival seems to have felt that he should leave. Arnold's dictum had been : remain for fifteen years or 'till you feel no emotion on receiving a new boy'. It is more likely that Percival was feeling the strain of his energetic years. He did not sound very optimistic about going to Oxford, where he had been offered the presidency of Trinity College, though it is possible that the university had never lost something of the glamour that it must have had for the boy coming up to the life there from the little northern town of Ambleside. It is also clear that by his schemes for putting knowledge within the reach of the working class, he had laid himself open to both opposition and censure. 'Like Arnold and Temple, Percival was a Liberal in politics and thought it was his duty to proclaim the fact with some of the aggressiveness and moral arrogance which sometimes characterises political reformers.'[7]

He remained at Oxford for only seven years before being called back to the school headship at Rugby. Space does not allow a detailed account of his career there, except to say that he was needed for a harder test than building up a school, for Rugby had fallen into something of a decline. He found dissension in plenty, the intellectual standard low and the moral tone weak. He eventually succeeded, by stern measures and exacting hard work, in raising the place, although many of the improvements, in scholarship for example, could be seen only long after his departure. But when he left, it could be said that there was a difference between the pre-Percival and the post-Percival eras. It was also said that he had done wonders for the school, but it was as well that his reign was a short one and right that he should go before his rigid system took too strong a hold. More succinctly, the verdict (which might have been murmured at Clifton too) was 'I grant you he harried us, but it was for our own good.'[8]

This saying might serve as a motto for all his lives. For Percival had definitely four consecutive lives, to each of which he gave himself utterly : school founder, college president, school headmaster and bishop. But of all these it was at Clifton that he lived most fully and happily, to Clifton that he so often went back as visitor, preacher or festival guest. It is fitting that in Clifton College chapel John Percival is buried.

A complete contrast to John Percival, the strikingly forceful puritan, whose career included the headships of two of the most famous public schools, is Henry Platt, whose work was done in one school only, a relatively unknown establishment. Dr Platt (a Doctor not of Divinity but of Law) went to Wellingborough in 1879, stayed there for twenty-eight years, and in his own way 'made' the school no less than Percival made Clifton or Thring his own creation out of that other Midland grammar school, Uppingham. When Platt went there, Wellingborough was not far from the moribund state to which it had been brought by a series of ill-paid clerics. These neither taught the boys themselves nor paid others to do so, but, perhaps understandably, pocketed the usher's pittance as well as their own miserable £13 6s. 8d. per annum. True, the school had revived somewhat under a couple of good headmasters, but the Taunton Commission in 1868 had only graded the Upper School as 'semi-classical', while the Lower School consisted mostly of boys under ten and was hardly 'secondary' at all. In 1876 the Charity Commissioners had put forward a scheme, but it was Platt who was going to transform the school and make the scheme work.

Platt was a product of All Hallows, Bloxham, itself a one-man venture, one of the rare examples of a private school which was in turn to achieve 'public' school status. (Its founder, the religious idealist, the Rev. P.G. Egerton, was one of the most interesting headmasters of the whole Victorian era.) Its curriculum, weighted to the 'modern side', was suited to middle-class boys. The Cambridge Local Examinations had been taken there from 1865, when Platt may well have been a boy at the school. This practice was admittedly followed largely to enable Bloxham to compare itself with other schools of the same type throughout the country. The excitement experienced on hearing their results read out shows how greatly the boys had been stimulated in this Age of Competition.

Much of the organisation of these examinations was probably done by Platt himself when he returned, having taken his degree at Cambridge, to become a teacher at his old school. He had had no other experience than his four years there when he became headmaster of the rather down-at-heel grammar school in the academically sleepy little Midland town of Wellingborough. The governors were obliged to find a new site for the school, and Platt persuaded them to take over a large open area outside the town. In his first two years, before the move, he had expanded the numbers beyond the capacity of the old Church Street (i.e. churchyard) buildings, and for a time the school held some of its classes in the old workhouse. No particularly noticeable rise had by then taken place in the population or industry of Wellingborough (a shoe-making town), but the numbers in the school rose surprisingly fast from 17 to 464. From one 'tumbled-down house in the High Street' the boarders expanded to fill the typical late Victorian boarding-houses built by the governors on the new site and whose names perpetuate Platt and his fellow-headmasters.

Understandably, Dr Platt introduced the same Local Examinations[9] as those for which Bloxham had been a 'Local Centre'. That school had, under his care, become one of the foremost in the country for results; Wellingborough was now going to claim this place and become a 'Local Centre'. At first selected boys, and later the whole number, seem to have taken external examinations as a regular practice. It would be interesting to know whether Platt had himself established, or whether he had merely adapted, the system of cramming (or 'preparation') which was so successful in producing both the Bloxham and Wellingborough results. The Wellingborough boys had test papers every month, on Saturday mornings, from quite an early stage. Later *The Wellingburian* would give the results. These could be summarised, for the benefit of parents:

> Upwards of ONE HUNDRED Certificates gained in each of the following years: 1895, 1896, 1897, 1898, 1899, 1900, 1901, 1902, 1903 & 1904.
> The greatest number of Senior Certificates gained by any school in 1893, 1894, 1895. . .
> The greatest number of Mathematical distinctions in 1895 [and] 1904, the number in 1903 being the greatest on record.
> THE FIRST SENIOR CANDIDATE IN PURE AND APPLIED MATHEMATICS (to whom was awarded the Exhibition . . . offered by St John's College, Cambridge) in 1886, 1893, 1894, 1905.

This is followed by no fewer than three pages of individual results, including

Position of the distinguished candidates
 e.g. 11th out of 2002 in English History
  13th out of 8585 in Mathematics[10]

Dr Platt had found something in which the school could build up a reputation and on which it could congratulate itself; writing twenty years later, the chronicler notes with pride that Wellingborough so often came 'first in all England' with its proportion of passes, and he quotes other distinctions. How a school's position in this context can be measured is not now very clear, nor should we now try, but on any reckoning Wellingborough's success was a creditable performance for a small provincial school. It gave the pupils a sense of achievement and self-respect.

Incidentally, it is interesting to see how some individuals spent most of their lives connected with the school in one capacity or another. Platt's successor, Fryer, probably held the record with nearly seventy years: as pupil (1882–89); as assistant master (1892–1907); as headmaster (1907–36); as governor (1943–50).

Platt was always conscious of what was appropriate in time and place. Examinations had been brought in at just the right moment. His discipline was authoritative without being excessively harsh, though, as was usual at that time, it included corporal punishment. His 'period' is perhaps indicated by the two things that were specially remembered as 'barred by the Doctor—cigarettes and motor-cars'.

In religious matters, the element of Dissent was very strong in Northamptonshire, and the High Church fervour of Bloxham did not appear at Wellingborough; in that Midland town the Middle Way seems to have been the successful one. Yet even in church-going, Dr Platt showed an idiosyncratic side which was characteristic of him: he did not insist on uniform during the week, but on Sundays the boys always went to morning service at the parish church in Etons and silk hats—an outfit which drew on them notice and missiles not always favourable nor comfortable. At night they assembled in 'Big Schoolroom' (the name, of course, adopted from public school tradition) where Dr Platt preached ('jawed' was the boys' word), one imagines in a style very different from Arnold's or Thring's. The only surviving account of any speech of his is that of his response at the magnificent celebration arranged for him and his wife on their silver wedding, which coincided with his twenty-five years' headship, when his work was recognised by boys, staff and governors. He was reported as being 'under considerable emotion' but the speech reads very cheerfully, with genial, unsophisticated jokes and the easy scriptural allusions of a jocular preacher, though with the ethical and emotional substratum which the first generation in this century would expect and appreciate. For example, in an outline of a code of public school behaviour, he exhorted his listeners : 'If your school is in any way great, see that it becomes greater. See that you never sacrifice your birthright for what may turn out to be after all a mere mess of pottage.'[11]

On this occasion Dr Platt and other speakers stressed the need for a school chapel, recognising that it would have to be built out of subscriptions. Neither Arnold nor Thring would ever have waited twenty-five years before establishing such a religious centre in the school, even granted the difference in affluence between their pupils and Dr Platt's; with them it would have been a matter of principle, with him it came lower in the list of things desirable. Presumably he felt his exhortations could be as effective in Big School.

Platt was not only a good organiser but an inspirer both in work and games. The pages of *The Wellingburian* are devoted not only to examination results but also to accounts of matches and comments on individual players—an indication that Platt encouraged the accepted prestige given to sport. But 'the Doctor' was also genial and open-handed and, above all, he was a 'character'. He played croquet and would call up a small boy to come and play with him, letting him go with what was regarded as a substantial tip. The following remarkable anecdote is recorded by William Whitehead, son of a racing trainer from Bedfordshire, probably Platt's own home county.

When I had been there a few weeks a master told me Dr Platt wanted me in his study. . . I was in a bit of a cold sweat. The interview was something as follows : 'Now William, I want you to understand distinctly I do not allow boys at this school to bet.' I told him I hadn't and would not, which was perfectly true. 'I'm glad to hear it,' he went on, 'but should you get a letter from home and they fancy one they may be running, bring the letter to me, and you are on, a pound to nothing. That's all I wanted you for. Good-night.' . . . A few days after, I did get a letter from home in which they told me they were running Worker at Nottingham the following week, and they fancied him very much. Obeying instructions, I took the letter into the study, gave it to the old boy, who read it, thanked me, and wished me 'Good-morning'. I thought no more about it until seven o'clock that evening, when I had another invitation to Dr Platt's study. There were eight sovereigns on his desk, and as he pushed them across to me, he remarked : 'Here you are, William. He won all right, at eight to one.' It was one of the surprises of my life.[12]

I quote this story because the attitude as well as the incident shows the gap between Platt and his predecessors earlier in the century. None of those 'very superior men' could have been the subject of such a tale—with the possible exception of the eighteenth-century Dr James of Rugby. And even if any of those early Victorian headmasters had taken a racing tip, they would never have put on the boy's money. It would have been unthinkable for Kennedy (too intellectual), for Arnold (too religious), for Thring (too moral) or for any of the clerics, good or bad, who governed the lesser grammar-turned-public schools. Platt, in a middle-class school in the midlands over which he had won complete ascendancy by driving his boys to undreamed-of results in work and sport, merely built up by such behaviour his image of open-handed unconventionality and increased his hold on their imagination.

For twenty-five years Dr Platt's good work was appreciated by boys, staff, parents and governors, and he himself obviously increased in popularity. It is sad to find that a cloud then arose. The cause of the disagreement with the governors is not very clear; it seems that, like some few other headmasters, he hoped to designate his successor. At any rate, he retired abruptly in 1907 and shook the dust of Wellingborough off his boots. It is interesting to note that he left £11,000 at his death seventeen years later, a remarkable sum for a headmaster at that time. Perhaps his pastime of racing continued to be profitable.

It should be noted that although there was an immense amount of feeling for and pride in the school, it was still Wellingborough Grammar School when he left. It did not appear in the H M C list till 1921, under Platt's less idiosyncratic successor. But it seems to have been generally acknowledged that it was Dr Platt who created this almost new entity of a school. In a curious individual way he seems to have embodied several characteristics of the turn of the century, that period of growing affluence, of ebullient cheerfulness, of upward thrust. His personal image could hardly be more concisely summed up than it is by D.C. Ulyatt in his unpublished *History of Wellingborough School*, the author being not much more than a boy himself when he set down this pleasantly naïve tribute :

> Dr Platt was one of the most famous and best headmasters the school has ever had—feared by the Juniors, loved by the Seniors, and worshipped by the Old Boys. He was a real sportsman, a good friend, a man of the world and an outstanding personality.

Not all attempts at reviving an old school or recreating it as a different type were successful even in the days of the nineteenth-century expansion. Henry St John Reade who attempted this at Oundle between 1876 and 1883 failed in his enterprise. It may be that the school was not ready for his transformation, or that his personality, attractive as it seems to have been, was not suited to the task, or simply that adverse circumstances were too strong. He had to deal not merely with apathetic governors but with men whose intentions, when they came to perceive where his policy was leading them, were contrary to his own. His experience at Oundle is a sad story of an adventure defeated.

Reade had been a boy at Tonbridge school under James Ind Welldon, who had done so much for the school. Welldon had previously taught at Shrewsbury under B.H. Kennedy and was therefore imbued with the traditions of a classical school, which passed on to Reade. But besides raising the standard of teaching at Tonbridge, Welldon had given the school new life, purposes and interests. There were new houses and a new chapel. A considerable proportion of time was allocated to games, gymnastics and athletics. 'Old boys' formed an association and came back to play matches. Young Reade got caught up with these new ideas and the prevailing atmosphere of pride in the school. He was captain of cricket (with colours) and he determined to carry the ideas which excited him into another school. After a short

teaching experience at Beccles, the tall, handsome young schoolmaster was appointed to the headship at Oundle Grammar
School, which seemed a place ready to his hand.

The school was in fairly good condition, but there had always
been complications about how it should be run. It had been
founded about 1566, with Sir William Laxton as its main benefactor and handed over to be managed by the Grocers' Company
of London, of which Laxton had been a Warden and Master. A
'court' of the Grocers' Company took the place of the customary
board of governors and had run the school (which consisted
chiefly, but by no means solely, of day boys) with varying success over the centuries. Laxton's will, however, had led to inter-
minable litigation and the existence of a second branch or
subsidiary school, later known as 'Laxton's.' The Company's
policy was anything but clear or consistent, and the townspeople,
who had little control over the school, were for the most part
indifferent to what went on, except that they were determined to
have their sons educated there at as little cost to themselves as
possible.

When Reade took up his post, he conceived a plan for a further
separation between the grammar school and the Laxton branch,
and intended to introduce a curriculum for the latter which
would in effect make it a 'Second Grade Modern School'[13] in a
separate building. He proposed to give 'a good and useful education to boys who leave school about the age of sixteen in order to
engage in Agricultural or Commercial pursuits'.[14] In effect, these
would be the day boys. The boarders would belong to the main
Oundle School, with a certain social distinction between the
leavers at sixteen and those at eighteen. For the latter, Reade
proceeded both in the curriculum and in the life of the school
to create what clearly had all the characteristics of a public
school. Carrying over the Tonbridge tradition, he laid stress on
games; he created houses: School, Dryden, Laxton and
Oppidans (the Oundle School day boys having their own house
for matches, etc.). There were trophies for games, examinations,
prize-giving at speech days; the monitors became prefects; the
sixth form wore 'mortar-boards'. A school magazine, *The
Laxonian*, was started, and 'old boys' came for cricket matches.
The 'classical side' of the school was evidently that which received
his special interest and congratulations, though there was not

only a 'mathematical side' at the top of the grammar school but also a non-classical department where mathematics and modern languages were taught to boys who stayed on whether they were going to the university—the goal of the classicists—or not. To this section of the school's academic organisation he gave the name 'Public Services Department'. The new idea evidently supplied a need among those boys who came as boarders, and the numbers shot up to over two hundred.

Reade's total organisation sounds a most sensible and forward-looking one. But he was quite clearly aiming at a school with all the accepted characteristics of a public school, and when this became apparent to the Grocers' Company, they did not like it. The school historian, W.G. Walker, records that 'As time went on and Reade began to make a success of it, they realised that his aim was to make, not a cheap school for poor men's sons but a great public school rivalling Uppingham as Thring had made it, and this at their [the Company's] expense.'[15]

Nor were the townspeople much better pleased, though what they chiefly deplored was that the governors raised the fees. Reade was caught in the cross-currents of argument and recrimination and made to retire. He had earlier jumped the gun by putting out a prospectus for Oundle School and another for the Laxton Modern School, and the governors considered that both this action and his creation of the second school were 'irresponsible'. For some time they refused to sanction the division and still referred to the two 'branches'. In the end, with arrangements made for transfer from one to the other and the proviso of having the same head for both, they did adopt Reade's plan, but he did not live to see it. He was a sick man before he left and died soon after his retirement in 1883. However, both the positive results of his work and his unrealised dreams were remembered with gratitude by the school.

Reade's career at Oundle was a brave experiment, but he lacked, on the one hand, the skill and charm to persuade and, on the other, the power to push his measures through. Another decade had to pass before the arrival of the man who really put Oundle School on the map.

The outstanding man who did for Oundle what Reade could not do—though Reade, unrecognised, had done much—was

6 Eranos, Rugby, 1898. Eranos was an exclusive literary society organised by the sixth form. Many of its members later achieved great intellectual prominence. Included in the group above are R. H. Tawney, the historian (seated, extreme left) and William Temple, son of Frederick Temple and future Archbishop of Canterbury (standing, extreme right).

7 The Governors of Wellington College, Speech Day, 1898. 'I say plainly . . . that those great means of blessing are the Aristocracy and the Christian Church.' (Thomas Arnold). Élitist institutions could be directed only by the élite: the Wellington governors comprised two princes, three dukes, three earls, three bishops, six knights and a former Prime Minister.

8 C. J. Vaughan, Harrow (1844–59).

9 Frederick Temple, Rugby (1857–69).

FOUR VICTORIAN HEADMASTERS

10 John Percival, Clifton (1862–78), Rugby (1887–95).

11 F. W. Sanderson, Oundle (1892–1922).

F.W. Sanderson, headmaster from 1892 to 1922. He may be ranked among the men who 'made' a school, so successful was he in moulding Oundle to his wishes. H.G. Wells, in *The Story of a Great Schoolmaster*, called him 'one of the most inspiring of living educationalists, and one of the greatest of headmasters the world has ever seen'.

This commendation of Wells's may not bear quite the weight now that it had in his own time, but it is far from negligible. It is also worth remembering that Wells sent his own two boys, one later becoming Professor G.P. Wells, to be under this head-master. Both his personality and his work need to be considered.

One remarkable thing is that he should ever have been appointed at all. Was it in fact his personality, or could it possibly have been foreseen that under his guidance this small grammar school, almost unknown outside its own locality, would become accepted as a public school with a particular character of its own? He is sometimes compared to Thring, and in one of his most important contributions to education—the insistence on providing opportunity for every individual boy ('strictly speaking, the dull boy does not exist')—he is completely in harmony with his great midland predecessor. But in background and temperament they were very different.

Sanderson, like Percival, was a Northcountryman, and his father had been employed in the Brancepeth estate office of Viscount Boyne. He went to the local village school and worked his way up as a student-teacher, not very different from an ordinary pupil-teacher, though perhaps he studied more. He won a theological scholarship to Durham University, where he took science and mathematics as well as theology, and then went to Christ's College, Cambridge, where he took a degree in mathematics as Eleventh Wrangler. After some years' lecturing, tutoring and examining at Cambridge, he took a post at Dulwich College. Here he developed the teaching of science, introducing chemistry and physics into the school curriculum for the whole of the 'modern side' and for the middle forms of the 'classical side'. He also developed, and persuaded the governors to equip in a very practical way an 'engineering side' for boys who would be going into engineering or manufacture. An old pupil thus sums up the convictions with which, after seven years at Dulwich, he came to Oundle :

G

He believed that Science could be made the basis for a true education. . . He was developing his ideas of a broad curriculum of education based on scientific method. He taught us by means of the simplest experimental apparatus, made by the boys themselves to a large extent in the workshop, to rely on experimental evidence for scientific facts, and to refuse to be satisfied with the pronouncements of authority.[16]

He was thirty-five years old when, rather to his surprise, he was elected to the headship of Oundle, then a school of ninety-two boys.

Not all headmasters have their portraits drawn by established novelists, so it is worthwhile to take advantage of H.G. Wells's description of Sanderson, remembering that he only knew him in the last eight years of Sanderson's life.

His complexion had a reddish fairness; he had well-modelled features, thick eye-brows and a thin moustache touched with grey, and he wore spectacles through and over and beside which his active eyes took stock of you. About his eyes were kindly wrinkles and generally I remember him smiling, often with a touch of roguery in the smile. Quick movements of his head caused animating flashes of his glasses. He was carrying a little too much body for his heart, and that made him short of breath.[17]

It was Wells who took the chair at, and later described, the last lecture Sanderson gave, which was characteristically entitled 'The Duty and Service of Science in the New Era'. This was given for the National Union of Scientific Workers, at University College, London. At the end of it, Sanderson, who had been ill for some time, died in his seat.

Wells, in his account of this 'bold, persistent, humorous and most capable man' who was transparently honest and free from vanity, refers to his hard work and wonderful teaching. But he and others add that Sanderson had a fiery temper which he never quite learnt to control, so that there were occasions when 'his smouldering indignation at the obstinate folly and jealousy that hampered his work blazed out violently'. In his early years at Oundle, he 'thrashed a good deal', often at white heat (he agreed with Bernard Shaw's maxim, 'Never punish *except* in anger') and the boys felt they were literally reaping the whirlwind. But he was genial by temperament, and punishments grew less and less, until his last years were almost free of beating or expulsion. He confessed to having changed his mind about the efficacy of punishment.

Yet sometimes he could meet opposition with great dignity and self-control. Early in his time at Oundle, when his ideas on the importance of science were being almost overtly opposed not only by the boys but by the senior members of staff, there was put on a satiric play 'full of the puns and classical tags and ancient venerable turns of humour usual in such compositions, against the Barbarian invader and his new Laboratories. . . It was the mock trial of an incendiary found trying to burn down the new Labs.' It was rehearsed before the headmaster, who sat there immobile listening to the little gibes against himself and what he stood and hoped for. At the end he made no comment except: 'Boys, we will regard this as the final performance,' rose, and quietly left them.[18]

'The strongest thing in all boys is their dislike to any change,' he is known to have said,[19] but there was more in the opposition than that. Sanderson was out of the tradition personally as well as educationally. He was considered no gentleman, no sportsman, no cricketer (his predecessor had been no mean performer in this respect) no (classical) scholar, not in orders—and he wore a made-up tie. By the end of his first decade there were only three members remaining of his original staff (he had brought two masters with him from Dulwich and four boys to finish their courses), and their going was not always without pain. The number of boys grew, but at first only slowly; by 1902 there were about 120; after that date the school increased as fast as the buildings would allow. But even in Sanderson's first decade the trend of his improvements was clearly discernible.

New laboratories were built, new subjects introduced . . . to meet the needs of such intellectual types as the school had hitherto failed to interest. There was a great development of biological and agricultural work. . . The attention given to art increased and there was great change and revolution in the history teaching.[20]

It was in the teaching of mathematics and mechanics, his own subjects, that the alterations came first. A new attitude to school work was given by his introduction of a 'science conversazione', an occasion for display of experiments and collections of almost any type, made in the pupils' out-of-school hours. Sanderson's programme for this innovation extends to some ten pages, and further schemes were outlined for everything from maps to music. The very fact that this does not now strike us as anything much out of the ordinary (apart from the curious name) simply shows how far we have all travelled along the path where Sanderson led.

Indeed, the three ideas which may be accepted as Sanderson's main educational principles have been so thoroughly accepted by later educationists as *general* principles that we may wonder at the opposition that they engendered, at the same time observing how far ahead of his age Sanderson was, and how near in some ways to our own. Briefly, he foresaw the importance of science and of technical education (and of introducing the latter into the public school curriculum); he wished to have every boy stretched to the utmost according to his talents, whether towards languages or towards practical work; and he tried to establish the principle of co-operation rather than of competition in their work.

Workshops were established as soon as he arrived and were expanded afterwards. But it was not only in practical work that Sanderson wanted to substitute for traditional class-teaching the method which he called 'investigation'—which so many educationists have so unadvisedly termed '*re*-search'. An assignment or scheme of work would be allocated, to be carried out with the use of books or apparatus, no less than it might be with tools.

> It is our duty [he said] to organise schools so that every boy weak or strong shall be able to make full use of his faculties. . . The school should be a place where a boy comes not to learn but to create. Mathematics, languages and the elements of science are not ends but tools and these tools a boy must accustom himself to use.[21]

This needed an enormous amount of organisation and a large staff, and Sanderson's main reason for delighting in the increase of numbers (which reached six hundred in his last year) was that it made possible the implementation of his scheme. He mentions 'masters for mathematics, physics, chemistry, mechanics, biology, zoology, anthropology, botany, geology, agriculture, economics, French, German, Spanish, Italian, Russian, Eastern languages, art, applied art, handicraft and music'.[22] It was, as he called it, 'a spacious staff'—though what is missing may give some cause for thought. But history, for instance, *was* taught by 'investigation', in which, as explained, Sanderson insisted on co-operation; we would call it 'group work'.

One might think that this insistence conflicted with another of his principles, that of bringing the school into contact with, and viewing it as a training for, adult life and the world outside. But, for example, he considered his workshop principles were a real training for management and, in a more general way, for leadership.

> We are entitled to say to the boy: 'When you go forth into life, perhaps to your father's works or business or profession, you must try to do for your apprentices and workers what we have tried to do for you. . . This is your real duty towards your neighbour.'[23]

We should not forget that, though never ordained as a clergyman, Sanderson had been a student of divinity. Perhaps what he said to the boys concerning the principles which should govern their conduct differed from the message of earlier headmasters less in content than in its realistic form. Sanderson's ideals on the essential role of the school may be summed up in his own memorable words:

> Schools should be miniature copies of the world we should love to have.[24]

Sanderson converted Oundle—boys, parents and governors—to his own ideas and made it a unique school. He built a bridge by which his boys could pass into the newer, technical, scientific world. How far he really influenced the public schools as a whole, it would be hard to say. Certainly, his main ideas, though their adoption at so early a period still strikes us as remarkable, are no longer regarded as the pioneering schemes they were when he launched them; that is the measure of his success in converting the academic world. Science subjects, group work, assignments, investigations—all these have been accepted as the stock-in-trade of progressive heads for the last half-century. Yet the effect of Sanderson's work has been greater in schools other than the public schools. For example, there is the influence of his views on the Hadow Report (1926) through which, in the long run, the present-day secondary modern and technical schools were created.

For it must be admitted that in the years between Sanderson's death and the end of the Second World War, no great multitude from the public schools passed over the bridge he had built. It is beyond the scope of this brief survey to do more than touch on the reasons: finance (no science department ever seemed satisfied, not even with a sum that would keep, say, a history department happy for years); prejudice (in spite of the example of men like Percival and Mitchinson, it took a long time to accept science as the *sole* academic background of a headmaster); method (the freedom in science teaching continued long to be regarded with suspicion); there were other reasons. The day of the Industrial Grants Committee was still far ahead when Sanderson died.

In the chapel at Oundle is placed a beautifully lettered memorial plaque. The text, appropriate to others besides himself, begins:

Here rest the ashes of
FREDERICK WILLIAM SANDERSON
Headmaster 1892–1922

To whom God granted grace
to revive this ancient school
which is itself his memorial.

By his vision and enthusiasm
he transformed the life of the School
promoted its vigorous growth
and enhanced its reputation.

Topics Fit for Gentlemen:
The Problem of Science in the Public
School Curriculum

A.J. Meadows and W.H. Brock

COMPARED with the practitioners of most other intellectual pursuits, very few eminent Victorian scientists emerged from the public schools. One of the rare exceptions was Charles Darwin, and we can find in his autobiography a brief but telling illustration of the public school attitude to science as it appeared at early Victorian Shrewsbury.

> Towards the end of my school life, my brother worked hard at chemistry, and made a fair laboratory with proper apparatus in the tool-house in the garden, and I was allowed to aid him as a servant in most of his experiments. . . The fact that we worked at chemistry somehow got known at school, and as it was an unprecedented fact, I was nicknamed 'Gas'. I was also once publicly rebuked by the headmaster, Dr Butler, for thus wasting my time on useless subjects.[1]

By 'useless' Butler did not, of course, mean that chemistry possessed no utilitarian value; on the contrary, to many public school men of the period chemistry was tainted as an educational subject by its commercial links. He meant simply that chemistry did not form a part of the liberal education that public schools were intended to provide.

The idea of a 'liberal education' was fundamental to much of the nineteenth-century discussion of school curricula. Although the exact implications of the term might differ considerably from one commentator to the next, there was general agreement that an education only qualified for the title 'liberal' if it developed all important aspects of the mind and the character. The significance of this concept for science teaching was that the sciences were commonly supposed to be of little value in the development of personality, whereas the traditional classical curriculum was regarded as nearly perfect. Whatever practical utility science might have, it could lay no claim to replace classics in the school curriculum.

This theme permeates much of the defence of the status quo throughout the nineteenth century. Thus a defender of the classical curriculum against the criticisms of the *Edinburgh Review* early in the century expostulated :

> Never let us believe that the improvement of chemical arts, however much it may tend to the augmentation of the national riches, can supersede the use of that intellectual laboratory, where the sages of Greece explored the hidden elements of which man consists and faithfully recorded all their discoveries.[2]

The same feelings were duplicated perfectly by Gladstone half a century later, when the classical curriculum was once more under attack from critics outside the system.

> What I feel is that the relation of pure science, natural science, modern languages, modern history, and the rest, to the old classical training, ought to be founded on a principle, and that these competing branches of instruction ought not to be treated simply as importunate creditors that take one shilling in the pound today because they hope to get another shilling tomorrow, and in the meantime have a recognition of their title. This recognition of title is just what I would refuse : I deny their right to a parallel or equal position; their true position is ancillary, and as ancillary it ought to be limited and restrained without scruple as much as a regard to the paramount matter of education may dictate.[3]

Curricular development in Victorian public schools can be viewed in one light as a record of the progress made in undermining the entrenched position of the classics. In this development the important advances occurred, as might be expected, far more readily when there were advocates of change within the system than when the pressures were entirely external. For example, the attacks by the *Edinburgh Review* mentioned above were largely ineffective since the reviewers tended to stand outside the English educational system as embodied in the public schools and universities.

It is therefore not surprising to find that the most significant change in public school curricula in the first half of the nineteenth century—the gradual extension of mathematics teaching—was stimulated by internal advocacy, notably at Cambridge. We may note that Whewell in the 1830s distinguished between permanent subjects (those with a static curriculum content) and progressive subjects (those where the content changed with time). He asserted that the former group—which consisted of classics *and* mathematics (i.e. Euclidean geometry)—provided a suitable basis for a liberal education, whereas the latter did not. Correspondingly, mathematics teaching at Eton can be said to have begun in 1836 when Stephen Hawtrey, a cousin of the then headmaster, was appointed to teach the subject.

The extent of this change must not be overemphasised. Mathematics at Eton was taken on a purely voluntary basis until the 1850s, and Hawtrey had to provide both the classroom and the assistant teachers out of his own pocket. Although defenders of the existing public school curriculum in the 1860s might speak of classics and mathematics where earlier they would usually have referred to classics alone, mathematics retained a markedly inferior position. This can be seen both in the number of hours per week devoted to it—usually three hours in school and about the same time in preparation during the 1860s—and in the small weight allotted to skill in mathematics in assessing a boy's ability. It was a common grouse of mathematics teachers at public schools that the form (or 'set') to which a boy belonged was determined almost entirely by how he performed in classics. As a result, the mathematical ability within a group might vary very considerably. This latter disadvantage existed not only in the older public schools but also in newer foundations such as Marlborough or Cheltenham. It is hardly surprising that when the Professor of Natural Philosophy at Oxford was asked his opinion of the mathematical attainments of public school entrants to Oxford, he replied: 'I do observe a very marked difference between young men coming to this University from the great public schools and from other schools or from private tutors, as to their mathematical attainments. The young men from public schools are far worse prepared.'[4]

Nevertheless, the acceptance of mathematics as a respectable ancillary subject for study in public schools did help pave the way for a new consideration of the claims of science. This arose partly from the existence of a breach in the classical facade; partly from the fact that mathematics in any case tended to overlap into physics; and partly it resulted from the appointment of mathematics teachers, some of whom were also interested in science. Thus at Eton, from 1849 onwards, the mathematics master, Hawtrey, put on courses of lectures in science. These were voluntary, given once a week only, and required the payment of special fees. But the lecturers were often eminent scientists, and it was possible to take a prize examination related to the course. By the early 1860s something like a hundred boys were attending the lectures.

This appearance of science in the Eton curriculum can hardly be called revolutionary : in the hierarchy of subjects it ranked somewhat below drawing. Yet Eton was ahead of Harrow, where no lectures were given and where the only encouragement consisted of a voluntary examination based on a set textbook. One of the masters at Harrow reported that he had known 'some boys get first in an examination after a couple of nights' hard reading'.[5] To see the public school attitude to the idea that science teaching should be taken seriously, we need only refer to the attempt to reform Winchester in the 1850s. The commissioners who were then investigating the college (in connection with their general inquiry concerning Oxford University) proposed that three of the fellowships should be set aside especially for physical scientists, only to be told by the Warden of Winchester (Dr Barter) that 'With respect to the proposal of devoting three of them to the promotion of physical science, we would only suggest the fear that first-rate men (and no others would, in the capacity of lecturers, be either for the honour or good of this College) would neither find sufficient employment nor enrolment.'[6]

The commissioners consequently enquired how the Warden proposed to provide competent and continuous instruction in physical science, and were assured that 'We would engage from time to time the best lecturers of the day in the various branches of such science, who should come to Winchester, and give our scholars successive courses of lectures.'[7] Doubtless glad to have this duty off their hands, the commissioners wrote back, warmly approving the Warden's suggestion—which amounted, in effect, to a more organised form of the practice at Eton.

The outcome was entirely predictable. When the Clarendon Commission examined the curriculum at Winchester in the early 1860s, it was noted that the science teaching

consisted simply in having a course of 10 or 12 lectures . . . on some branch of natural science delivered once a year in the summer. . . All the boys were required to attend, but it appears that attendance was not enforced very strictly. There have been no examinations, and no prizes or rewards for attention to, or proficiency in, the subject. We cannot refrain from observing that less could hardly have been done consistently with the narrowest and most literal interpretation of the Warden's letter.[8]

George Moberley, the headmaster who had been mainly responsible for the original idea of retaining occasional science lectures at Winchester, was quite unrepentant. The Clarendon Commissioners recorded his opinion that

For a school like Winchester, and taught in the only way which he thinks practicable at Winchester, it [science] is 'worthless'. Several of the boys, he admitted, derived much good from the lectures, and gained an interest in the subjects of them which outlasted the lectures themselves. But 'Except for those who have a taste for the physical sciences, and intend to pursue them as amateurs or professionally, such instruction', he repeats, 'is worthless as education'.[9]

The creation of the Clarendon Commission in the early 1860s was a reflection of a new wave of pressure to reform the public schools. It is on the attempts to change the public school curricula during this period—the 1860s and 1870s—that the present examination will concentrate, since the item heading the list for incorporation at this time was science. The headings under which the existing curriculum was attacked were much the same as in previous years. The standard criticism of narrowness and inefficiency can, for example, be found spelt out in Thackeray's apostrophe to the students of an agricultural college in Ireland during the early 1840s.

You are not fagged and flogged into Latin and Greek at the cost of two hundred pounds a year. Let these be the privileges of your youthful betters; meanwhile content yourselves with thinking that you *are* preparing for a profession while they are *not*; that you are learning something useful, while they, for the most part, are not: for after all, as a man grows old in the world, old and fat, cricket is discovered not to be any longer very advantageous to him—even to have pulled in the Trinity boat does not in old age amount to a substantial advantage; and though to read a Greek play be an immense pleasure, yet it must be confessed few enjoy it. . . Stout men in the bow-windows of clubs (for such young Etonians by time become) are not generally remarkable for a taste for Aeschylus.[10]

In fact, an inquiry into the courses of study at the older public schools was not the primary aim of the new commission—it was first and foremost concerned with their finance and administration—but there was an important reason why the curricula also needed scrutiny. As a result of reforms in the mid-1850s, entrance to the civil service and the army had come to be via competitive examinations. Although classics and mathematics counted for the most marks in these examinations, a fairly wide range of subjects, including the sciences, could be taken. For example, in the entrance examination for Sandhurst two science subjects—called the natural sciences and the experimental sciences—were available, and, together, they counted for two-thirds of the marks allotted to classics.

Hardly surprisingly, the teaching at the older public schools was found to be inadequate for these new, broader-based examinations. Attempts to remedy this deficiency met with variable success. Thus Eton established an 'army class' to provide the additional teaching required; however, both its prestige and its standards were low, and, according to a subsequent report, 'Boys who attended the class—most of them very young—were generally among the idlest in the school, and lost what interest they had previously taken in the regular work.'[11] This type of deficiency was much in the minds of reformers in the 1860s.

The attacks on public school curricula during the 1860s and 1870s concentrated on the lack of science for two main reasons—one negative, one positive. On the negative side, two subjects strongly advocated for inclusion earlier in the century—mathematics and modern languages—had by this time been incorporated in the curriculum, albeit very partially and incompletely. (The difficulties which beset the gradual rise of modern languages were, if anything, even greater than those which had accompanied the acceptance of mathematics.) Science seemed to many external observers to be the next subject on the list.

But more importantly, on the positive side, the scientists themselves were by the 1860s intellectually in the ascendant. It is, in fact, possible to discern at this time the formation of a scientific pressure group—men with roughly similar ideas on education, well acquainted with each other, whose voices were listened to not only by their fellow-scientists but also by a much wider public. One of the acknowledged leaders of this unofficial grouping was T.H. Huxley, whose views on the public school curriculum may be regarded as representative. These may be briefly summarised by his remark that the major public schools should 'be made to supply knowledge, as well as gentlemanly habits, a strong class feeling, and eminent proficiency in cricket'.[12] This was not far removed from Thackeray's earlier opinion; however, if the sentiments were similar, the attack was now pressed home in much greater depth.

We have seen that the theoretical bulwark of the public school curriculum was the concept of a liberal education. What happened during the 1860s was that the scientists began to argue more and more strongly that a classical education did not provide a full training for the mind : such a training could only be obtained by the inclusion of science. An exemplification of this point is provided by the account of Faraday's examination by Lord Clarendon, chairman of the Clarendon (Public Schools) Commission.

CLARENDON : You probably are aware that what our great public schools profess and aim at most is to give a good training to the mind, and it is there considered, perhaps, as you were saying just now, from habit and from prestige, that that is effectually done by the study of the classics and of pure mathematics, and that in that way they furnish the best training of the mind that can be given. Now I would ask you whether you think, supposing the training of the mind is the object of public schools, that that system of training the mind is complete which excludes physical science?[13]

Faraday replied without hesitation that he had found many of the best minds, educated at public schools, to be quite incapable of comprehending scientific matters. Clarendon now pressed him further:

> You would not consider that the minds of such men as you allude to, who have been highly trained and who have great literary proficiency, are in a state readily to receive such information as they are deficient in? You do not find any peculiar aptitude in those minds for grasping a new subject?
>
> FARADAY: I do not.

The issue here was, of course, whether or not learning was transferable. It had always been argued in favour of the classical curriculum that the intellectual skills it imparted could be used in other situations. But the scientists were now urging that, as far at least as their own subject was concerned, this was not true. No amount of classical study would assist in the acquisition of scientific knowledge. Study of science trained areas of the mind left untouched by the classics (or even by mathematics).

The arguments of the scientists clearly convinced the Clarendon Commissioners, as is evident from the section of their report dealing with science teaching.

> Natural science . . . is practically excluded from the education of the higher classes in England. Education with us is, in this respect, narrower than it was three centuries ago, whilst science has prodigiously extended her empire, has explored immense tracts, divided them into provinces, introduced into them order and method, and made them accessible to all. This exclusion is, in our view, a plain defect and a great practical evil. It narrows unduly and injuriously the mental training of the young, and the knowledge, interests, and pursuits of men in maturer life. . . It is perhaps the best corrective for that indolence which is the vice of half-awakened minds, and which shrinks from any exertion that is not, like an effort of memory, merely mechanical. With sincere respect for the opinions of the eminent Schoolmasters who differ from us in this matter, we are convinced that the introduction of the elements of natural science into the regular course of study is desirable, and we see no sufficient reason to doubt that it is practicable.[14]

Since the majority of leading Victorian scientists were not products of the public schools, and therefore stood outside the system, it might be expected that their arguments would have relatively little impact. While this is undoubtedly true to some extent, the situation is by no means so clear-cut. For during the 1860s some members of staff in the older public schools accepted part, or even all, of the scientists' case. They were not themselves outstanding scientists, indeed they might not be scientists at all in the sense of having carried out research work, but they had in one way or another—often by reading mathematics at university—developed an informal interest in the contemporary scientific scene, and they were frequently acquainted with members of the scientific pressure group. For example, F.W. Farrar at Harrow devoted a good deal of time in the mid-1860s to the advocacy of science teaching in public schools. In 1867 he edited an influential book, *Essays on a Liberal Education*, which attacked the current state of the curriculum in public schools. One of the essayists in this volume, E.E. Bowen, also at Harrow (and one of the three Fellows of the Royal Society on the staff at this time), was given the task two years later of organising a 'modern side' there. More significantly still, some of the emerging generation of headmasters—Henry Montague Butler at Harrow, Frederick Temple at Rugby, George Ridding at Winchester—were personally interested in science.

Thus, although much of the stimulus to curricular change in the 1860s came from outside the public schools, a good deal of the action was engendered internally. But a master who wished to introduce science teaching still faced considerable problems. Such difficulties were clearly apparent in the early career of J.M. Wilson (1836–1931), who was appointed to the staff at Rugby in 1859 and twenty years later became headmaster of Clifton. In terms of background, family connections, etc., Wilson was a fairly typical public school master, but his mathematical studies at Cambridge—he was a Senior Wrangler—had already led him to an interest in science. This interest was made use of at Rugby. Although he was primarily engaged to teach mathematics, it was also proposed that he should give occasional lectures in science to replace those formerly provided by itinerant lecturers. Initially these science lessons were given in the cloakroom of the town hall. (A new science laboratory was built

shortly afterwards, but it held too few boys to be of great use.)
Systematic teaching was almost impossible, since boys joined
and left each term, attendance was voluntary, and the time
available for science amounted to a couple of hours a week.

Nevertheless, Rugby was already ahead of the other major
public schools in at least two respects. In the first place, the
trustees were prepared to spend money on the development of
scientific facilities in the school; and secondly, Wilson took his
science teaching very seriously, consulting frequently with leading
scientists of the day (e.g. J.D. Hooker, P.G. Tait, A.W. William-
son). Despite these advantages, progress in the early years was
slow, and the Clarendon Commissioners felt bound to comment:
'It is impossible to feel that the immediate results are as yet quite
proportionate to the place which is now formally given to
the study [of natural science] in the arrangement of the School,
and to the expenditure which the Trustees have devoted to
it.'[15]

Wilson, however, was fortunate in his headmaster. With
Temple's agreement, the number of boys receiving some training
in science was increased during the 1860s, and subsequently the
facilities available for practical work were also extended. As a
result, Rugby by the 1870s was in high favour with the pro-
science lobby. Indeed, by this time Wilson himself had become
a highly regarded member of the pressure group. It is a noticeable feature of the Victorian period that, because the number of
public school teachers interested in science was small and their
calibre high, they could mix freely with scientists of all degrees
of eminence. For the same reason, science teaching in public
schools, if minimal in quantity and hampered by restrictions,
could yet be of high quality. As Wilson remarked to his friend
John Tyndall: 'At present science is only taught by clever and
enthusiastic men, who could teach anything. But when it is
taught by everybody there will be another story.'[16]

Wilson's work at Rugby led him to become regarded as the
leading expert on science teaching in public schools: he appeared,
for example, as a witness before both the Clarendon Commission
in the early 1860s and the Commission on Scientific Instruction
(the Devonshire Commission) in the early 1870s. Indeed, the
latter commission incorporated his ideas into the part of their
report headed 'Opinions in favour of the Teaching of Science in

12   Malvern College Artillery Cadet Corps, about 1900.

13   Sherborne Cadet Corps in Camp, Aldershot, 1906.

14 'The Last of the Squirrel Hunters'. This illustration is from a history of Marlborough published in 1893.

Public and Endowed Schools'. A summary of Wilson's views thus provides a reasonable indication of the main arguments that were pressed upon the public schools during the 1860s and 1870s. They can be grouped together in the following way.

(1) The traditional classical curriculum did not provide all that was needed educationally. Despite the time and energy devoted to the teaching of Greek and Latin, it could not be denied that many boys were still mainly ignorant of these subjects when they left public school. Different types of mind were attracted to different subjects: science might have a strong appeal for those boys who were not attracted by the classics.

(2) The experiences of the best schools abroad indicated that a broader curriculum produced better-educated people.

(3) Science had its own contribution to make to the development of the mind: it stimulated the curiosity. Wilson claimed that science therefore led towards self-education in later life. Nor was this the only new contribution it made to the curriculum; its emphasis on exact knowledge introduced another element not provided by classical studies.

(4) Science had an immediate practical value, not only in the obvious sense that it could be of use in a future career, but also in the sense that it led to lofty ideas of the universe and so supported religious belief. This final point was the only one which the scientific pressure group of the time would not have supported unanimously. Huxley or Tyndall would have agreed that a study of science induced lofty ideas, but would have denied that these supported any religious belief. However, they were in this respect not altogether typical of their peers: a large number of working scientists in the 1860s agreed with Wilson. Certainly the close connection between the public schools and the Church implied that most scientific sympathisers on the staff of public schools agreed with him. Wilson himself took holy orders in 1879 and later became a canon of Worcester cathedral, while his mentor of the 1860s, Temple, who held similar views on the connection between religion and science, eventually went on to become Archbishop of Canterbury.

If Wilson was able, as an 'insider', to discern the most telling points in support of science teaching at public schools, he was necessarily also aware of the practical objections raised by defenders of the status quo. We can extract from his writings

H

four themes that were frequently pressed against the introduction of science.

(1) The lack of encouragement to curricular change offered by Oxford and Cambridge.

(2) The difficulty of obtaining suitable science teachers.

(3) The expense of teaching science.

(4) The difficulty of finding time for the study of science within the existing curriculum.

Of these, the most important was certainly the first. It was acknowledged, even by the scientific pressure group, that a clear move towards science on the part of the ancient universities would be more likely to produce a shift in the same direction in public schools than would any other single action. In 1867, when members of the group were drafting a report for the British Association on science teaching, they agreed to stress that 'Schools are so much influenced by the Universities that reform in the subjects of teaching at schools must come from above.'[17] (Huxley actually objected to this draft statement—but on the grounds that it appeared to have a theological connotation.) The importance of establishing this base in the universities is reflected in the acceptance of mathematics by the public schools. As the report of the Clarendon Commission pointed out, 'Mathematics at least have established a title to respect as an instrument of mental discipline; they are recognised and honoured at the Universities, and it is easy to obtain Mathematical Masters of high ability who have had a University education.'[18]

Both Oxford and Cambridge, as part of their reforms in the early 1850s, had introduced the possibility of taking examinations in natural science. Initially, these were hedged around with so many restrictions that their practical significance was very limited. But gradually, as the century progressed, the position of science teaching in the two universities became more secure, and their science professors felt able to stress the educational value of their subject more strongly. An interesting illustration of this occurred at Oxford in the 1880s. By then some chemists were beginning to claim that their own subject was as capable of laying the foundations of a liberal education as classics. It was proposed that prospective chemists might be allowed into Oxford without a knowledge of Greek, but the Professor of Chemistry refused to endorse the scheme until the university as a whole publicly admitted that a complete liberal education could be obtained without studying Greek. Such agreement was not, in fact, forthcoming until the twentieth century; but even at that early date it was clearly felt by the chemists to be purely a matter of time.

The delay in instituting science courses at university level was directly responsible for the second of the practical objections raised—the lack of suitable science teachers. In this respect, as the Clarendon Report had indicated, science compared very unfavourably with mathematics, whose early acceptance in the universities had led to the production of a sufficient number of potential mathematics teachers. To be suitable for employment in a public school, a master was expected to have been educated at Oxford or Cambridge, and, often, to have been at a public school himself. These requirements drastically limited the number of potential science teachers until late in the nineteenth century. The opinion of one headmaster, quoted by the Devonshire Commission, illustrates this attitude exactly.

> I do not think I could improve upon the teachers who might be selected from Oxford and Cambridge. . . I would here observe that a mere chemist, geologist, or naturalist, however eminent in his own special department, would hardly be able to take his place among a body of masters composed of University men, without some injurious effect upon the position which science ought to occupy in the school. . . In preferring the two older Universities, I do so only by reason of their stronger general sympathies with public school teaching. I am aware that, if I merely wanted a high scientific man in any branch, I might find him equally at Dublin, London, or a Scotch University.[19]

Equally, the average public school master did not wish to change his main teaching interest and take up science teaching, though, as has been shown, some mathematics teachers were prepared to do so. Not only was there the difficulty of learning a new subject, but also the educational background of most public school masters was naturally such as to make them doubt the value of science teaching. The Clarendon Report also emphasised this aspect. 'School education alters slowly, and runs long in the same groove; a master can only teach what he has himself learnt, and he is naturally inclined to set the highest value on the studies to which his own life has been given.'[20] It is certainly noticeable that opinion against the introduction of science teaching was found to be strongest amongst the schoolteachers themselves, both by the Clarendon Commission and the subsequent Taunton Commission. (We may note in passing that the use of mathematics masters to teach science was not always an unmitigated blessing. Mathematics teaching in England, especially in schools, had become excessively formalised by the latter part of the nineteenth century. Some of this formalism rubbed off on to the science teaching, so that, for example, some schools concentrated on the more boring aspects of physics, whereas Wilson had found that boys responded best to botany, geology and astronomy.)

During the 1860s schools also had the problem of finding suitable science textbooks for use in class; for this was an area of publishing where previously there had been no demand. However, during the decade this deficiency was noted by the group of scientists who were pressing for an increase in science teaching. More particularly, Alexander Macmillan, who was closely involved with Huxley and his fellow-scientists, recognised this as an area of need, and commissioned some of the leading scientists of the day to write elementary science texts. Consequently, by the early 1870s, up-to-date and readable school science books were becoming available. The Devonshire Report analysed the science books in use at a number of public and endowed schools and found that many were already employing Macmillan's new textbooks (some of which, incidentally, were written by scientists involved in the work of the Devonshire Commission itself).

The third main objection to the introduction of science teaching in public schools was the question of its cost. This, too, was investigated in some detail by the Devonshire Commission. They concluded that although considerable sums of money could certainly be spent on the construction of suitable laboratories and lecture theatres, it was not essential to do so : ordinary buildings could be adapted for the purpose at relatively little cost. Furthermore, the running expenses of laboratories could be kept reasonably low : thus Manchester Grammar School, which placed considerable emphasis on the teaching of science, spent only £100 per annum on such expenses. The report concluded that most probably 'science can be introduced at one-tenth of the cost which is usually supposed to be that which is absolutely essential'.[21] In any case, the sums of money involved would hardly have embarrassed the older and wealthier foundations, which generally seem to have spent appreciably less than Manchester Grammar School.

The final practical objection concerned the difficulty of inserting science into the existing syllabus. The weight of this argument varied very considerably from school to school. Contemporary opinion agreed that some schools had a crowded, even an overcrowded, curriculum. This was especially true of the ones which prepared a large proportion of their boys for the civil service or army examinations. The following *cri de coeur* came from Marlborough in the early 1870s.

> The boys' time is already absorbed by studies which have of late years been largely multiplied, and which in most cases they know to be essential to their future prospects in life, seeing that most of them will have to be examined in all those subjects. It is not merely a question of the time taken up by the other subjects; the boys are absolutely distracted by them, and cannot approach a new subject, and especially such a new subject as Science, with that undivided attention which is absolutely necessary, if any advance is to be made in it.[22]

Most critics of public schools, including the members of the scientific pressure group, agreed that there was not a great deal of room to insert much science into the Marlborough curriculum. But then, most of them were not asking for a great deal: a typical figure they might have in mind was three or four hours per week. In any case, the argument of an overcrowded curriculum could hardly be advanced by the older public schools, which formed the main target for attack. We may compare in this regard the moderately sympathetic attitude of the Devonshire Report towards the problems of Marlborough with the following comments of the Clarendon Commission on the older foundations.

> It may, perhaps, be objected that there is not time for such a course of study as we have described, and that it could not be attempted without injury to classics; that the working hours are already long enough; that not more than a certain quantity

of work can be put into a certain number of hours, and that a boy's head will not hold more than a certain quantity of knowledge. It is not, of course, a conclusive answer to this objection that it has been urged before against changes which have been made, and made successfully. Until a few years ago, there was no time for mathematics. . . Yet scholarship is none the worse, and general education is much the better, for the introduction of mathematics. . . There would be reason therefore to distrust the objection, had we no other means of judging of it. But we are persuaded that by effective teaching time can be found for these things. ₂ . We are satisfied that of the time spent at school by nine boys out of ten much is wasted, which it is quite possible to economise. . . The great difficulty of a public school, as every master knows, is simple idleness, which is defended by numbers and entrenched behind the system and traditions of the place, and against which, if he be active, he wages a more or less unequal war.[23]

Following the reports of the Clarendon and the Taunton Commissions, the Public Schools Act of 1868 and the Endowed Schools Act of 1869 appointed special commissioners to examine and, where necessary, change the statutes and the governing bodies of the schools concerned. The former act, in particular, was bitterly opposed in the House of Lords, one of the points at issue being the question of science teaching at public schools. The opposition was to some extent successful; the activities of the commissioners were more restricted than the supporters of science teaching had hoped. Nevertheless, the special commissioners appointed under the 1868 act proceeded to insist that the older public schools should build laboratories and should also appoint at least one science master for every two hundred boys.

It thus appeared that the efforts of the scientific pressure group were beginning to pay off : the public schools were officially committed to the teaching of science (including practical work), and such teaching had acquired some influential advocates within the public schools themselves. Yet when the Devonshire Commissioners published their survey of public and endowed schools in 1875, they concluded that

The Evidence thus placed before us conclusively proves that in

our Public and Endowed Schools, Science is as yet very far
from receiving the attention to which, in our opinion, it is
entitled. For instance, the Returns furnished to us show that,
even where Science is taught, from one to two hours' work
per week may be regarded, with very few exceptions, as the
usual time given to it in such Classes as receive Scientific
Instruction at all. Moreover, the Instruction in Science is
generally confined to certain classes of the School.

Among the 128 Endowed Schools from which we have
received returns, Science is taught in only 63, and of these
only 13 have a Laboratory, and only 18 Apparatus, often very
scanty.[24]

Why was so little progress being made? The Devonshire Commissioners considered the various practical difficulties we have
discussed above, but evidently believed that in many instances
these merely concealed a basic reluctance on the part of the
schools to countenance science teaching. The main conclusion
of the report made dismal reading for scientists.

On a review of the present state of the Public and Endowed
Schools, it appears to us that though some progress has no
doubt been achieved, and though there are some exceptional
cases of great improvement, still no adequate effort has been
made to supply the deficiency of Scientific Instruction pointed
out by the Commissioners of 1861 and 1864. We are com-
pelled, therefore, to record our opinion that the Present State
of Scientific Instruction in our schools is extremely unsatis-
factory. The omission from a Liberal Education of a great
branch of the Intellectual Culture is of itself a matter for serious
regret; and, considering the increasing importance of Science
to the Material Interests of the Country, we cannot but regard
its almost total exclusion from the training of the upper and
middle classes as little less than a national misfortune.[25]

This lack of progress was not simply a delay in implementing
the recommendations of the 1860s, for, despite the additional
pleas of the Devonshire Commission, no really fundamental
progress in the position of science teaching in public schools took
place throughout the remainder of the nineteenth century. Of
course, individual advances did occur during these decades. We

might, for example, note the emphasis Thring at Uppingham came to place on practical science, and the similar interest of Sanderson at Oundle a little later. But these were isolated instances; moreover, the emphasis was developed in each case purely as a means of moulding a particular aspect of the boys' character, rather than for the sake of the subject-matter itself. The advocates of science teaching continued their campaign throughout this period, and helped achieve a noticeable improvement in the amount and standard of science teaching throughout the school system as a whole by the end of the Victorian era. But the main peaks of this achievement, such as the Technical Instruction Act of 1889, exerted little or no influence on the public schools. On the other hand, in the realm of mathematics teaching, public school masters played a predominant and creative role in the Association for the Improvement of Geometrical Teaching (later the Mathematical Association), which 'modernised' Euclid and injected algebra and trigonometry into syllabuses.

If, then, the practical objections raised to science teaching in public schools were not, except in a few instances, genuine deterrents, how can the reluctance of the public schools to incorporate science teaching be explained? Why was their inertia so great, faced as they were with pressure from the intellectual community (not only scientists), from Royal Commissions, and from within their own fold?

There seem to be two points that were fundamental to this underdevelopment. The first was the lack of pressure on public schools in favour of science from their ultimate constituency— the fee-paying parents. This appears with particular clarity in the evidence submitted to the Devonshire Commission. One of the questions headmasters were asked was : What departments of science are preferred by parents? A typical answer (from Rossall School) was : 'Parents exhibit complete indifference to the whole subject, with the exception that they occasionally object to their sons devoting any time at all to it.'[26] This parental indifference stemmed partly from snobbery (the 'science-is-for-tradesmen' attitude) and partly from a lack of any obvious urgent need for science in their children's careers. (Even by the end of Wilson's stay at Rugby, probably less than ten per cent of the boys could be said to have required any knowledge of science for their future careers.)

But fundamentally the indifference went a good deal deeper than this, and reflects what may perhaps be counted the basic reason for the public school attitude to science. All those who argued in favour of science teaching stressed its intellectual and utilitarian value. But the opponents of science teaching were generally talking of character building and the inculcation of moral behaviour. As a result, the two groups were as often talking past each other as at each other. Howard Staunton, in one of the more substantial books concerning public schools written in the Victorian age, explained to his readers:

> They [the public schools] are the theatres of athletic manners, and the training places of a gallant, generous spirit for the English gentleman. This is the highest merit claimed for them by the warmest and most discerning of their admirers. England will, doubtless, in due time succeed in creating institutions aiming mainly at stimulating and storing the mind; but by no process of transfiguration are the great Endowed Schools likely to be rendered institutions of this stamp.[27]

The same public school spirit was casually adverted to by the Clarendon Commissioners when discussing the introduction of new subjects into the curriculum.

> It is not easy to win steady attention from a high-spirited English lad, who has the restless activity and love of play that belong to youth and health, who, like his elders, thinks somewhat slowly, and does not express himself readily, and to whom mental effort is troublesome.[28]

To people raised in this sort of tradition, the joys of science, as described by its supporters, were not only for the most part unattractive : they were positively repulsive. Science was necessarily divorced from humanity. It neither fostered 'athletic manners', nor inculcated 'a gallant, generous spirit for the English gentleman'. What, then, was its *raison d'être* in the public school curriculum? Even Temple, despite his sympathy for science, felt bound to stress the point to the Clarendon Commissioners :

> The real defect of mathematics and physical science as instruments of education is that they have not any tendency to humanise. Such studies do not make a man more human, but simply more intelligent.[29]

So long as John Bull remained the model for the British public school boy, any subject that merely made him more intelligent had little hope of making headway. Real progress in the teaching of science in public schools had to await the twentieth century.

The Ideal of Manliness

Norman Vance

'THERE is a manliness which is identical with virtue; and there
is—as usual—a certain spurious semblance of manliness—the
Devil's counterfeit of it—which I call mannishness.'[1] The headmaster of Marlborough, writing in 1874, was fully aware of the
ambiguity of manliness. It was a concept that was always changing in the Victorian public school; its history is, in a sense, the
history of the age.

What kinds of manliness would a Victorian schoolmaster or
schoolboy have in mind? We can probably distinguish at least
four basic types : the chivalric, the sentimental-benevolent, the
sturdy English, and the moral.

The chivalric ideal of courage, loyalty, self-sacrifice, stainless
integrity and protection of the weak, was the medieval ideal of
manliness. It has been argued that this stemmed from an attempt
to make nobility of deeds match nobility of birth, or even take
its place. In *The Romance of the Rose* 'Nature' is, in a way,
spokesman for this tendency when she insists that 'gentility of
lineage is valueless when it lacks goodness of heart'.[2] Chivalry
reappears in many guises in the Victorian era, following in the
wake of medieval popularisers such as Sir Walter Scott, author
of *Ivanhoe* and *Quentin Durward*, and Kenelm Digby, who
entered a plea for a new knightliness in *The Broad Stone of
Honour* (1822). In an industrial age, when power and wealth
were passing more and more into the hands of the middle classes,
the debate between intrinsic and merely inherited nobility was
again relevant. Disraeli's wealthy bourgeois Millbank wins
through to a true nobility as well as the aristocratic Coningsby.
In *Sir Percival* (1886) J.H. Shorthouse, a Birmingham manu-
facturer, sought to recall the religious idealism of Arthurian
chivalry in an increasingly agnostic age. In *A Knight of the*

Nineteenth Century (1877) the Rev. E.P. Roe was using a familiar rhetoric when he detailed the moral redemption of an over-indulged young man in terms of a rise to knightliness. The *Saturday Review*, in its obituary of the solid but rather unromantic Prince Consort, spoke up boldly for the new bourgeois chivalry: Albert was an example of honour and manly virtue, prominent in

> all those benevolent enterprises for the relief of misery, and for improving the lot and character of the people, which are the prosaic but solid substitutes for the visionary enterprises of knight-errantry in forming the character of a gentleman at the present day.

Albert's achievement was, in fact, mainly as a benefactor, and this calls to mind the second kind of manliness historically available to the Victorians. The latitudinarian divines had claimed that man had a hope of perfection, and that his endeavour should be directed towards the practice of loving his neighbour and generally improving society. Isaac Barrow claimed in a sermon that 'walking as Christ did' involved not monastic seclusion and asceticism but everyday acts of generosity and charity.[3] Richard Steele, best known for *The Spectator*, had shown the same practical attitude in *The Christian Hero* (1701), advocating works of charity supported by generous feeling in the face of the cold neo-Stoicism of his age. It was on this model that Fielding too had developed some of his most sympathetic characters, such as the kindly Allworthy in *Tom Jones* and Parson Adams in *Joseph Andrews*. In the same tradition, Henry Morland, in Henry Brooke's *The Fool of Quality* (1766–72), devoted himself to the poor and oppressed, animated by a 'passionate and tearful sensibility'.[4]

But Brooke's hero is a manly prototype not only for his benevolence but for his sturdiness—the third kind of manliness I have identified. Neglected by his noble parents, he finds his own recreation wrestling with pigs and boxing with village boys, so that he is neither 'physicked into delicacy, nor flattered into pride' by the effete fashionable society of the time. This shaggy manliness is part of the English national legend. It has many manifestations: archery on the village green, foot-races at fairtime, the gladiatorial football matches in Lakeland described by

Hugh Walpole, the vigorous cricket of the healthy country boys in Miss Mitford's *Our Village*. Wellington's supposed comment about Waterloo has immortalised the playing fields of Eton, but even before this, in the Peninsular War, he upheld the manly English sporting character by bringing out his foxhounds and hunting behind the lines of Torres Vedras during lulls in the fighting. Popular works such as Pierce Egan's *Boxiana* (1818–24) and *Book of Sports* (1832) and R.S. Surtees's memoirs of a sporting grocer, *Jorrocks' Jaunts and Jollities* (1838), were available to remind the English public of Victorian times of their manly heritage.

Unfortunately, this kind of manliness was at times questionably moral, associated as it was with violence, gambling, intemperance and other forms of dissolute behaviour. Maria Edgeworth, whose educational children's stories were popular in the Victorian nursery long after her death, insisted on the distinction between manly exercises and achievements and manly character. There was a place for the former : in *Frank* (1822) it is agreed that Frank must go to school to be 'roughed about among boys, or he will never learn to be a man, and able to live among men', and physical courage and strength are encouraged by pursuits such as riding. But sturdy moral qualities are required as well to produce a manly character : Frank must show strength of mind, persistence, fearless truthfulness and consideration for others.

Under the influence of the Evangelical revival, moral manliness became a common subject of discussion.[5] The man who became a new creature in Christ was more truly a man, it was claimed, and true manliness became the description of his moral character. The virtues of the chivalric and sentimental ideals were often incorporated in this rather more severe conception, while the qualities and vocabulary of the unregenerate sturdy manliness were a rich source of metaphor and analogy. It was a favourite preacher's trick to emphasise the close connection between 'virtue' and *vir* ('man'). Many school sermons were to stress the message and example of St Paul, who had talked of running the race with patience and fighting the good fight of faith and who could therefore be regarded as the prophet of manly Christianity.

How were these different concepts of manliness reflected in the ideal of manliness in the Victorian public school? This was something the Clarendon Commissioners were aware of when they reported on the nine 'great schools' in 1864. They were convinced that the public school system fostered high standards of manliness and gentlemanly conduct, and to this they attributed the greatly improved moral standards at the universities. Their definition of manliness appeared to be 'manly virtue', though the term came to denote much else in the schools, and they gave full credit for the spread of this admirable quality to the great schoolmasters, especially Arnold of Rugby.[6]

Arnold was the greatest exponent of moral manliness. He used the rhetoric of sturdy manliness and of chivalry like his contemporaries, but his ideal was more generous than the meagre pietism offered by some of his Evangelical fellow-clergymen. It owed something to the religious speculations of the poet Coleridge, whom Arnold greatly admired. In *Aids to Reflection* (1825) Coleridge rejected the sentimental benevolence of the eighteenth century as shallow emotionalism, an inadequate style of manliness. In its place he insisted on the moral life dictated by the Divine Reason linking God and man through the Divine Logos. This developed a

> manhood or manliness, strength of character in relation to the Dictates of Reason; Energy of Will in preserving the Line of Rectitude tense and firm against the warping forces and treacheries of temptation.[7]

In Arnold's case some have argued the line of rectitude became a tightrope. Certainly Stanley, his biographer, gives his hero an almost mythical status as an embodiment of terrible righteousness.

> That ashy paleness and that awful frown were almost always the expression . . . of deep, ineffable scorn and indignation at the sight of vice and sin.[8]

But although Arnold insisted that manliness was moral maturity, he was a more liberal schoolmaster than is generally believed. He realised that moral earnestness was not to be achieved through cloistered virtue fostered by rigid supervision. He may have agreed with the exaggerated opinion of John Bowdler,[9] that 'Public Schools are the very seats and nurseries of vice', but his policy for changing this was to try to foster self-respect among the boys by showing them respect. They should be treated as gentlemen and rational beings, he maintained, and trusted to do as much as possible for themselves. The severest punishments at Rugby were for breaches of trust, such as a lie to a master. This attitude was reflected in Arnold's teaching methods : he imparted little direct information, except as a reward for an intelligent answer, preferring to let a boy's own interest prompt him to find out for himself and to formulate his own opinion. In the same way, discipline was administered largely by the boys themselves, through the praepostors, in whom Arnold placed implicit trust. He has been accused of overstraining his best pupils, making them men before their time, and this is probably true in the case of gifted individuals such as Clough, but he was anxious to anticipate 'the common progress of Christian manliness' by encouraging self-reliance and unselfishness as opposed to childish dependency and thoughtlessness. If a boy failed to grow out of this moral childishness he was regarded as unfit for public school life and was recommended for removal from Rugby.[10]

Ironically, Arnold's chief problem at Rugby was partly the result of his policy of trusting the boys with a measure of independence. His greatest enemy was 'the spirit of combination in evil within the school'. Schoolboy society, left largely to its own devices, had its own pursuits and enthusiasms, its own games and its own code of values, which remained largely impervious to the higher morality he was trying to foster. The sturdy, rough-and-tumble manliness of the games-field and the poaching expeditions could easily lend itself to the 'lawless tyranny of physical strength', and its conformity to schoolboy tradition rather than the example of Christ distressed him deeply. For him, the manly hero was not the athletic champion, as it would be for the boys, but he who 'struggled against the stream of school opinion' in the interests of truth and right. Arnold would watch the boys' games from the sidelines, and he conceded that they had an important auxiliary role in the school in developing physical health and strength to enable the boys' minds to function properly, but his ideal of manliness owed little to the games-field.[11]

The same could be said for Dean Farrar, author of the immensely popular *Eric, or Little by Little*, whose ideas to some

extent reflected Arnold's and whose dictum on manliness was
quoted at the beginning of this chapter. For many years an assistant master at Harrow, and later headmaster of Marlborough,
Farrar had little real interest in sport, though he was prepared
to be tolerant since the boys enjoyed it. His school novels acknowledged physical courage as a value : Eric risks his life to save a
friend marooned on a sea-stack, and Walter Evson, hero of *St
Winifred's, or The World of School* (1862), traverses a perilous
mountain path in thick mist to fetch help for his companions.
But moral courage is shown to be far more important. Farrar's
public school heroes achieve manliness in the resolute pursuit of
righteousness in the face of temptation and unpopularity, manifesting the 'courage which braves opinion in the cause of right'.
Arnold would have made boys of this quality his praepostors.
But Eric's moral development is rather uncertain, and this gives
Farrar's novel the bizarre excitement of a spiritual cliff-hanger :
'Now Eric, now nor never ! Life and death, ruin and salvation,
corruption and purity, are perhaps in the balance together.' This
florid style could easily adapt the rhetoric of militarism and
chivalric idealism for moral purposes : Farrar constantly
reminded his pupils in the school chapel that there was 'no dis-
charge in the War Against Sin', and tried to kindle their enthusiasm by constant reference to Christian heroes who 'into the next
age, if not into their own . . . flash an epidemic of nobleness'.
This appeal to the hero-worshipping instinct was both understandable and politic in an age which was still hearing Thomas
Carlyle trumpet forth the supreme significance of great men in
the history of the world.[12]

But Thomas Hughes, whom Carlyle wakened to an energetic
sense of social responsibility, combined manliness and hero-
worship in the public school more acceptably in *Tom Brown's
Schooldays* than Farrar managed in the strained moralism of
Eric. Hughes made his work a best-seller by relating his preaching much more directly to the sturdy variety of manliness, which
was certain to make interesting reading. Hughes had been a
pupil of Arnold's and later became his great populariser, but
David Newsome is right in saying that *Eric* is closer to the spirit
of Arnold than *Tom Brown*.[13] Yet *Tom Brown's Schooldays* is
characterised by a sort of demotic Arnoldianism. The ideal of
the English Christian gentleman is equally present to Squire

Brown and Thomas Arnold, though it is not expressed in the same way. But for Hughes the moral earnestness of the Doctor is best blended with the more palatable sporting manliness, the common theme of Tom's early experience of Berkshire games and pastimes, and football and cricket at Rugby. Hughes is conscious of the wicked spirit of combination in the school just as Arnold was; he tries (unsuccessfully, perhaps) to bridge the two moralities—the discrete worlds of sturdy schoolboy life as he remembered it, and Arnoldian moral earnestness as it appeared to his more mature awareness. Arthur, the moral focus of the book, comes perilously close to a pious milksop and is not redeemed by being put in the eleven for Tom Brown's last match. Old Brooke tries to tell the school that iniquitous school custom and tradition should yield to Arnold's reforming zeal, but even the bombast of house-match enthusiasm with which he indulges his audience fails to get the message across. Brooke is an athletic hero as well as a moral hero trying to resist the evil of school custom, and Tom Brown, from the moment he protects Arthur at his prayers, follows in his footsteps. But the very enthusiasm with which Hughes describes the games and boisterous unofficial activities of the boys undermines the fragile synthesis of sturdy manliness and Christian morality, because the inevitably sober sermonising jars with the lively tone of the rest of the book.

Thomas Hughes has been made the prophet and high-priest of the games cult which swept the later Victorian public schools. The empty catch-phrase 'muscular Christianity' used by his early reviewers[14] was sometimes applied to this later development; often it had little to do with Hughes, and even less to do with Christianity. Hughes and his friend Kingsley, whose novels were popular reading among schoolboys in the 1860s and long after, preached a Christian manliness which gave full and enthusiastic recognition to the physical in man. But this was part of a wider theological perspective, owing much to F.D. Maurice, in which the things of the present world, the ordinary affairs of men and the appalling social evils of the time were the proper sphere of man's God-given responsibility. Manliness was not simply game-playing: it had affinities with Plato's notion of *thumos gennaios*,[15] 'spirited nobility'—the sublimation of passion and energy in a righteous vehemence directed against wickedness

I

and injustice, both in the individual and in society. Unfortunately, the more adult aspects of this concept of manliness, spelt out in more detail in *Tom Brown at Oxford*, were less easily assimilated by posterity. *Tom Brown's Schooldays* virtually founded a genre of juvenile literature. The book's popularity lay in its muscularity rather than its morality, and thus the school-story modelled on it both reflected and encouraged an ever-increasing tendency to glorify school games.

How did the 'games cult' develop? The Clarendon Commission found plenty of evidence in 1862 that games were popular. This was, of course, a perfectly natural phenomenon. Games were usually organised by the boys themselves (though masters occasionally participated) and were a voluntary, unofficial recreation. But the Rev. C.O. Goodford, provost of Eton, sounded a prophetic note of warning. There were professional games coaches available at Eton to give instruction to any boy who wanted it, and Goodford was uneasy about it: under their régime games were becoming a science rather than a recreation, and they were taking up so much time that some enthusiasts who also showed intellectual promise were falling behind in their academic work. The popularity of athletic heroes in the school, which Hughes had made use of in his novel, could also be a source of irritation to some of the masters. Oscar Browning, later to become a noted educational reformer, resented the fact that intellectual distinction alone no longer gave a boy much influence in the school. He came to regard the 'rising tide of Philistine athleticism' as disastrous for the school and the country.[16] R.A.H. Mitchell, who had captained the Oxford eleven for three successive seasons, was largely responsible for creeping athleticism at Eton, because for perhaps the first time the natural interest of the boys was shared and stimulated by an infectiously enthusiastic master who was not afraid to proselytise. At Harrow also there was a keen athletic spirit in the 1860s, with some sort of official support: it was one of the few schools of the time with compulsory games.

The ideal of manliness took a new turning, and perhaps not for the better, when Edward Warre, another sporting master at Eton who later became headmaster, tried to rationalise and justify his enthusiasm to the Clarendon Commissioners. Eton games were, he claimed, morally beneficial in that they provided a healthy antidote to vice and extravagant luxury, and kept idlers away from sloth and temptation. Manliness was moving from the chapel to the changing-room, and *Tom Brown* was only one factor in the transition. The freedom which Arnold had preserved for his pupils was now considered dangerous. Charles Wordsworth, nephew of the poet, himself a distinguished athlete and schoolmaster, had claimed that 'An idle body is a house swept and garnished for the indwelling of an unclean spirit,'[17] and had recommended compulsory games as an obvious solution to this problem. What had been a pleasure and a relaxation now tended to become an instrument of official policy in the schools, and a nightmare for the unathletic.

From the mid-nineteenth century athleticism spiralled to prominence.[18] The universities had always provided ample opportunity for developing sporting interests, and in the 1850s and 1860s it was easy for athletic Etonians and Harrovians to communicate their enthusiasm to other undergraduates, to the disgust of serious-minded dons like Mark Pattison, Rector of Lincoln College, Oxford. On going down, university graduates were able in their turn to diffuse this mounting enthusiasm in the various schools where many of them found masterships. And there was an increasing demand for organised games in the schools. Established schools were discovering that official sport was an efficient and generally popular way of keeping boys out of mischief, and the newer public schools, founded to educate the increasingly important middle classes, were often anxious to establish themselves on a sound footing by performing well in the new inter-school championships. The same opportunism was sometimes evident in the universities. E.S. Talbot, first Warden of Keble, helped cement the myth of muscular Christianity : the new college's associations with the Oxford Movement and its continuation gave it an ecclesiastical complexion, while Talbot ensured its rise to acceptance in the university and the country by developing its sporting reputation. St Edmund Hall, which was late in acquiring full collegiate status, has seen a similar development in the present century.

Parents often encouraged the schools to concentrate more on games than all the masters might have wished. The sons of newly rich manufacturers might well be sent to the public schools in the hope that they would rise into the ranks of the gentry, and if they could not distinguish themselves academically they could be put under considerable pressure to achieve eminence on the sportsfield. G.E.L. Cotton, one of Arnold's assistants, had no particular interest in games himself. But in 1852 he went to be headmaster of Marlborough, a school of recent foundation which had got off to a disastrous start. He was pragmatist enough to realise that the official institution of a great sporting tradition would materially help to reduce indiscipline and occupy spare time and energy that might otherwise be devoted to lawlessness, or even to plotting rebellions such as the one his predecessor had faced.

Edward Thring, headmaster of Uppingham and founder of the Headmasters' Conference, was another who was prepared to use the current enthusiasm for games as a method of building up a decayed school and bringing unruly energies under control. He refused, however, to go the way of other headmasters along the line of least resistance. He held out against the appointment of a cricket professional for as long as he could, and he would not countenance the reform of the old Uppingham football game so that the school could enter for the inter-school rugby competitions. Even so, the games cult gradually took hold of the school. Cormac Rigby, in his unpublished study of Thring, has even suggested that if this had not been disrupted when cholera in the town forced Thring to evacuate the whole school, there was some danger that Uppingham would have slipped from his control into the hands of the philistines and athletes and would have slumped to the level of a second-rate tuft-hunting academy.

More and more, manliness declined from the moral strenuousness of Arnold's conception and approximated to the cult of the physical. This was not always simple athleticism. H.H. Almond, headmaster of Loretto in Midlothian, was chiefly interested in moral and physical health : he inaugurated a 'Sparto-Christian' ideal of temperance, courage and *esprit de corps* supported by a regiment of all-weather exercise, cleanliness, comfortably informal dress, and fresh air. Like many later Victorian headmasters, he had read Herbert Spencer's popular works on education and wholeheartedly agreed with him that it was absurd that men should try to breed fine bullocks and horses but have no interest in raising fine men. The effect, though not the chief object, of this endeavour was a phenomenal run of athletic success in inter-school competitions, and between 1880 and 1890 there were usually at least three of his former pupils playing football for Oxford or Cambridge. By these means Loretto acquired the status of an English public school, and sturdy sporting manliness, with a simple morality attached, was transplanted to the rather alien soil of the Scottish lowlands from the games-fields of the Sassenach.[19]

Almond was quick to point out the moral value of games, and so did many other apologists of sport. In particular, the old spirit of combination which had baffled Arnold could be transformed into team spirit and a corporate enthusiasm for the athletic fortunes of the school in which both boys and masters were actively involved. There were voices raised in protest: Matthew Arnold inveighed against sporting barbarism in the schools, deeming it a threat to culture, and Wilkie Collins protested against athleticism in his novel *Man and Wife* (1870) by representing a so-called muscular Christian athlete as a savage brute and a murderer. The defence—which becomes tediously familiar—was that athletic manliness was in fact morally valuable, though to what extent always remained a moot point. A writer in the *Journal of Education* (1884) claimed that the delight of exercise and the glory of play submerged tensions and hostilities at school, developed dignity, courtesy and the spirit of brotherhood and co-operation. In this activity, he claimed, one had a glimpse of one side of the highest good: 'There lives more soul in honest play, believe me, than in half the hymnbooks.'[20]

The same writer also claimed that part of the fascination of games was the simple aesthetic pleasure of watching a beautiful run at football. As agnosticism and aestheticism began to supplant theology and moralism in the latter part of the century, so did the so-called muscular Christianity yield a little to muscular Hellenism. Goldsworthy Lowes Dickinson was one of the most eloquent Hellenisers: in *The Greek View of Life* (1896) he epitomised the new attitude when he indicated his admiration for the Greek ideal of the perfect soul imaged in the perfect body. Arnold once referred, rather casually, to Plato's ideal blend of gymnastic and music; later headmasters took it much more seriously. With a predominantly classical curriculum, boys and masters knew their Herodotus and would recall how Solon told Croesus that the happy man was 'whole of limb, a stranger to disease, free from misfortune";[21] they would also remember how the poet Simonides had extolled health and beauty as the highest good.

John Addington Symonds had not enjoyed his schooldays at Harrow, and though a keen mountaineer he was never an athlete, but his lectures on the Greek poets, originally delivered to the boys of Clifton College (1873–76), were a fine example of the new Hellenism. Symonds was able to communicate his love of Pindar, who had supremely achieved the translation of vigour and energy into art and beauty. An agnostic himself, he expressed the mood of post-Christian manliness in wistful quotation from Pindar's sixth Nemean ode:

> We are not unlike immortals either in our mighty soul or strength of limb, though we know not to what goal of night or day fate hath written down for us to run.[22]

William Johnson Cory, master at Eton and author of *Ionica*, was the poet of agnostic, aesthetic manliness. Shrinking from the void of an unknown hereafter, he clung like a true Grecian to the fleeting beauty of the earthly and the physical, giving

> Whate'er he had to give
> To freedom and to youth.

Too short-sighted to participate himself, he watched the games of his pupils with a loving enthusiasm. He celebrated the exploits of river and rifle corps and defined a pagan ideal of patriotic, fearless nobility in classically elegant verse. In the succession of valiant and admirable youth in the school he found an intimation of immortality denied him by religion.[23]

The militarist strain in Cory's verse links him with another late Victorian development in the ideal of manliness. The poets of imperialism such as Alfred Austin and Sir Henry Newbolt urged that manliness was more than simply playing the game: it included a heady aggressive patriotism, recalling the chivalric ideal in a new form.[24] Newbolt urged boys and men

> To set the Cause above renown,
> To love the game beyond the prize;
> To honour, while you strike him down
> The foe that comes with fearless eyes.

But for all their trumpetings, the last years of the reign saw a certain flagging. Aestheticism had begun to take over from moralism as the rationale of sport and the substance of manliness, but aestheticism and the decadence, Pater and Oscar Wilde, were closely linked, and elegant lassitude crept into fashion. Only under the stress of world war did the manly aspect of aestheticism flicker into life again. Rupert Brooke was a magnificent athlete at Rugby. But at school his celebration of the vigorous and the beautiful was deeply shaded with elegiac despondency:

> . . . the startled soul
> Flutters and fails before the darkness that is God.

In 1914, however, God

> . . . caught our youth, and wakened us from sleeping,
> With hand made sure, clear eye, and sharpened power,
> To turn, as swimmers into cleanness leaping.[25]

H.A. Vachell's novel *The Hill* (1905) tried to establish a clear link between the hectic manly enthusiasm of the playing fields of Harrow and the battles of the Boer War, but the formula was losing its old appeal. Rudyard Kipling, writing at almost the same time, found the games-field irrelevant, a symbol of the irresponsibility of a nation under stress yet wilfully blind to its danger:

> . . . then ye contented your souls
> With the flannelled fools at the wicket or the muddied oafs at
> the goals.

In Kipling's novel *Stalky & Co.* (1899) a ranting appeal to the patriotism and military ardour of the boys at the Imperial Service College disastrously misfires, though the boys are neither unpatriotic nor anti-militarist. They are, in fact, made resentful by the blatant attempt to exploit their strong but essentially private manly feelings.

Perhaps this signals the beginning of the end. As the world war approached, and Officer Training Corps were established in the schools, manliness tended to be diverted more and more into military channels. Militarism fused with, or even supplanted, the games cult as the chief manly ideal. The fervent enthusiasm, the stirring possibilities of (apparently) immediate transfer from

games-field to battlefield, had in the end an exhausting effect
and burnt out. The grim realities of war gradually undermined
the manly enthusiasm which had become so narrowly defined.
Siegfried Sassoon, whose earlier career as a cricketer at Marlborough and a fox-hunting man made him a typical representative of the sturdy, sporting variety of manliness, eventually threw
his Military Cross into the sea. Alec Waugh's remarkable novel,
The Loom of Youth (1917), written when he was still an adoles-
cent, describes the weakening of the ideal of manliness. Under
the shadow of the European conflict the fanatical insistence on
games and the mystique surrounding them tended to become
strained, unreal, irrelevant. There were none to replace the 'lost
generation'—the manly cricketers and rugby-players who died
in the trenches.[26]

In the Victorian public school manliness passed from moral
earnestness into vigorous 'muscular Christianity', games mania,
Grecian aestheticism, and finally a recruiting campaign. It
reflected the changing atmosphere of Victorian society and largely
disappeared, with some of the last vestiges of Victorianism, in
the mud of the Somme.

Militarism and the Victorian Public School

Geoffrey Best

It is only the young that depart from life without pangs. They are not as yet fettered to this earth by the thousand threads that civil life weaves round us. They have not as yet learnt to be sparing of the hours of life. The enigma which they are curious to solve still lies before them as a closed book. They mount the hill without perceiving the abruptness of the precipice on the other side. Their love of adventure rouses their eagerness for battle. Rest and enjoyment, the aim and inspiration of riper years, are as yet far removed. They advance into battle with joy and light-heartedness, two very necessary qualities for the bloody work before them. *The strength of a nation lies in its youth.*

THESE words come from the 1898 edition of a best-selling book which was first published in 1883. The book, *The Nation in Arms*, was a classic of pre-1914 militarism, and the passage in question is a typical example of what was being written at that time about the nation's youth and their role in its wars. Its viewpoint would therefore appear to be an excellent starting-point for an investigation of the subject of militarism and British public schools. Yet the book was written not by a headmaster in late Victorian England but by a German general, von der Goltz.[1] The passage quoted calls to mind an incident in another German book, this time a classic of anti-militarism, which was written in 1929 and very quickly banned in the country of its origin. This book, on which was based the film 'All Quiet on the Western Front', begins with a scene in which a schoolmaster urges his boys in an extraordinarily moving speech to immolate themselves on the altar of their Fatherland.

Did such exhortations have a parallel in British public schools

towards the end of Queen Victoria's reign and in the years leading up to the outbreak of world war in 1914? Exactly how did
the patriotic headmasters and other leaders of British youth seek
to influence the boys in those schools where the officer élite of
the British army was being trained? What ideas about war and
military service did boys get in those schools? Such questions are
important, not only in the study of the public school system, but
also in an understanding of far more profound and diffuse
questions such as the nation's conventional attitudes towards war,
and its prevalent ideas about the use of violence in the solution
of problems. When these topics are considered within the context
of international history, it may be possible to detect the underlying factors of the militarism which was such a conspicuous
element in pre-1914 European thought and which, far more than
'incidents' and assassinations, telegrams and ultimata, were responsible for the causation of war.

By the later Victorian period the public schools were educating
the top echelons of the country's governing élite. Therefore, they
must have had some connection, either directive or reflective,
with the formulation of government policy and the cultivation of
the British national ideology (i.e. the dominant ideas about
patriotism, legality, social deference, manliness, etc.). Moreover,
the general recognition in the non-public school world of the
élite's supremacy and of the superior value of its cultural ideals
enabled those ideals to filter downwards and outwards until they
permeated the whole of society. Proof of the diffusing power of
the public school ethos is provided by the extraordinary popularity of 'public school' fiction—frequently found at immense and
ridiculous removes from reality—among boys in 'state' elementary
and secondary schools, or by the fact that the British Borstal
institution, a successful device for the disciplining of juvenile
criminals in the inter-war period, was modelled expressly on the
public school house system and ideals of personal conduct.[2] It
explains why men from every non-public school walk of life,
fighting for their country and empire in the Great War, so readily
accepted, without the resentment or resistance that might have
been expected, the leadership of very young public school men
(many of them little more than boys) in the trenches and battle-
lines.

It is first of all necessary to establish some basic facts, such as the physical connections between the public schools and the army in the Victorian period. Perhaps the most obvious fact that emerges from any investigation is the exceptional part played by Eton throughout the nineteenth century in providing a much larger number of officers for the army than any other school. This was undoubtedly so before Victoria's accession too. The Duke of Wellington had been at Eton, although there seem to be no good grounds for believing that he ever attributed his greatest victory to its playing fields. In fact he spent only three years there, disliked it very much, learned little, and never returned to it willingly. He learned much more that was useful to him in his profession at the Military Academy in Angers in France, one of the best of a species of European institutions to which professionally ambitious young Britons were going during the eighteenth century. Only one of his top generals had been to a school whose title as a public school was beyond dispute : Picton, to Westminster. Of course, many officers must have been to the few public schools of that pre-Victorian, pre-Arnoldian epoch, but nothing resembling military instruction or experience could have been acquired there. If you wanted serious military education in the nineteenth century you went from school to the Royal Military Academy at Sandhurst, the Royal Military Academy in Woolwich for the artillery and engineers, or the college at Addiscombe founded in 1809 to train officers for the East India Company's army; those were the three institutions at which professional military instruction was offered after the first decade of the century.

The foundation of these institutions had a very limited effect on the recruitment of officers to the army. For what were called the departmental officers—engineers and the artillery men, well understood to be a socially inferior group to the line officers of the infantry and cavalry—Woolwich became essential. You did have to know a little trigonometry etc. to be able to manage the business of engineering, and you did have to know some element-ary physics etc. to be an efficient artillery officer. (There seems to have been no limit to what you didn't have to know to get into the infantry or the cavalry.) From quite early on in their histories, certain public (and probably other) schools began strongly to specialise in the training of boys for admission to the professional military colleges. Cheltenham and Marlborough from very early on were prominent in this business; Wellington and Clifton seem to have become prominent by the 1880s. But Sandhurst was not as indispensable for the infantry as might be thought, because you only went through Sandhurst if you could not afford the gentleman's and rich man's mode of entry: purchase of a commission. Before entry by purchase was at last abolished in the 1870s, a proportion only of infantry and cavalry were entering the army through its professional military institution. The rest were all entering either from school directly or by two other post-school means which continued into the early twentieth century, and whose importance may easily be underestimated.

One of these was the 'crammer'. Crammers seem to have been extremely important. Between school and the competitive examinations which to an ever-increasing extent were confronting boys seeking gentlemen's careers, there loomed the papers of the civil service examiners, and few schools seemed to have been able to jack boys up to sufficient levels to be sure of getting them through without spending three or six months at a crammer *en route*. Churchill, for example, had to go to Captain James's crammer in the Cromwell Road in the 1890s.

> It was said that no one who was not a congenital idiot could avoid passing thence into the Army. The Firm had made a scientific study of the mentality of the Civil Service Commissioners. . . They fired a large number of efficient shot-guns into the brown of the covey, and they claimed a high and steady average of birds. Captain James—if he had known it—was really the ingenious fore-runner of the inventors of the artillery barrages of the Great War. . . He did not need to see the enemy soldiers. Drill was all he had to teach his gunners.[3]

The crammer did for Churchill what Harrow failed to do. It got him into Sandhurst. We must not forget that public school men *en route* for the officers' mess were likely to have experience of the crammer as well.

Another post-public school military experience that lasted until 1908 was 'the backdoor into the army' via the Militia. If you couldn't get through the Sandhurst examinations, not even with Captain James's help, you could still get in through the Militia backdoor. But it was the usual practice from 1874 onwards that Sandhurst should process officers for the infantry and cavalry, and Woolwich for the artillery and engineers. No doubt some large proportion of these men came from the growing number of public schools. At the time of the Boer War a check was made on the proportions supplied by different public schools.[4] If we accept the figures produced by this survey, we may note which schools supplied the most officers in that war. The artillery, the senior departmental service, got 84 officers from Cheltenham, 62 from Wellington, 46 from Clifton, and 43 from Harrow; the numbers then tail off. The Engineers recruited 26 from Wellington, 24 from Cheltenham, 16 from Clifton, 15 from Marlborough, 11 from Harrow. (Not a single Etonian in engineereering!) The Royal Army Medical Corps called on other schools: 17 from Clifton, 16 from Edinburgh Academy, 13 from Dulwich, 13 from St Paul's. Lastly the infantry: 610 from Eton, 281 from Harrow, 280 from Wellington, 217 from Cheltenham, 191 from Charterhouse, 191 from Marlborough.

If we next examine the quantity and kind of military experience which these trainee officers would have had by the time they arrived in the army's colleges, it is surprising to find that the school corps played a considerably lesser part than might be supposed. Perhaps one gets a wrong impression about the public schools from the fact that there was always, it seems, a school sergeant. It is scarcely possible to read any public school fiction in which a school sergeant does not appear somewhere. Foxy in *Stalky & Co.* is perhaps the best-known example. It seems to have been usual, from some quite early date, for public schools to appoint ex-army sergeants. What exactly did they do? Sometimes they were porters and janitors, and often they taught gymnastics, along with which drill often figures; even for boys not in the corps some elementary experience of drill under the school sergeant is heard of, apparently considered as part of gymnastics, which in those early days were restricted to dumbbell exercises and similar practices of the most mechanical kind. But the corps was what mattered most.

What did the boys get out of the corps? One reads of cadet corps and rifle corps; sometimes these terms were interchangeable but they sometimes denoted separate organisations. The rifle corps was the more significant because it involved competition and therefore 'interaction' with other schools. Shooting matches appear in the school magazines along with the other competitive and interactionary sports; they became the subject of growing national interest after the establishment of the National Rifle Association's Wimbledon Common competitions in 1860. But what military experience did it and the cadet corps (if that was something different) provide? The answer varies very much from school to school, but in the early days of the corps, before the 1890s at the very earliest, it hardly seems to have given any significant military enthusiasm and expertise. The early accounts of school corps, as far as can be judged from school histories and magazines, are usually of small, piecemeal, often rather embarrassed beginnings, and of unremarkable growth in face of a good deal of indifference and some hostility. In some cases it was explicitly the sports side of the school which feared distraction and competition from corps enthusiasm. In other cases it seems to have been a more intellectual or moral objection to militarism and the military as being or as representing something of dubious value in a British Christian nursery. But clearly there were immense differences between schools.

Eton, under Dr Warre, who was quite a militaristic character, was unique. It had a proper Volunteer Corps of its own, which was flourishing in the 1880s and 1890s, according to evidence given to the 1904 Royal Commission on the Militia and Volunteers.[5] The headmaster was very keen on it. (He even advocated compulsory military training for schoolboys throughout the country.) The boys were said to have a parade every morning during chapel time and they had three field days a year, a greater number than is recorded for any other school corps. Rugby in 1904 had 220 boys, just over a third of the school, in the corps. The commanding officer admitted to the 1904 Royal Commission that some of them only joined it because it enabled them to get off school work, and he spoke of the strong opposition that he had met among some of the staff at Rugby—opposition such as might, he said, be met in every other school in the United Kingdom.[6] The headmaster of Westminster told the Ward Committee in 1907 that they had a corps at his school—admittedly a very recent one—but that the boys were reluctant to join it because it was 'necessarily officered in the main by boys who are not very good at games, and consequently they are not quite so much respected'.[7] From Glenalmond, Scotland's most army-conscious school and an undoubted public school by every test, about one-tenth of the boys went into the army. A rifle corps was founded there in 1875. Their shooting was always first class and they were equal to the best in England in the Ashburton Shield and other competitions at Bisley. But the *Glenalmond Chronicle* (a very good school magazine, much more cultivated than its Fettes or Loretto counterparts) yields disquieting intimations that the corps was not all that efficient. For example, a letter to the editor in April 1888 complained: 'Could not the Corps sergeants learn the bugle call? It is a little awkward when, after a bugle call, you hear "Retire!", "Fire!", "On the centre, close!", "Halt!" all at once.' In 1898 (two-thirds of Glenalmond's boys were in the corps by then) we find in the report on the corps that signalling and cycle sections—up-to-date, modern innovations—had been added to the corps but subsequently abolished. The *Glenalmond Chronicle*, however, expressed the belief that 'The latest development, an efficient band of pipers and drummers, seems more likely to last.'

Wellington was a particularly army-conscious school, and the history of its corps raises an interesting question about the connection of the public schools with the army through the medium of the Volunteers, that somewhat independent-minded and high-spirited branch of the army's auxiliary forces constituted in 1859 under some kind of War Office supervision. About half Wellington's boys came from military families, and most of those boys were going to be ploughed back into the army. Its corps was started in 1882, and by 1895 it was efficient enough and contained a sufficient number of senior boys to meet the War Office requirements (a minimum of ten fully trained cadets aged seventeen or over) for it to be affiliated to the Volunteers and to be eligible for a small grant towards the expenses of the annual camp. This and similar corps therefore had a definite, if loose, connection with the War Office. We should, however, be wary of reading too much into this as evidence of any serious connection between the public schools and the army, as the Victorians tended to draw sharp social and functional divisions between the army and the Volunteers.[8]

By the time of the Boer War the cadet and rifle corps of the public schools had a regular round of more or less prestigious activities. There was the annual camp, taken with other public schools, and there was a big annual public schools camp at Aldershot, a kind of a rally for most of the southern and midland English schools and for Glenalmond too, whose relatively wealthy boys could afford the fares. There were field days, often organised on an inter-school basis; there were the numerous shooting matches, public appearances at local shows and festivals, and occasional national events like the 1887 Royal Review at Aldershot and the 1897 one at Windsor. But despite all this, it is unlikely that the corps played a very big part in most public schools' lives until after 1900. Certainly it cannot be said of the pre-Boer War public school that the corps was by definition an important and admired central part of its system. At very few schools (Marlborough, Cheltenham, Wellington, Glenalmond—and also, of course, Eton) was it that important. It was always voluntary; it was small beer beside games; in some schools it was small beer beside work as well; and rarely can it have attained marginal efficiency in a realistic military sense.

The change came around the time of the Boer War. Corps were then quickly founded where they had not existed before, and increasing proportions of boys enlisted in them. The swelling numbers were accompanied by a greater keenness shown for corps work, more time allocated to the corps in the school timetable, and constant pressure and encouragement by visiting grandees from the Navy League and the National Service League, the big pressure groups campaigning for conscription so that Britain, like every other major power of Europe, would have a large conscript army ready to fight the next war. Lecturers from the Navy League and the National Service League were making the rounds of the public schools, no doubt with the object of arousing enthusiasm. Tirpitz would have been intrigued by the Navy League's propagandists among the Scottish public schools. 'Dr Rogerson of Merchiston . . . confined himself to the Tudor period of our history.'[9] Mr Johnstone of Edinburgh Academy talked to Fettes about the navy between 1603 and 1780, to Loretto about 'the various methods of fighting and manoeuvring for the windward berth'.[10] This new interest in military matters is, of course, part of that movement, well known to historians, which derived new impetus from the sense of relative inefficiency and

15 Upper School at Eton.

16 Charterhouse, from the playground.

17 Old Quadrangle at Rugby.

18 City of London School.

(despite Mafeking) humiliation during the Boer War, and which was linked with older-established causes for concern about Britain's performance relative to her international rivals. It promoted a many-sided movement for greater industrial and educational efficiency and military strength, spawning military and pseudo-military organisations of all sorts. It also produced Fisher's naval reforms and Haldane's army reforms; and to Haldane's reforms of 1908 can be traced the beginning of the Officers' Training Corps, the OTC, knitting together (the official phrase) the universities and the public schools into an efficient part of the military system for providing officers for the regular army or the new auxiliary army, the 'territorials'.

In this militarisation of the public schools, one man seems to have been pre-eminently influential: Lord Roberts. The hero of India, the victor of South Africa and the National Service League's trump card in its campaign for conscription, Roberts was touring the public schools from the moment he got back from South Africa. Public school records are full of him: 'Lord Roberts came to review the corps', 'Lord Roberts came to give the prizes', 'Earl Roberts came to open the Boer War Memorial', and so on. Other military grandees were doing the same thing, but Roberts seems to have been far and away the chief of them. Visiting Glenalmond in 1906, he told the boys that they must all prepare themselves for a share of the business of national defence.

> I look to you public school boys to set an example. Let it be your ambition to render yourself capable of becoming leaders of those others who have not your advantages, should you ever be called upon to fight for your country. . . Public school training inculcates just those qualities which are required in leaders of men: self-reliance, determination, and a certain amount of give and take, exacting obedience to authority more by an appeal to honour and sound common sense than by severity, and by a happy mixture of prudence and audacity.[11]

In turning from the institutional aspects of the question to the ideas which underlay and permeated those institutions, it is probably safest to follow the example of the authors of an

K

excellent article on 'Militarism'[12] in a recent social sciences ency-
clopaedia by starting with some dictionary definitions of that
rather complex term. 'Militarism' can mean 'the prevalence of
military sentiments or ideals among a people', 'the predominance
of the military class in government and administration' and 'the
tendency to regard military efficiency as the paramount interest
of the state'. How might the public schools and their teaching
relate to these definitions?

In considering 'the prevalence of military sentiment or ideals'
in Britain, we must not be misled by the pacific appearance of
British Victorian history and, in particular, by the celebrated
fact that Britain was engaged in only one European war between
1815 and 1914. For all that, it is surely true that Victorian society
evinced a very widespread consciousness of the army and the
navy, at least in their historical roles, although no doubt men
like Thomas Hughes would be much more ready to feel vibra-
tions about them than men like Richard Cobden. Then there
is that amazing cult of the Iron Duke which continued throughout the nineteenth century. Other heroes of the French wars were
admired too, notably Nelson, whose biography by Southey seems
to have been a common item on school prize lists by the end
of the century.

But the Victorians had heroes of their own. There was a constant trickle of imperial and colonial wars right through the
period, and these too produced their military heroes, leaders sufficiently popular to have figured in folk art such as Staffordshire
pottery. Another aspect of the Victorians' interest in military
ideals is their cult of the Christian warrior and their notions of
the marriage of strength with virtue; as a recent excellent article
on 'Christian Militarism' has pointed out, this was by no means
a phenomenon of late Victorian times.[13] It is present in all its
elements by the 1850s. Some heroes of the Indian mutiny were
famous evangelical Christians—religious heroes as well as military ones. General Gordon is perhaps the best example of this
type of figure. Finally, there is the Victorians' predilection for
playing at soldiers, to which they seem to have been as addicted
as any of their continental counterparts. Anyone who goes around
military museums may be puzzled by the magnificent displays
of military paraphernalia. Where did it all come from? How did
so many different and often gorgeous uniforms, badges, helmets,

etc. originate within so small a military power as Britain? The answer is that most of these are not the uniforms of regular soldiers at all. They are the uniforms of the Volunteers, the Militia and the Yeomanry. It seems to have been a natural spare-time occupation for the aristocracy and gentry, especially for those all of whose time was spare, and for many bold bourgeois and artisans too, to belong to these organisations and to participate in the prestige and public appearances which appertained to them. (Surtees's humbug Jawleyford had his portrait painted in the uniform of the Bumperkin Yeomanry.) Although the Militia, Yeomanry and Volunteers were of questionable military value, they put on some show of being military, and constituted part of a general awareness of military things which the Victorians had and which we may too easily miss. The public schools come just onto the fringes of it by means of their cadet corps.

The second definition of militarism had to do with the pre-dominance of the military class in politics or government. This certainly does not apply to Victorian Britain. If there was a European country in which the military class was *not* predomin-ant in politics or government, it was Britain. This was partly because of the admirable principles of the Duke of Wellington, who might have left a legacy of militarist ideas behind him, but actually left the very opposite, it being among his main principles that the soldier should be put firmly under the civilian's orders, that the object of war was to restore peace, and that that soldier most succeeded who never had to fight a war at all. The Duke's principles combined with central constitutional traditions to keep the generals in their proper places. Was there a change, though, shortly before the Great War? There is some evidence to suggest that there was. So many of the top brass of the armed services just before the Great War, in Britain as everywhere else, were bitterly and explicitly contemptuous and resentful of the politicians—'those bloody frocks', as Kitchener used to call them. Such attitudes and language came readily to strong men of a ruling class when they regarded the style of parliamentary politi-cians and the ways of politics. The public school magazines and biographies give some grounds for supposing that the young men and boys in the schools were likely to share this impatience and contempt. If distaste for democratic politics plays into the hands interest, then maybe the public schools were contributing to something of that sort before 1914.

Militarism might also mean 'military efficiency as the paramount interest of the state'. That, of course, was a common European concern from the 1880s onwards (if not from earlier still). Britain, like every other country, experienced an impulse to strengthen national security, improve the national ability for self-defence, and to modernise industry.[14] The public schools cannot be seen as having originated any part of it. They simply reflect the dominant trend. Perhaps they reflect it with a special brightness because of their ethos. But what direct contribution to military efficiency did the public schools make? The answer has to do partly with *character*. If there was one thing all public schools believed they were good at and agreed on as their *raison d'être*, it was the education of character. So by testing the products of the system against its own emphasis on character, it should be possible to discover contemporary military evaluation of the direct usefulness to the army of public school education. Cardinal to the principles of that education was the distrust of mere intellect. Character was there to correct the excesses and foibles of intellect; 'cleverness' was something to be wary of.

However, it is also apparent that some shrewd military experts of the time felt that the public schools were not doing enough in the intellectual line to promote the military efficiency the country needed. Colonel G.F.R. Henderson, for example, one of the best military writers of the time who served successively on the staffs of Sandhurst and the Staff College between 1889 and 1900, was professionally worried about the insufficiency of brains in the army, and ready to salute military brains wherever he found them. Henderson knew enough about the realities of modern war to want British officers to learn from the vulgar drunken, democratic Grant as well as the pious, gentlemanly Jackson. Henderson's periodical articles, collected in 1905 into a five-hundred-page book, *The Science of War*, returned again and again to the topic of brains, but he did not find it necessary to discuss the public schools. They simply did not come into his ideas about increasing the proportion of intelligence in the army. He had something to say about Woolwich, about Sandhurst, about Oxford and Cambridge, he even looked at crammers, but what was happening in the public schools did not seem to interest him. They seem to have been below the level at which he thought it sensible to start.

Another contemporary commentator was Spencer Wilkinson, who became the first Chichele Professor of Military Science at Oxford. Questioning the Rugby School cadet corps commander at the 1904 Royal Commission, and agreeing with him that corps could do more than games to make men of boys, he went on to remark that corps and games alike reduced, or distracted boys' attention from, the cultivation of their intelligence—the most important thing for those who were going into the army. His preference was obviously for less talk about character and more concentration on the mind. Finally, there was Colonel F.N. Maude, who held a variety of part-time jobs teaching military history and who was a clever, prolific and influential, if peculiar, periodical writer. Unlike Wilkinson, he was not so worried about the lack of intelligence, while at the same time being intensely concerned about character. He was a vigorous and outspoken opponent of the public schools' concentration on classics. He was against classics from the prep school upwards. First of all, he argued, the modern soldier needed to spend more time on living languages, mathematics, and so on, the staples of those less prestigious 'modern sides' of public schools. But beyond that, classics seemed to him morally damaging. Clean minds in healthy bodies should be the British ideal. 'But how can we hope to attain either when we place in the hands of boys, at the most critical period of their lives, a knowledge of languages which unlocks the door to about the lewdest literature in Western Europe—indeed in the world?'[15]

There was a clear relationship between militarism and sport in the British public schools. Sport concerned the military in two ways: firstly, as the straight road to physical health and strength, indispensable to the good soldier; secondly, because of the special value attributed to team games in training the essential qualities of the officer and leader. The first of these is indisputable in a general sense, though there seems little evidence to suggest that German and French officers got out of breath quicker than the British—somehow or other they must have attained physical fitness without having played rugger. The second is more subtle and interesting and was undoubtedly the aspect of sport that mattered most to the keen public school master, who really believed that rugby and cricket were schools of morals, manliness and leadership. At no school can they have been more highly estimated than Loretto.[16] Its great headmaster, H.H. Almond, was one of the grand examples of the fanaticism for sport and physical toughness which swept across the public schools from the 1860s and 1870s. So fanatical and keen was he as a sportsman that in his later years he had to be restrained from watching school matches because the excitement was bad for his heart. This celebrated Scottish public school had no corps until 1910. They held it off as long as they possibly could. The school legend is that they were reluctant to compromise over open-necked shirts which, Almond insisted, were perfectly suitable for schoolboys. But another ground of Loretto's resistance may have been Almond's belief that a school which possessed a rugby field had no need of a corps. No doubt there were many other sports-minded masters who felt the same. The simple, straightforward notion that a lad who has had a good rugger training at school is well on the way towards the command of troops was certainly one that appealed to a good many soldiers as well. Colonel O'Callaghan-Westropp, a military member of the Royal Commission on the Militia and Volunteers (1904) thus pressed a reluctant public school corps commander : 'I will put it this way. Situations may arise in a good cricket or football team requiring as quick decision, perhaps a shade quicker, than a company commander with his line of skirmishers in the field.'[17] As the Duke might well have said, if you can believe that, you can believe anything.

A curious phenomenon that provides a graphic example of the connection between sport and warfare in the public school mind is the sports terminology which is such a noticeable feature in all public school speech and writing on military matters. Indeed, it may be more a national than an upper-class peculiarity. Churchill remarks in his *Early Life* that war had seemed to him at Harrow, and still seemed to him in India, an extension of school games. The Dulwich College football song sang of 'Fifteen fellows fighting full, Out for death or glory'. Letters from the front in the Boer War and Great War (school magazines published a lot of them, some written straight to the headmaster or the housemaster) very frequently used sports language to describe the action. The practice extended to the highest-ranking officers : General Lord Horne, in an introduction to a book on sniping, wrote : 'It may fairly be claimed that when hostilities ended on 11 November 1918, we had outplayed Germany at all points of the game. Perhaps as a nation we failed in imagination, possibly Germany was more quick to initiate new methods of warfare or to adapt her existing methods to meet prevailing conditions. Certainly we were slow to adopt, indeed, our souls abhorred, anything unsportsmanlike.'[18] The ideal of sportsmanship on the battlefield was echoed by Captain Nichols, RFC, when he told Loretto that 'the German Flying Corps is the only part of that degraded nation's military machine which "plays the game", and hoped that the good feelings which existed between the German and English Flying Corps would always be kept up.'[19]

In conclusion, it is necessary to consider loyalty, a most important element of the public school ethos found, of course, both on playing field and battlefield, but not there alone. Sport is certainly relevant as the supreme means of inculcating submersion of individual interest into the common good of the team, the community, the nation. The educational theory of sport was that it trained you out of individualism into corporate membership and loyalty and devotion to your microcosmic nation. Anyone can see how this led very easily into training for the ultimate team : your country's army fighting for national life and death. The loyalty syndrome which was such a prodigious part of the public school ethos began with loyalty to your house (which in some cases seems to have been at least as great as loyalty to your school), and rose through loyalty to your school (a paradigm of the nation) to loyalty to your country, faith and leaders. Public school boys, expressing in their letters and diaries their sense of purpose or obligation in the Boer War and Great War tended to say that they were glad to be bringing credit to the school, they wouldn't let the school down or forget 'the loyalty to Queen and country which I first learned at school'. A good example of just how it was first learned at school is provided by a verse from the amazing Glenalmond marching song written by their headmaster, an excellent man called Skrine. Skrine was not at all a militarist or a philistine, but this was what he thought fitting for the rifle corps :

Fair mother, thy waters and walls
Far hence to thy soldiers will come,
In the hush ere the hurricane falls,
In the dread ere the beat of the drum.
O, safe with thy soldiers up-grown
Is thy honour, high Queen of the Glen,
And the battle shall seal them thine own,
Glenalmond, right mother of men.

Chorus :
Oh by lilt of the kilt, by the swinging foot free,
By twinkle of sporran adance at the knee,
By flutter of bonny hill-bonnets alee,
'Tis Glenalmond, Glenalmond is out![20]

Loyalty to school and loyalty to country march close together;
and if loyalty to school sometimes did come closer than loyalty
to country, that would have been nothing strange to soldiers at
least as well accustomed to fight for the honour of the regiment as for their Queen.

With loyalty the wheel of the public school's ethos comes full
circle. Its claims go beyond those of life. Duty, devotion and
sacrifice—loyalty's fellow-travellers—called from beyond the
grave. The prospect of death in service must always have been
within the public school boy's horizon. The risk of early death
in the careers at which many public school boys aimed must
have been greater than nowadays, even if the youthful school-
leavers were not going directly into the armed services. They
knew it from family tradition, religious principle and imperial
folklore. Men might assume, rather than explicitly state, that
death was something anyone might meet along the road. If you
went into the Indian civil service or any part of the colonial
service, you were scarcely more likely to come back than you
would be after the Great War. But more important is that cultivation of the idea of dying nobly for your country, which is
usually part of militarist theory. Militarist writers commonly
hold the noblest death to be that achieved in fighting for the
fatherland/motherland/*patrie*—a death more desirable by far
than staying mouldily alive in some ignoble commercial or
materialist way of life. Something of this is certainly apparent

in the public school ethos. One meets that note of contempt for the commercial, 'mere money-making', home-staying bourgeois sort of existence again and again. Those are the kind of things public school boys could easily learn to shun, for they were the objects and styles of life more appropriate for grocers and grammar school boys.

General Sir Ian Hamilton was one of the party who toured the public schools with Lord Roberts. He was attached to the Japanese army in the Russo-Japanese War and later wrote a very interesting book about it. Visiting Glenalmond in 1905 to unveil the Boer War memorial tablet, he explicitly recommended to the boys the Japanese spirit of self-sacrifice : meeting death *pro patria* 'as a bridegroom who goes to meet his bride'. He wondered if such a spirit could overcome the money-loving luxury of Europe, and concluded with an adjuration to the boys to be ready to work and fight 'for Glenalmond, Scotland and the Empire'.[21]

The same mixture of patriotism, sacrifice, idealism, and anti-'materialism' appears with pathetic force in the *War Letters of a Public School Boy* (1918), put together by the father of a Dulwich boy, Paul Jones, who had been killed in his tank near Ypres in 1917. These letters are the more interesting for Jones's having apparently been no mere stereotyped public school product. For one thing he was an ardent liberal admirer of Lloyd George, which got him into a good many fights behind the gym. Furthermore, he did not like classics, and escaped from them as soon as he could, to such good consequence as to win a history scholarship to Balliol. But two parts of his public school education had gone deep into Paul Jones. One was sport : he was captain of rugby and captain of athletics, and fairly fanatical about both. The other was a distaste for 'materialism' and 'ordinary' life. This is explicit in many of his letters. As one of his fellow-officers wrote to his father after his death, he 'was not built for a mercenary age'. Paul Jones himself put it rather differently in a long letter to his younger brother, about to go into the army :

Have you ever reflected on the fact that, despite the horrors of the war, it is at least a big thing? I mean to say that in it one is brought face to face with realities. The follies, luxury, selfishness and general pettiness of the vile commercial sort of existence led by nine-tenths of the people in the world in peace-time are replaced in war by a savagery that is at least more honest and outspoken.[22]

There speaks the true voice of the highest-minded spirit of militarism. It could come straight from Clausewitz or any of his more modern disciples. Rather war and death than 'ignoble' peace and life. For the historian of the public schools it calls to mind that passage from *The Hill* (1905) which David Newsome quotes at the end of *Godliness and Good Learning*

> To die young, clean, ardent; to die swiftly, in perfect health; to die saving others from death, or worse—disgrace; to die scaling heights; to die and to carry with you into the fuller ampler life beyond, untainted hopes and aspirations, unembittered memories, all the freshness and gladness of May—is not that cause for joy rather than sorrow?[23]

So we find ourselves close to General von der Goltz after all.

9

Athleticism:
A Case Study of the Evolution of an
Educational Ideology

J.A. Mangan

THE OBJECT of this chapter is to trace the rise of an educational ideology—athleticism—in one English public school, Marlborough College, in which its influence was profound.

It is important to appreciate that in many English public schools, including Marlborough, during the second half of the nineteenth century athleticism was not merely a term signifying a liking for healthy outdoor activities: to use Robert Nisbet's striking phrase, it was 'a neologism born of moral passion' operating at the level of an educational ideology. Through it, physical exercise (team games in particular) was indulged in considerably and compulsorily in the belief that it was a highly effective means of inculcating valuable instrumental and expressive goals—physical and moral courage, loyalty and co-operation and the ability both to command and obey—the famous ingredients of 'character training'. As such, it was enthusiastically embraced by many pupils, masters and parents. Though not unopposed, it was widely supported as a favoured ethos, and in many public schools it appears to have exerted a considerable influence until after the Great War. Today the term still serves as the descriptive label of this once powerful and now extinct educational ideology.

The cult of athleticism is faithfully enshrined in much of the contemporary literature, and it is worthwhile to take the following examples from two famous nineteenth-century novelists of boyhood in order to supply a period flavour of the educational and moral certainty surrounding games-playing. First, Charles Kingsley, that clerical paladin, furnishes an illustration of the commitment of a Victorian apologist:

Masters and boys alike know that games do not, in the long

run, interfere with a boy's work—that the same boy will very often excel himself in both; that the games keep him in health for his work; and the spirit with which he takes to his games when in the lower school is a fair test of the spirit with which he will take to his work when he rises into the higher school; and that nothing is worse for a boy than to fall into that loafing, tuck-shop-haunting set, who neither play hard nor work hard, and are usually extravagant, and often vicious. Moreover, they know well that games conduce, not merely daring and endurance but better still, temper, self-restraint, fairness, honour, unenvious approbation of another's success, and all that 'give and take' of life which stands to a man in such good stead when he goes forth into the world and without which, indeed, his success is always maimed and partial.[1]

Dean Farrar, novelist, theologian and headmaster of Marlborough from 1871 to 1876, could scarcely be considered one of the protagonists of games-playing, which, to paraphrase his own words, was not even of tenth-rate importance compared to things of the mind and soul; yet he too had some kind remarks to make on the subject.

Even from your games, you may learn some of those true qualities which will help you to do your duty bravely and happily in life. No one can be a good cricketer who does not practice—who does not take trouble—who is not glad to amend faulty ways of playing—who does not attend to rules. And in a yet better and higher sense, no one can make a first-rate cricketer if he is not ready, and steady, and quick, and bold; if he is not trained to bear a reverse with a perfectly good-humoured smile; if he is not free from self-consciousness which is usually called being nervous; or he has not the pluck, and the patience and the good humour and the self-control to play out tenaciously to the very last a losing game, ready to accept defeat, but trying to the end to turn it into victory. Well, believe me, you want the very same good qualities in the great cricket-field of life.[2]

It is fashionable today, and to a degree wise, to look askance at such a naïve faith in the educational qualities of the playing field, but at the same time it is as well to remember that we are reacting, possibly predictably, with extremism to extremism. It is perhaps salutary to recall that English education has embraced the belief in the efficacy of sport for character building since Tudor times.[3] The fault of the late Victorian and Edwardian public school, as this investigation of Marlborough College will reveal, was that of excessive and procrustean emphasis.

Marlborough College opened on 20 August 1843. The brutal frog-hunt of the first hours aptly symbolises the pupils' main recreational habits for almost a decade. Games were neither an integral part of the curriculum, nor the main leisure activities of the boys. Under its first headmaster, the Rev. M. Wilkinson, the college was firmly in the tradition of public schools of the time. Staff were scholars. Sport was the boys' concern. However, Marlborough boys for the most part were the sons of country clergy, since the school was founded to provide an élitist education at reasonable cost for the offspring of this relatively poor middle-class clientèle. In consequence, recreational pursuits were rural. Edward Lockward is perhaps suitably representative of the unacademic boy—the majority of pupils. No scholar, he naturally sought escape from the meaningless existence of the classroom on the banks of the Kennet and in the glades of Savernake Forest. His ancestors, as he wrote, 'so far as there is any record of them, appear to have been sportsmen'.

Lockwood, in fact, clearly located a powerful factor in the rise of athleticism once these country pursuits were proscribed. 'I had not the faintest idea what the Latin grammar was all about, and as no one made the faintest attempt to explain anything, I gave up all hope of understanding it, and passed my time during school hours in other ways than acquiring classical knowledge.'[4] In other words, the aridity and restricted nature of the academic curriculum and the brutality of the pedagogy played an important part in the attractiveness, first of the countryside, and later of the playing field. Nearly thirty years later, when athleticism was nearing its peak, Leslie Stephen sought to explain the extreme interest in sport at Oxford in broadly similar terms.[5]

'Chiefly recruited from the bucolic counties,' as one pupil later recounted,[6] these Marlborough sons of country vicarages were far from angelic in action and personality and 'developed naturally into poachers, rat-catchers and even raiders of poultry-yards'.[7] The 'squaler' (a piece of cane topped with lead used in the hunting of rabbits and squirrels) was as much the unremarkable sporting equipment of early Marlburians as the cricket bat was to be in later days. More inoffensive physical activities were not unknown. Cricket and football were played by enthusiasts; there was eventually hockey and pole-jumping, racquets and fives and an interesting assortment of playground games including marbles, peg-tops and 'fly the garter'. At least one assistant master, John Sowerby, was a keen sportsman. The fact that his sporting efforts were mainly holiday activities and not an important school contribution shows how games were far from being symbols of an official educational ideology. So it remained from the school's creation until the appointment of G.E.L. Cotton as headmaster in 1852.

With the arrival of Cotton the informality and relative unimportance of games ended. They were elevated from being a minor preoccupation of the boys' culture to being a central concern of headmaster, staff and pupils, and were embraced for the first time within the framework of formal school objectives. Cotton himself provided one explanation for this innovation in his famous circular to parents at the end of his first academic year. 'The mass of the School', he wrote, 'are not trained up to cricket and football at all, which as manly and healthy games, are certainly deserving of general encouragement.'[8]

There is, however, another side to the coin. Cotton inherited a discontented and failing school.[9] A major responsibility, therefore, was the production, through coercion, persuasion or both, of an amenable clientèle. Coercion had failed under Wilkinson, and Cotton, leaning on his Rugby experience, adopted a dual strategy to achieve his ends. He brought with him the Arnoldian prefect system and drove a wedge into the pupils' ranks. In conjunction with this simple policy of 'divide and rule', he introduced a policy of 'involvement' to seduce the boys away from the Wiltshire countryside through the provision of better games organisation and by the recruitment of young, athletic masters who won the pupils' affection through their prowess with bat and ball. This latter action showed a wise recognition of the fact that successful social relationships are often the most effective mechanisms by which new ideas become accepted.

Foremost among these new men were E.A. Scott and C.H. Bull. Scott accompanied Cotton from Rugby and was a major figure in the development of rugby football, racquets and fives. It was in his time at Marlborough that colours and house matches were initiated. Bull was a younger protégé of the headmaster who had been in Cotton's house at Rugby, and, in the words of a pupil, 'at football made us work. Every fellow played for all he was worth. So did Bull.'[10] These masters 'who became boys out of doors' were the 'stormtroopers' of Cotton's new principle of social order.

Meanwhile in his sermons Cotton established a sublimatory educational rationale for his innovatory instrument of social control. From the chapel pulpit he expounded a Christian version of the Graeco-Renaissance concept of 'the whole man' :

> God, who gave us our immortal spirits, is the Creator also of our bodies, and our minds. All our powers and faculties, the limbs which are so strong and healthy, the understanding which is strengthened and developed by our daily studies, are equally the workmanship of Him who has also reunited us to Himself in Jesus Christ. And, therefore, in gaining wisdom and knowledge and bodily strength, we are carrying out his gracious purposes no less surely, though more indirectly than when we are reading the Bible or kneeling before Him in prayer.[11]

At the same time in Cotton's value-system games became a vehicle for the creation and reflection of Christian excellence.

> Of one thing there is no doubt : that both intellectual and bodily excellence are only really blessed when they are a reflection of moral and religious goodness, when they teach us unselfishness, right principles, and justice.[12]

In this and similar utterances can be clearly discerned the origins of the moral fervour associated with the athleticism of later decades. Cotton also made modest claims for the practical value of games as a producer of manly vigour and as an occasional aide to mental application.

With such arguments he drew games into the school curriculum and pedagogy, but he was always a realist where boys were concerned. Not surprisingly, therefore, he early anticipated an

over-enthusiasm for the 'pleasures of the playing field' and
solemnly warned against the dangers of such indulgence.

> Undoubtedly there is a danger lest at this particular season
> the due proportion of work and relaxation should be inverted,
> lest your interest should be so absorbed in this particular excite-
> ment that you forget the main business for which you have
> been sent to this place. Such an inversion, such an engrossing
> occupation of the mind, by an employment, which however
> salutary, is after all, a mere amusement, cannot take place
> without great injury to yourselves. Perhaps its least evil is, that
> it retards the course of that education which is to fit you for
> doing your duty to God and man. It must also engender a
> certain amount of self-will, a feeling of self-importance, a
> desire for self-indulgence. The applause here bestowed upon
> success in games is apt to blind a person to his own ignorance,
> to make him indifferent to the faults of his character, to prevent
> him from realising the fact that he will be judged very differ-
> ently when he passes from boyhood to manhood. Above all
> this immoderate interest in mere amusement is inconsistent
> with the sober spirit of watching unto prayer. It intrudes not
> only into the time of study, but into times intended for yet
> holier occupations. Thus by a strange perversity we employ
> God's gifts for our own injury.[13]

But Cotton was spitting into the wind. His strategic capitula-
tion to the 'boy culture' through his open support for games,
together with his policy of recruiting muscular assistants in an
attempt to reduce the 'generation gap', were to have dramatic
and unintended consequences. The pied piper played his tune,
and the response was an eventual stampede.

What is intriguing in the subsequent decades is not the popularity of games among the pupils—boys have always liked
vigorous physical activities—but their considerable importance
in the life of the school. At a time when in British society there
was a gradual realisation of the need for occupational competence
and a growing distrust of the patronage system of appointment
(the same decade in which Cotton reformed Marlborough recreations, for example, saw the introduction of competitive examination for posts in the Indian civil service and for entrance to the
army training establishments of Sandhurst and Woolwich)

19 King Edward's School, Birmingham: the grammar schoolroom.

20 Marlborough College: C-House.

21 Wellington College.

Marlborough and the other public schools actively promulgated the anti-industrial educational ideal of the 'gentleman' with its strong emphasis on liberal education and outdoor activities. The influential Clarendon Commission on the public schools which reported in 1864 both publicised and sanctioned this ideal.

It is not easy to estimate the degree to which the English people are indebted to these schools for the qualities on which they pique themselves most—for their capacity to govern others and control themselves, their aptitude for combining freedom with order, their public spirit, their vigour and manliness of character, their strong but not slavish respect for public opinion, their love of healthy sport and exercise. These schools have been the chief nurseries of our statesmen; in them and in schools modelled after them, men of all the various classes that make up English society, destined for every profession and career, have been brought up on a footing of social equality, and have contracted the most enduring friendships, and some of the ruling habits of their lives; and they have had perhaps the largest share in the moulding of the character of 'the English Gentleman'.[14]

Yet Britain was the foremost industrial nation in the world at this time and owed her great wealth to this industry. The production of technically knowledgeable leaders to maintain industrial success was a major educational requirement. The next thirty years marked Britain's growing inability to counter the competition of the emerging industrial nations of Germany and the United States. With some justification it has been suggested that a large portion of the blame can be laid at the door of English public schools with their unrealistic curriculum and ideals and their self-appointed role as the mechanism by which the '*arriviste*' middle classes were transformed into gentlemen, for whom the professions and public and imperial service were the only suitable careers.[15]

Why did Marlborough flourish when it largely ignored its nationally logical role as a training institution of skilled managerial manpower for the world's leading industrial nation? There are several reasons. To cater for the hard-headed and to mollify the critical, public school education was, in fact, becoming less

L

occupationally dysfunctional. In particular, the new schools
created in the middle of the century provided for those concerned
with earning a living, through their 'modern sides', which
offered subjects directly related to occupational futures.[16] Furthermore, the growing emphasis in the schools on outdoor activities
had its practical aspect. The development of robust health
(physical and moral) took on a fresh significance from this time
since it became intrinsically linked with expanding imperialist
careers. No less a figure than a professor of philosophy in a book
suitably entitled *The Making of Character* consciously or un-
consciously provided the imperialist rationale for the time spent
on sunlit cricket squares and muddy football fields.

> If we are apt to have misgivings about the long hours and days
> given in boyhood to games, we must not think too exclusively
> of the immediate results. We must think of the heavy drafts
> which arduous vocations make in after years on bodily vigour
> and endurance, and not least of that sense of insurance against
> whatever the future can bring which comes of the conscious-
> ness of calculable physical fitness.[17]

Whether or not the hours so spent had a beneficial effect is of
little account. What is of importance is that those at the time
believed that they did. In addition, Marlborough, as a leading
public school, constituted an élitist initiation centre : its pupils
were specialised into recognisable behavioural norms which
served as guarantors of acceptable personal qualities, attitudes
and mannerisms; and these in themselves were important job
qualifications.[18]

But the essential attractiveness of Marlborough and the other
public schools was that they offered their own kind of technical
training which was available nowhere else—a training in the
style of a traditional, leisured élite rather than the skills of an
industrialised society. The gentleman's education comprised the
gift, as Kitson Clark has put it, of a 'legacy of the old English
aristocratic class to a larger class'. It proved a seductive offering.
Ironically the practical and scientific model of education of the
'dissenting academies' was now ignored by many of the English
middle class and Dissenters themselves became Church of England gentlemen.[19] Two distinguished educational historians, in-
elegantly calling a spade a spade, have declared that the motive

for this metamorphosis can be summed up in the one word—snobbery.[20]

Thus the reasons why the educational paradigm of the 'gentleman' was successful at Marlborough and its ilk were a curious mixture of sensible realism, understandable vanity and downright shortsightedness on the part of the clients. Since the embryonic gentlemen played games in order to learn how to become gentlemen, at Marlborough after Cotton the moral discipline supposedly imbued by diligent use of willow and puntabout became as legitimate an educational concern for subsequent generations of staff and pupils as the mental discipline supposedly developed through the construction of polished classical iambics.

The ideological seeds of athleticism sown by Cotton in his sermons germinated rapidly. By 1867 its tenets had become sufficiently crystallised and formidable to produce an encomium in the *Marlburian* by one who signed himself 'Trebla'. His extravagant claims for the virtues of athleticism were perfectly seriously made, if occasionally verging on the ridiculous. It fostered courage, active and passive; it developed the quality of self-abnegation (since it offered the opportunity to deny oneself rich foods); it generated patriotism, for while excellent Latin and faultless Greek did nothing to promote *esprit de corps*, a house team was united by the indissoluble ties of common hopes, sympathies and aspirations; it encouraged a love of a life of action (and those ambitious of immortality were reminded that the Temple of Fame was gained through activity, not mere speculation). But above all, it fanned

> that noblest, and purest and highest of all earthly worships—hero-worship: that worship which has lain at the root of half the greatness that ever existed in this world's history, which overcame the frivolity and scepticism of Alcibiades, which stirred the fiery emulation of Alexander, which led the high-born gentlemen of England to pour out their blood like water on the fields of Naseby and Marston Moor.[21]

If this was not enough, 'a truly chivalrous football-player . . . was never yet guilty of lying, or deceit, or meanness, whether of word or action'.

This article provoked an interesting response from an early

Marlburian pupil aesthete who deprecated the hero-worship of mere brute force and of the least deserving who abused the influence their prowess gave them.[22] Trebla counterattacked such heretical views. It was not his intention, he retorted, to glorify brute force. Only the moral qualities of courage, patriotism, hero-worship and self-denial need glorification. Those who opposed athleticism saw only animalism. But exercise could be gained with dumb-bells and parallel bars; he had chosen football rather than gymnastics precisely because it supplied a *moral* training.[23]

If Trebla upheld an ideal, Dean Farrar, who had been an assistant master at Marlborough under Cotton and in 1871 was to become headmaster, was critical of the reality as he saw it. In a forthright lecture to the Royal Institute in the following year, he pleaded for the introduction of more science, English literature and modern studies in the public school curriculum, and, in language familiar to the readers of *Eric, or Little by Little*, bewailed the rise in the public schools of 'extravagant athleticism' : 'The marble which is brought to us is white and precious, and it is the fault of our method and our system if the statue which we hew out of it is so often, not a Zeus or a Hermes but an Adonis or an athlete.'[24]

Farrar's ideological alternative was a heady pot-pourri in which the ingredients were the ideals of 'virtuous Christianity' and 'intellectual endeavour'. The former clearly took precedence over the latter. 'The object of a school, that above all must be a Christian school,' he exclaimed to his Marlborough boys, 'is as far as we can to teach you from the first to do God's will, not your own, until God's will is your own.'[25]

Trebla's article and the subsequent exchange are significant. As early as 1867 we find a paean to athleticism as a builder of character in preference to muscle, and the establishment of a simple, linear relationship between games and moral virtue. No less significant are the equally early misgivings of Farrar. Despite his protests and his proffered ideological alternative, however, in the next three decades athleticism at Marlborough was to take on the features of a Mannheimian 'total ideology' and powerfully affect the lives of many boys. Two major forces were critical in the development of this process—the requirements of British imperialism and a fundamental anti-intellectualism.

Imperialism, militarism and athleticism in the last quarter of the nineteenth century became a revered secular trinity of the upper-middle-class school. A recent historian has written : 'By the end of the century it was not the public school system in general but the playing fields that were associated with the imperial battlefields.'[26] These lines from 'Carmen Marlburiense', a college song, bear local witness to this general phenomenon.

Be strong, Elevens, to bowl and shoot,
Be strong, O Regiment of the foot,
With ball of skin or lead or leather,
Stand for the Commonwealth together.

Whatever its intellectual limitations, the association *had* a basic soundness, as Rupert Wilkinson has suggested in his comparative survey of the training of two imperial élites : 'In public school England, the traits of the educational community, with its monastic barrack-room living, were also those of the military regiment. The same resemblance between education and military service did not exist in Confucian China. There virtue was sought through scholarship rather than athleticism; and moral suasion was preferred to muscular evangelism. Not surprisingly the Chinese held professional soldiering in low regard, and imperial defence suffered accordingly.'[27]

One writer, with justification, has labelled the cultivation of the physical as an educational aim 'the public school, colonial ethic' and has written : 'The colonising tradition centres round the code of the frontiersman; of its ideals the most outstanding were courage and endurance, the vital frontiersman virtues.'[28] Certainly from 1870 onwards the exciting pioneer world of Empire was regularly publicised in the *Marlburian* through the contributions from former pupils with such titles as 'The Personal Narrative of a Fortnight's Service with the Attacking Force in the Khybar', 'Shooting in Travancore', 'Fire in Tasmania' and 'Pleasures of the Veldt'.[29] Hortatory letters from Old Marlburians urged emigration, exploration and missionary work. The arduous but satisfying physical nature of life overseas was made clear, and an obvious and logical connection was drawn between the development of sound wind and limb, stamina and physical courage on English playing fields and pioneering in Canada, soldiering in Burma and baptising in Melanesia.

The 'Anglo-Saxon' suspicion of intellectual brilliance has been closely analysed.[30] At regular intervals Marlborough headmasters voiced their conviction of its essential soundness. Cotton, while anxious to jolt his pupils out of their narrow, parochial world and keen to raise the academic tone of the school, took pains to lecture the less intellectual about their qualities and warn the clever of the dangers of their talents. While those of ordinary merit, he insisted, were often blessed by strength of character, steadiness, calmness and clear judgment, the brilliant were often unsettled, dissatisfied, self-conscious, vain and morbid. In his view, normal ability harnessed to a dutiful nature and spirit of self-improvement were most beneficial to a school. While undoubtedly this type of comment is a good example of a compensatory rationalisation, it was not calculated to ensure the school intellectual a secure status, and no doubt this attitude served in part to produce the Marlborough boy who, when asked to write an essay on the most useful citizen—political-economist or professional cricketer—chose the latter on the grounds that he gave pleasure, while the other 'few understood and was dull'.

Farrar praised the honourable, well-mannered, serious-minded pure-hearted boys who often performed a higher service to their country than those of conceited, worthless brilliance. Intellectual gifts, he warned the school congregation, might be precious but they were also perilous.[31] The *Marlburian*, too, expressed a dislike of the clever. 'Knowledge puffeth up' an editorial trumpeted in 1888. Learning, it continued, gave a wrong idea of the relative importance of things. Those with any sort of learning were in great danger of despising everything else and looking down on those without it. Such anti-intellectualism, combined with the imperialistic mood, points to the accuracy of Harold Laski's later philippic on the product of the public school, the 'English gentleman' who, if true to type, was suspicious of thinkers and sceptical of dwellers upon heights, and who played games in the belief that their cultivation was the secret of national greatness.[32]

We can, in fact, ask essentially the same question of the whole species of public school boys of the late Victorian-Edwardian era as Correlli Barnett asks of the public school writers of the Great War, namely, who would guess from their cloistered introversion that Britain in the pre-war years was a nation of searing social inequality and gross injustice?[33] Most Marlburians looked inward

within the college walls or into the far distance—to tropical rain-
forests or the undulating savannah, never to the industrial deserts
of the English north or midlands. They hardened their muscles,
took their knocks and developed their 'pluck' for England across
the seas, because this was how aspiring and actual gentlemen
behaved.[34]

The apologists for athleticism became increasingly sophisticated
in argument, constructing a moral value-scale for games, but the
central dogma remained the same. Thus when a contributor to
the *Marlburian* in 1873 discussed the relative value of football
and cricket as vehicles of moral education in an essay on comparative athletics, he came to the happy conclusion that, although
football was morally superior to cricket, both games encouraged
patience, endurance, enthusiasm, fidelity to one's side, coolness
and watchfulness. He must have delighted Trebla (who, incidentally, may have been a master, since he was still at Marlborough). In the same year Trebla produced a 'Ruskinian Study'
in which he hymned the virtues of a rugby ball. In a passage
discussing the individual's responsibility as a member of the
college community he declared :

> Football is his first work. Into that he has put as much of
> human patience, commonsense, forethought, experimental
> philosophy, self-control, habits of order and obedience, careless
> courage, careful patriotism, unity of purpose and harmony of
> aim as can well be put into a space of six inches in diameter
> and eighteen in circumference.[35]

Support for rugby and cricket was apparently as unequiv-
ocally strong among the majority of boys of the period, if at a
more prosaic and less philosophical level of involvement. The
editors of the *Marlburian* in December 1875 lamented the fact
that hundreds of fellows passed through the college without a
thought for anything except games, and possibly work. An im-
penetrable curtain of philistinism, they complained, reduced the
sounds of political life to the faintest echo, while literature, history
and social questions were smothered. Did these chroniclers exag-
gerate? In the light of Farrar's comments, it is reasonable to
suppose that they did not. Of course, it would be purely fanciful
to suppose these 'hundreds of fellows' played games for their
moral attributes. Their interest in the main was undoubtedly

apolaustic; nevertheless, the consecrated ideology of athleticism allowed, excused and 'explained' their indulgence.

Comments from other quarters throw light on the grip of the games ideology. In the previous year the theologian J. Llewellyn Davies had used the college pulpit to remark 'that educational good sense was beginning to protest against a predominance of bodily exercise that had to be checked'.[36] But the energy of many, it would appear, was determinedly focused on games and discussion about games above all else. One clear indication of this was a continuous spate of letters in the correspondence columns of the *Marlburian* on a wide range of internal sporting topics. Fierce controversies raged—the relative merits of rugby and association football, the desirability of hockey, the debilitating effects of casual suburban cricket on the school eleven. In contrast, despite the first editors who had the best of literary intentions, the literary element of the college magazine languished. Editorials bewailing the paucity of quality articles were a recurrent feature.

From time to time in the *Marlburian* there emerged protesters against the games emphasis—infrequent, feeble voices crying faintly in a dangerous wilderness. Protests often served merely to reveal the crushing impact of the ethos. Several examples may be cited. 'Sloper', a young correspondent who had no skill at football, which in his own words was 'the sole passport to a happy life', wrote baldly that a mind as rich in learning as Croesus in gold was small value in a school world ruled co-equally by football and cricket.[37] One Marlburian editorial[38] contained extracts from a 'manuscript' of a mythical lunar creature, a student of man and his institutions. From him we learn that the culmination of English folly at this time was the public school system with its concentration on outdated knowledge and with games the great desideratum and sole source of conversation. Such was the grip of this system, however, that protesters earned hatred and unpopularity and were regarded as 'little less than maniacs'. The editors recorded that the manuscript ended abruptly as though the author was beaten by the maligned 'after the manner of the place'.

Those champions of the playing field who were permitted extra terms at school incurred the wrath of an indignant young academic because they held back the able in the lower forms, but it was made quite clear to him by a subsequent correspondent that his was definitely a minority view and that he had failed to appreciate the contribution these gentlemen made to the school.[39]

In the last three decades of the nineteenth century Cicero and Virgil continued to be translated at Marlborough; the 'modern class' beckoned the less able and the obviously vocational; Oxford and Cambridge scholarships were consistently won; the college natural history society and debating society attracted devotees, but the evidence, incomplete though it must be, clearly reveals that games-playing—ostensibly for character development in the forty-eight years between Cotton's innovatory headmastership and the turn of the century—had acquired formalised rituals of involvement and a considerable importance beside which, for many of the boys at least, the rival ideologies of the 'dutiful Christian' and 'intellectual endeavour' paled into relative insignificance. By the mid-1890s it seemed undeniably true that as a jejune, anonymous Marlborough poet wrote,

> . . . one athletic rage,
> Has seized Marlburians of every age,
> Now, filled with frenzy, cricket all will play,
> Now, all-absorbing football rules the day,
> Where'er you go, the topic is the same,
> And all our talk at tables is 'the game'
> I, who-so-oft renounce athletics, lie
> Not, 'B-v-'s' self e'er tells more lies than I
> When sick of football, tired, bruised and sore,
> We swear to our best friends we'll play no more,
> We wake next day, prepared for what you will,
> And long for games again, to show our skill.[40]

Fittingly in the Marlborough centenary celebrations pageant— the Centenary Cavalcade—the year 1894 was chosen to symbolise the zenith of the games movement, and the chorus sang of the era with absolute credibility :

> Rugger, hockey, cricket, fives
> Racquets—the centre of our lives.[41]

The three headmasters who succeeded Cotton—G.G. Bradley (1858–70), F.W. Farrar (1871–76) and G.C. Bell (1876–1903)—

all accepted the ideological emphasis on games with differing degrees of enthusiasm, although Bell had clearly lost patience with philathleticism by the end of his long sojourn. In a series of prize-day speeches from 1898 to 1901 his enthusiasm for college sporting performances was consistently lukewarm. In 1898 he felt moved to suggest a corrective to the imbalance, as he saw it, in the recognition accorded to athletic and intellectual achievement: 'We have a very full equipment of challenge cups and shields and it does not seem desirable to add to their number. We offer quite enough stimulus to athletics. I have often wished to see a challenge prize of a similar kind to one awarded in another school to the house which had most distinguished itself in the studies of the school.' The following year, after a reflection that athletics was a great deal talked about by schoolmasters, foreign observers and the press, came the cool comment 'I will only say that games and athletics vigorously pursued, well organised and, let me add, not too much talked about are generally estimated to be excellent helps towards school discipline and good tone.' The year 1900 brought a note of resignation: 'Following the order of our school *"virtuti, studio, ludo"*, it is time to say a word about games *I suppose*' (emphasis added). And in 1901 came the excuse: 'My watch tells me that I have left little time in which to refer to games.' In retirement three years later Bell himself donated an *academic* challenge cup which was suitably entitled the Bell Trophy, and in 1906 as a guest speaker at the annual prize day he uttered a now familiar *cri de coeur* that sufficient was done for the body but not for the mind.

Athleticism as a moralistic ideology was increasingly under attack at an official level in the early years of the twentieth century. No doubt because of the wide audience it attracted, the annual prize day was utilised to redefine educational objectives and priorities. In 1906 not only Bell but a distinguished Old Marlburian, T.L. Papillon, used the occasion to voice unease at the power of games and issued a warning to the boys not to put their whole trust 'in the machinery of athletics'.

Times were changing once more. The Balfour Education Act of 1902, with the subsequent systematisation and expansion of secondary and tertiary education, increased both academic and occupational pressure upon the public school boy[42] at the expense of his athletic activities. The games cult suffered an additional

blow at Marlborough with the appointment, as Bell's successor
in 1903, of Frank Fletcher, whose attitude towards the idolised
athlete was one of unequivocal hostility. His distaste for the pre-
eminence in school life of the muscular philistine and his 'saurian'
endeavours is recorded in his own account of his life as a schoolmaster.[43] At Marlborough he was determined to encourage
greater intellectual effort, widen cultural horizons and reduce
the status of the athlete. The *Marlburian* records that on his
arrival 'He found that the cult of games had weakened the
position of the Marlborough prefects until they had become the
rois-fainéants of a community in which the captains were the
Mayors of the Palace. He set himself to right this Merovingian
condition and gradually, against much opposition, the ball made
room for the book.'[44] Thus Fletcher challenged the sporting
establishment and asserted the position of the prefect over the
athlete. There is a certain irony in a headmaster coming directly
from Rugby, like Cotton, and having to ensure the domination
of one of his famous predecessor's two strategies over the other.
That Fletcher had to overcome the resentment of staff as well as
boys nicely illustrates the inversion of Cotton's involvement
strategy that had occurred in the interim.

After a struggle lasting several years Fletcher was eventually
convinced, as he put it, 'that brain and strength were working
in harmony . . . but in the right order of preference'.[45] In fact,
by reducing the domination of one ideological commitment he
appears to have exacerbated relations between two opposed sections of the boys. An interesting struggle now comes to light
between the supporters and detractors of athleticism. No doubt
the long oppressed non-athletes were encouraged and fortified by
the new headmaster's official support and his criticism of the
hitherto inviolable. In all probability their resistance stiffened,
and consequently their provocation became more overt. This is,
of course, conjecture, but it is undeniably true that a long, bitter
and eventually well-publicised battle between 'aesthetes' and
'hearties' was seriously joined in Fletcher's time and remained
a prominent feature of Marlborough life for the next thirty years.

However, as regards the mass of pupils and their housemasters,
it is at least questionable whether the pro-intellectual evangelism
of Bell and Fletcher greatly changed institutional priorities immediately. In one house certainly, that of T.C.G. Sandford, there

is evidence that the athletic ethos continued little diminished in intensity. Sandford, 'a prodigy of physical energy' is an archetypal figure of the athleticism movement—a symbol of ideological purity. An Old Marlburian himself, in his youth he had been a noted schoolboy athlete 'who learned early how to train others . . . and became a very successful and rather terrific Captain of House and School'. He became in due course a man of simple values and dominant personality. His contribution to the college, stated his obituarist, 'lay in a career of athletic service . . . unequalled in the school's history'.[46] A traditionalist and the last Marlborough master to keep a cane beside his desk, it was as housemaster that he displayed his 'fullest power and will' in defence of bodily fitness. 'He coached and beat and cared' for his house with devotion and the products were 'tough but not hooligans'. Athletically, Sandy's house dominated the school. Within the house, according to an ex-pupil, Ulric Nisbet, writing of Marlborough before the Great War, athletics dominated the boys.

> The Spartan discipline that he inflicted upon himself was reflected in our own customs and doings. There were two pairs of hanging rings in our long dormitory, and upon these each Saturday night new boys, and sometimes those not so new, were made to carry out an excruciating exercise called 'pull-through'. Failure was punishable with three strokes—in pyjamas. Panic always produced failure; otherwise it was knack rather than muscle that accompanied the feat. I was once tapped in dormitory possibly for failing on the rings, but more of my contemporaries suffered regularly (notably poor C, too tall for his years) till their seniority or a compassionate prefect saved them from further disgrace.[47]

Only in the worst conditions did members of T.C.G.S.'s house wear overcoats. When occasionally released from their own games to watch a school match they could always be recognised, shivering in football kit. The conditioning was apparently successful. 'Those with an ambition for glory', wrote Nisbet, 'could conceive of nothing more illustrious in those days than a place in the eleven.'

The stupefying tragedy of the Great War, however, stilled momentarily the developing internal 'aesthete-hearty' struggle for ideological supremacy. For month after month and year after year the pages of the *Marlburian* were filled with the obituaries of Marlborough dead. Even in death the sportsmen often attracted the most attention, and a superior sort of immortality for their skill with bat and ball.[48] If intellectualism was slowly in the ascendant, the lost boyhood heroes of the playing field were mourned with an intensity peculiarly and uniquely representative of the era.

> A King was he of high degree,
>   King of the boys who love,
> The lads they know can tackle low,
>   And the lusty lads who shove.
>
> King of them all, and King of the ball,
>   Whatever the colour be;
> Red, white and brown, they owed his crown,
>   And King of them all was he.
>
> Good was his name, he played the game,
>   And he made the red ball hum,
> A King beloved as he stood and shoved,
>   Or burst through the reeking scrum.
>
> Farewell, young King, away you fling,
>   All in the flush of youth,
> Playing the game, the grand last game,
>   For England and for Truth.[49]

Despite the understandable reincarnation through verse of the brave and the beautiful, the Great War proved a watershed. After it, as a consequence of increasing academic and occupational pressure from the state-educated and various internal pressures of an aesthetic and intellectual nature, the college authorities continued the pre-war shift towards an extension of both the objectives and ingredients of public school education. Athleticism, once arrogantly assertive, moved first on to the defensive and then began a gradual retreat. By the second half of the twentieth century a new ideology had emerged—individualism. This is well illustrated by a prize-day speech by the headmaster, F.M. Heywood, in 1951, in which he outlined the characteristics of the good school as he saw it. They make interesting reading and included respect for individuality, freedom (including freedom for leisure) and variety. Service, physical courage and group loyalty did not receive a mention.

During its heyday in the late Victorian period, it is important to recognise that athleticism was not an exclusive ideology. Other ideologies existed—central and peripheral, overt and covert. Some have been recorded, others possibly have not. The other major educational ideologies have been mentioned earlier—those of the 'English gentleman', the 'dutiful Christian' and 'intellectual endeavour'. These at one and the same time coexisted, openly competed and overlapped with athleticism. The present survey, therefore, is a study of emphasis not exclusiveness. The extant evidence leaves little doubt that in the decades immediately before and after the turn of the century games fanaticism at Marlborough was pronounced, heavily involved the majority, and this involvement was underpinned and legitimated by a powerful and explicitly formulated educational rationale. In the main, during their years at Marlborough, many boys played rather than studied or prayed.[50] In this respect the college conformed thoroughly to the contemporary stereotype of the English public school.

The apparently dominant social image of the English public school of late Victorian times fits Marlborough like a glove. However incredible this image may seem now, it is well recorded by J.H. Simpson, a public school master and antagonist of athleticism, who wrote in 1900 :

A great many people think of the public schools, when they think of them at all, as being primarily places where boys learn to play games. . .

I believe that anyone who has observed public school life from inside for several years without allowing his prejudices to be altogether enlisted on the side of tradition will concede that the popular impression *is in this matter broadly true.* The cult of games and athletic success does remain the liveliest interest of the great number of boys. This cult is, both for good and bad, one of the most choice products of the public school system. A study of athleticism, to use an ugly word, is a necessary part of the structure of the system as a whole.[51]

Despite Simpson's observation, no specific study has yet been made of public school athleticism, and this investigation of Marlborough College is an attempt to rectify the omission. For, as an educational ideology, athleticism at Marlborough had several important roles: it was used by Cotton as a form of pseudo-reasoning which permitted the obscuring and rationalising of his real motives for games; it served as a set of beliefs which legitimated and sustained a preoccupation with physical activities in this small society; and for Trebla and his successors it constituted a number of value-judgments presented as truths to strengthen their impact and ensure their acceptance. Its emergence was due to a natural enthusiasm of the 'boy culture' for physical pursuits, to the anti-intellectualism of the upper middle class, to the restricted nature of the curricular and extra-curricular activities, to the strenuous nature of imperial service and, above all, to Cotton's calculated exercise in human relations.

The Origins of Modern Football and the Public School Ethos

Eric Dunning

THE BIRTH of modern sport may be traced to that fundamental transformation of leisure patterns which accompanied industrialisation, a process in which Britain led the way. But what might be called the prehistory of modern football—which started as a 'folk-game' during the pre-industrial era—unfolded in the Victorian public schools of the mid-nineteenth century. These were the 'social loci' of the birth and early development of the prototypes of modern rugby and association football, and to this institutional setting may be traced the ethos dominant in British sport until the 1950s. Indeed, it still survives in rugby union, since 'old boys' of public schools have maintained their original dominant influence in that sport.

Cricket began to undergo a process of modernisation a good deal earlier, from the mid-eighteenth century, mainly under the aegis of the aristocracy and gentry. But a century later the process of industrialisation was well advanced, the ascendant bourgeoisie exercised growing power, and this was to have a decisive influence on the development of modern football, as indeed, on modern sport generally. Much the same might be said of the public schools themselves, and in this connection Arnold's Rugby figures prominently. It was at Rugby, in about 1830, that football first began to emerge as a strictly organised, complex and elaborate, controlled and 'civilised' sport.[1]

There are various ways in which to approach an analysis of the public schools and their activities. Here they will be treated as social systems whose development is bound up with that of society at large. The central focus will be on the nature of power and authority relations at each level; that is, on the 'balance of power' between masters and pupils, among the pupils themselves,

22 Lancing College Chapel.

23   Clifton College.

24   Fettes College.

and between different social classes in the wider society as this impinged upon the public schools.

The types of football played by public school boys in the eighteenth and early nineteenth centuries were local adaptations of the general 'folk' tradition, that is, loosely and informally organised, locally variable games played according to oral rules. There were no referees or linesmen, no restrictions on the number of participants, few limitations on the size of the playing area, and games were rough and wild. But one crucial point differentiated the public school variants of folk-football from the forms played in society at large : the game was closely bound up with the prefect-fagging system, the system of pupil 'self-rule' which had grown up in these schools. This epitomised the prevailing system of authority, and the boys themselves adopted and ran their football as a leisure activity, sometimes in defiance of the masters. Samuel Butler endeavoured to prohibit at Shrewsbury a game he described as 'fit only for butcher-boys' or better suited to 'farm-boys and labourers than young gentlemen'; he met with some success, but from about 1830 it was played by stealth, and under the next headmaster it came into its own.[2]

David Newsome has suggested that many masters of this period had an educational ideology grounded on the 'deeply respected tradition' that boys should be free to use their leisure as they wished. This may be, but the choice of such an educational value probably reflected the inability of earlier generations of masters to direct leisure-energies into chosen educational channels. Certainly the history of the public schools between about 1750 and 1832 is punctuated by rebellions which indicate the relative powerlessness of the authorities. This was a period when aristocratic entrants became socially, if not numerically, dominant within the schools, thus creating an ethos which relegated masters of inferior social status to the position of paid dependants. Since such pupils had no need of qualifications and parents tended to value most the relations formed with other boys, there were few barriers to this form of pupil power. The situation was highly conducive to the development of a pattern of authority among the pupils which would fill the 'power vacuum' in the schools; not unnaturally, this took the form of the well-known prefect-fagging system.

Particularly relevant to the evolution of school games is the

M

fact that the older and stronger boys acted in relation to the younger and weaker according to whim, unchecked by anything other than the customs forged among themselves. One of the customary duties of small boys was 'fagging out' at football. In other words, they were relegated to 'keeping goal' for their seniors, i.e. ranged *en masse* along the base lines, or, as at Winchester, also around the sides of the pitch. The 'uncivilised' character of the game at this stage, in particular the roughness of older towards younger boys, may be illustrated by some reminiscences. At Westminster in the 1850s, according to Captain Markham, 'the enemy tripped, shinned, charged with the shoulder, got you down and sat upon you—in fact might do anything short of murder to get the ball from you'. Charterhouse played a game called 'football in cloisters' in the course of which fags in goal 'were sent spinning head over heels for five yards along the stones'. 'Scrimmages' in this game sometimes lasted for three-quarters of an hour, during which 'shins would be kicked black and blue; jackets and other articles of clothing almost torn into shreds; and fags trampled underfoot'. The roughness of the game was aggravated by the wearing of special iron-tipped boots. This was also the case at Rugby, where such boots were called 'navvies'. The latter are described as having 'a thick sole, the profile of which at the toe much resembled the ram of an ironclad'. At Winchester not only were junior boys placed in lines around the pitch to demarcate boundaries, but two fags standing, one at each end, with their legs apart, served as 'goal-posts'. Football at Shrewsbury went under the name of 'douling', the term also used for fagging and reputedly derived from the Greek word for slave.[3] There could hardly be a clearer indication of the direct link between the public school game at this period and the hierarchy of authority among the pupils.

Versions of the game varied, and changes in it took place at varying rates in different public schools during the second quarter of the nineteenth century. Such changes were dependent largely on changes in the structure of the schools which, in turn, were dependent largely on changes in the structure of society at large. These wider developments can be summarised, briefly if somewhat crudely, by the sociological concept of 'bourgeoisification'. It is usual to denote as the 'mid-Victorian compromise' the period when the power of the ascendant middle classes was approximately equal to that of the established aristocracy and gentry; and the development of the public schools, notably within the Arnoldian pattern of reform, can be seen as one aspect of the resultant fusion of values. It was in that context that the modernisation of football gained ground.

Mack describes the controversy about the structure and functions, indeed the very existence, of the public schools during the early years of the century, the decline in numbers (severe at all schools except Eton and Rugby) and the positions taken up by conservative, liberal and radical reformers. In the outcome the emphasis was on moderate reform, if possible from within the system, but this met with little success until Arnold produced a compromise solution which approximated closely to the new social realities. As is well known, the instrument he turned to new use was the prefect system, which he endeavoured to transform into a regularised scheme of indirect rule. While considerable autonomy remained with the boys, the rights and obligations of prefects and fags were more clearly and formally defined, to some extent in written form, with due recognition of the authority of staff and headmaster. Newsome has suggested that the subsequent increase in numbers at Rugby gave rise to increased problems of discipline. That is not unlikely. In any case, attempts at reform usually tend to meet with resistance in greater or lesser degree. It is a measure of Arnold's success, however, that, under his régime, the refractoriness of the pupils never reached the heights of rebelliousness endemic in public schools in the eighteenth and early nineteenth centuries. There was, T.W. Bamford notes, almost an open revolt in 1833 when Arnold, after a complaint from a local landowner, expelled six boys for fishing in the Avon—a step indicating how far the imposition of discipline checked former aristocratic licence. But his favourite prefects defused the situation, and his friend Thomas Carlyle, after visiting Rugby in 1842, described it as 'one of the rarest sights in the world, a temple of industrious peace'.

Arnold is said to have resolutely excluded aristocratic entrants when Rugby gained a new reputation: 'Aristocrats tried, and tried in vain, to make him open its door for the admission of pupils from the higher classes.'[4] Meanwhile, in consultation with local farmers, he waged war on such formerly favoured activities as hunting, shooting and fishing and destroyed the pack of hounds kept by the boys.[5] Accordingly there was more time for school-based games, football included. Arnold took a 'hearty interest' in these, seeing them 'as an integral part of education' according to the head boy at Rugby at the time of his death, and this 'put him in sympathy with all that was good, even in the least intellectual of his scholars'.[6] His ban on traditional gentlemanly sports and his positive encouragement of the team game were a spur to the development of football at Rugby. The formal endorsement of school games recalls the other aspects of education emphasised by Arnold—intellectual, moral, religio-political—which provided the general context into which games must fit. It was not, however, Arnold himself but later school-masters who espoused an ideology which placed organised team games in the forefront as an instrument of moral education.

The influences brought to bear on the evolution of football operated at different levels. For one thing boys were now able, if not constrained, to devote more time and attention to a game which, since it was confined to the school premises, had to be played within circumscribed spatial limits and could benefit from more explicit rules. More generally, the Arnoldian reforms created social relationships conducive to this development. As a result, football grew quite rapidly in complexity, while at the same time becoming 'domesticated' into a more controlled and orderly game. Detailed evidence is lacking as to the manner of this 'civilising process', but two hypotheses may be advanced. Either leading boys acted entirely on their own initiative or, as seems more likely, there was encouragement from the staff to regularise the organisation and rules of the game and eliminate some of the more barbaric features. Both these alternatives suggest new social relationships at work.

There were other social changes in the school which had significant effects on the development of football. One of these concerned the function of the school 'levée'. Games had for some time been organised, in common with other activities, by a system of informal assemblies known as 'levées'—a term presum-ably borrowed from the pattern of absolute monarchy to cover a prefectorial summoning of subjects to receive orders. Under Arnold, according to one historian of Rugby, the levées became more formal, orderly and 'democratic', as the boys learned 'the necessity for order and decent procedure'. Arnold's son William later wrote of an imaginary levée called to fix the opening of the football season in terms which may well have reflected his father's approach : 'This law and legislating in all its degrees, this constitutional settling of these excited questions by a recognised authority, is very good and humanising. . . All orderly and proper now : plenty of excitement, but under decorous restraint.' Levées were held at four levels : school, house, Upper School, sixth form. It was a sixth form levée that in 1845 produced *The Laws of Football as Played at Rugby School*, the earliest rules of the game committed to written form. William Arnold was one of the three drafters of the pamphlet in which they appeared. It was divided into two sections : the first dealt with matters of discipline and general organisation, the second with the main rules governing the playing of the game itself.[7]

It is usual to ascribe the first rules to 1846, when, in fact, a different set was printed deriving from another source, though under the same title. This time, only rules relating to the playing side of the game figured, that is, the experimental rules of 1845 as sanctioned, with one or two alterations by an Upper School (or Big-side) levée. The point is important in so far as it denotes that prefects, even if acting as the main initiators of change, had now to submit directives to the Upper School as a whole. The 1846 rules had a short preamble :

> The following set of rules is to be regarded rather as a set of decisions on certain disputed points, than as containing all the Laws of the Game, which are too well known to render any explanation necessary to Rugbeians.

At this stage, then, there was no attempt to codify the game completely; written rules were only perceived as necessary with respect to disputed points. Since the written rules numbered thirty-seven, it seems that considerable controversy could arise. Evidently this occurred mainly in relation to 'offside', the types of physical force regarded as legitimate, and 'fair' means of controlling and propelling the ball. In each of these respects rugby football, becoming more elaborate, had begun to develop characteristics differentiating it from forms played elsewhere. It had also clearly attained a level of complexity with which the earlier customary controls could no longer cope.

The principal function of the new rules was that of 'conflict regulation', minimising the possibility of disputes. The rules defining legitimate types of physical force were, of course, particularly important, since disputes in that connection are likely to have escalated into 'real' fighting more readily than those concerned with other aspects of the game. The earlier unwritten rules had allowed a good deal of roughness and violence, particularly on the part of older and stronger boys. Scars inflicted by 'navvies' had been a source of pride. The introduction of written rules, with the corresponding increase of objectivity, helped to remove the game from the caprice of the most powerful and place it under a recognised authority, and in so doing to regularise it by circumscribing and prohibiting certain forms of activity. Four rules may be cited as examples :

> Rule xi : No player being off his side shall hack, charge, run in, touch the ball in goal or interrupt a catch.
> Rule xvi : A player standing up to another may hold one arm only, but may hack him or knock the ball out of his hand if he attempt to kick it or go beyond the line of touch.
> Rule xxv : No hacking with the heel or above the knee is fair.
> Rule xxviii : No player may wear projecting nails or iron plates on the soles or heels of his shoes or boots.

These rules did not eliminate entirely the opportunity of taking part in a 'manly' physical struggle. They permitted a degree of violence considerably greater than is allowed today and continued to do so for several decades, but after this initial period the game began to take on more of the attributes of a 'mockfight'. Thus, beginning as a group contest incorporating, to a considerable extent, 'real' fighting, football was regulated into a form of physical struggle which extended the players but which had a diminishing chance of inflicting serious injury. In other words, brute force came to count less, the use of skill more. Here was a significant step towards the modern form of rugby football which involves an intricate balance of strength and skill, spontaneity and control. As has been suggested, this accorded directly with other changes under way at Rugby at the time and served to bring the game into line with prevailing educational aims, thereby preparing the way for the eventual elevation of football, as one of the chief team games, to the level of an educational value in itself.

To turn, by way of conclusion, to a specific point, rugby football is supposed to have developed its distinctive form as a result of a single deviant act by an individual. A commemorative tablet in the school close records the exploit of William Webb Ellis

Who With a Fine Disregard For The Rules of
Football, As Played In His Time,
First Took The Ball In His Arms and Ran With It,
Thus Originating The Distinctive Feature Of
The Rugby Game
A.D. 1823.

To attribute so much influence to a chance occurrence would seem mistaken.[8] Matthew Bloxam first initiated the story, sixty years after the event, in the school magazine *The Meteor* (no. 157, 1880), in an article recalling his own schooldays in old age. However, he had left the school in 1820, and his hearsay account might well have faded into obscurity had not outside developments favoured its adoption in defence of the later version of the rugby game. By the 1890s football was developing as a commercial spectacle, with players and spectators drawn primarily from the industrial working classes, particularly in the north of England, and in 1895 came the split into the semi-professional game of rugby league as against the wholly amateur rugby union. It was in that very year that a pamphlet issued by the Old Rugbeian Society, *The Origins of Rugby Football*, resurrected the Bloxam story and that the commemorative stone was erected—an attempt, no doubt, to reassert proprietorship in face of encroachments by 'outsiders' in all senses of the term. For, had it been the overriding intention to explain the development of the game, there were equally distinctive features which should have been explained, such as use of the oval ball, the H-shaped goals, scoring above the crossbar and by tries as well as goals. Possibly Rugbeians, initially in rivalry with other public schools, deliberately added to the distinctive characteristics of their game. Certainly it brought the school to attention, as in 1839, when the Dowager Queen Adelaide paid a visit and one of her principal requests was to watch a game of football. When in 1849 football rules were committed to writing at Eton, a principal rival, several were diametrically opposed to those recorded at Rugby a few years before.[9] It is interesting to note that central among these is a taboo on the use of hands, now the main distinguishing mark of association football or 'soccer'. It may, therefore, be that the incipient bifurcation of the rugby and association games was connected with status rivalry between Eton and Rugby in the 1830s and 1840s. Several attempts were made during the next decade and the early 1860s to develop a uniform football code but, owing to the intensity of 'old boy' rivalry, particularly between Etonians and Rugbeians, they proved a total failure.

The bifurcation was only to be firmly institutionalised at a national level with the foundation in 1863 of the Football Association and in 1871 of the Rugby Football Union. 'Old boys' of public schools were primarily responsible for the formation of both these associations, at a time when the games cult was becoming predominant within these schools. By this route the concept of 'character training' became central to the ethos which developed in British sport generally in the later nineteenth century. The cricket and football fields were seen as arenas for the learning and display of gentlemanly ideals: 'character', 'style', 'good form', 'fair play', 'group loyalty', 'self-control', and a host of others. The amalgam is indicative in so far as style, good form and group loyalty may be classed as values of the landed classes; self-control and competition—an essential ingredient of the organised team game—as those proper to the ascendant bourgeoisie.

A new element was to be added when both brands of football spread downwards to the working classes, while also becoming increasingly professionalised and commercialised, if not 'proletarianised', with, as the obverse, the eulogising of the amateur player whose supremacy is inherent in his pursuit of the game for its own sake and nothing else. But this final stage in the diversification of the game occurred largely outside the Victorian period, and entirely outside the public school system. For the purposes of this study, it serves merely to remind us that a game which was once regarded as the arcane diversion of a favoured few eventually became the common property of the masses.

The Architecture of the Victorian Public School

Malcolm Seaborne

THE MOST obvious way to deal with the architectural aspect of the Victorian public schools would be to show the stylistic development of the schools, illustrated with examples taken chronologically. In fact, there is a coherent development, beginning with schools built in the classical style in the early decades of the century, succeeded by what we might call 'scholastic' Gothic and then 'ecclesiastical' Gothic, with some variations of style after the manner of Christopher Wren, merging into the Queen Anne style after 1870.

However, it is also important to look at the rationale which lay behind the building of the Victorian public schools and to probe into the educational and economic reasons why schools were built when and where they were. Educationally speaking, the 'heroic' period for the building or rebuilding of the public schools was during the first half of Victoria's reign, from about 1840 to 1870. This was the time when new educational and social class changes made themselves felt in their most uncompromising form. Old schools were rebuilt, new and ambitious schools were founded, and the inherited educational system underwent enormous changes. As only one index of this, we may note that of the 200 schools which today belong to the Headmasters' Conference, 85 were founded during the nineteenth century, and 45 of these were founded in the thirty years 1840–70.

The best starting-point for a survey of public school architecture at the opening of Victoria's reign is provided by the series of aquatints produced by Ackermann in 1816.[1] Eight of the nine 'great schools' were depicted, as was Christ's Hospital, which occupied a class by itself approximating to 'great school' status. (Shrewsbury was not included, since it only began its revival under Butler and Kennedy early in Victoria's reign, and was not at that date considered to be in the top flight of public schools.)

Ackermann's prints help to show that in virtually all the public and grammar schools at the beginning of the reign all the teaching took place in one or two very large schoolrooms. In the bigger schools the boys were divided into classes under separate masters or ushers, but they simply sat in different parts of the one large room. The time-honoured system by which the master called upon individual boys to construe, or to come and stand before him to 'say' the lesson, i.e. recite what had been learned, still held sway. Boys in class worked individually or in pairs, and there was little or no expository teaching or lecturing by the master.

The arrangements for dining and (in the boarding schools) sleeping were also communal in character. Usually the boys ate in one large dining-hall and slept in large dormitories. There was virtually no individual privacy, and the masters took little interest in the social life of the boys, who in many cases developed their own self-governing republics ruled over by the senior boys or prefects.

An examination of the 'great schools' indicates that the architectural inheritance was a very mixed one. Winchester had been founded in the fourteenth century, and at the beginning of Victoria's reign was still using the 'new' schoolroom built in the 1680s. Eton, founded in the fifteenth century, had its Lower School in the original buildings of 1479 and its Upper School in a building dating from about 1690 (*Plate* 15). Westminster had since 1602 used as its schoolroom the former monks' dormitory, and this continued as the main place for teaching until the early 1880s. Charterhouse also occupied a former monastic site (*Plate* 16), with a new schoolroom built in 1803 but on wholly traditional lines. St Paul's had been rebuilt on its original site in 1670 and again in 1824, but the design was entirely traditional. Merchant Taylors' continued to occupy its 1675 building until 1875. At Harrow, the early seventeenth-century schoolroom was extended in 1819, but the numbers attending were small until after the appointment of Vaughan as headmaster in 1844. Shrewsbury continued to occupy a relatively complex set of buildings which dated from the early seventeenth century.

The two other major schools, later examined by Royal Commissioners—Christ's Hospital and Rugby—were notable for having more recently acquired new buildings, in the second and third decades of the nineteenth century, and they exemplified certain new architectural and educational principles which were later to find expression in many other schools.

Before discussing specific schools, however, it is necessary to examine in more detail the new principles making themselves felt in the early nineteenth century. First and most obvious was the problem of larger numbers, resulting from the increase in population and the growing demand from the new industrial and commercial classes for secondary education. The earlier response to increased numbers—as at Winchester and Eton in the late seventeenth century—was simply to build another large schoolroom, dividing the boys roughly according to age and their proficiency in classics, into 'upper' and 'lower' schools. A further device, exploited particularly at Eton but also, to a lesser extent, at the other schools, was to take over private houses for teaching and sometimes domestic use. Indeed, at Eton most of the actual teaching in the early nineteenth century went on in the 'pupil-rooms' of the masters, and not in the main schoolrooms.[2] Another advantage of using private houses was that it was possible to adapt readily to fluctuating numbers: it is remarkable that numbers at Eton more than doubled (from 364 to 806) between 1800 and 1860, with relatively little major rebuilding.

The development of Rugby before the advent of Arnold is interesting on two counts. Firstly, in the absence of a tutorial system on the Eton model, increasing numbers were catered for not merely by building a new 'Big School' but also by building separate classrooms (still called 'schools', however). Thomas James, who really began to build up Rugby as a leading school towards the end of the eighteenth century, had been driven to convert barns and outhouses for use as classrooms, and it was soon after this that the governors, who owned valuable land in London and had an accumulated surplus of £40,000, decided to rebuild the school. It was also fortunate that they had the advantage of a large existing site. Henry Hakewill was commissioned as architect, and rebuilding went on from 1809 to 1816, comprising what are now known as the 'Old Buildings'. Tradition was followed in forming the various rooms around a quadrangle, and it is interesting to note that the Tudor Gothic style was chosen in an attempt to emulate the architecture of earlier academic buildings of the great period of educational expansion during the sixteenth and seventeenth centuries (*Plate* 17). However, the plan, by providing for separate classrooms and individual studies for the boys, was much in advance of its time.[3] In the scale of its rebuilding Rugby was also important, and can be compared at this period only to Christ's Hospital, which was rebuilt during the years 1825–32 by John Shaw and his son, surveyors to the hospital. They, too, built in Tudor Gothic and on the grand scale, as was the tradition with this important school associated with the merchants of London. These buildings were used until 1902, when Christ's Hospital moved to Horsham, after which they were demolished.[4]

More important than increasing size, however, was the introduction of new subjects and of expository teaching methods. In this respect it was the private schools and the secondary schools of Nonconformist origin which led the way. A pioneer school of this type was Mill Hill, whose building of 1825 was in the classical style invariably preferred by Free Churchmen of that time; however, instead of the single large schoolroom, it contained separate classrooms, and English, mathematics, French and natural philosophy were taught in addition to the accepted classical curriculum. The architect was Sir William Tite, who also designed the Scottish Presbyterian Church in Regent Square (1824–27), Nine Elms Railway Station, Battersea (1838) and the Royal Exchange, Threadneedle Street (1841–44). The best example, however, of the influence on school design of the introduction of new subjects was the City of London School, which was a new foundation with a custom-built school completed in 1837 at the expense of the city corporation to the design of J.B. Bunning, later city architect and designer of Holloway Prison (1849–51) and the Coal Exchange, Lower Thames Street (1847, now demolished). This building remained in use until 1882, when the school moved from Cheapside to the Victoria Embankment. The design included specialist teaching rooms, and the school claims to have been the first in England to give practical science lessons (1838). Its restricted site necessitated a four-storey building, for which the Tudor Gothic style was adopted (*Plate* 18).

The opening years of Victoria's reign were indeed notable for a number of important new school buildings in the major provincial towns. King Edward's, Birmingham, was rebuilt in New

Street in 1838 to the design of Charles Barry and A.W.N. Pugin (*Plate* 19), and although this building no longer survives, there are good examples of the early Victorian period at Leicester, Sheffield, York, Cheltenham and Liverpool.[5] It is interesting to note that while the Anglican foundations adopted the Perpendicular Gothic style revived by Hakewill and Shaw, the Nonconformist schools continued to build in classical style. As one of the speakers at the opening of the Nonconformist Proprietary School at Leicester in 1837 put it, the Gothic style was suitable only for those 'whose associations fondly clung to the dark Monastic exploded institutions of our country, who love to dwell rather on the gloomy periods of our history, than to contemplate the blaze of light and knowledge which has since burst upon the world'.

Yet this was, of course, during the same period as the publication of Pugin's *Contrasts* (1836) and only a few years before the appearance of *Tract XC* (1841). The religious controversy aroused by the Oxford Movement was naturally reflected in the field of education and produced some very interesting school buildings. It led to the revival of far more adventurous Gothic architecture than the rather tame 'scholastic' Gothic of Hakewill's buildings at Rugby or Bunning's at the City of London School. Only in a few cases were major schools of outstanding architectural merit built in non-Gothic styles, and, after the controversy had died down, one finds a reversion to milder Gothic forms, later merging into equally 'safe' neo-Georgian.

There was, of course, one important precondition before school architecture could be further developed. An effective demand, involving increased numbers and a modernised curriculum, could not by itself bring about the erection of new buildings: it was also essential to have sufficient capital resources. The schools built in the late 1830s and 1840s were financed on the proprietary principle by which shares were raised by public subscription. Only when such schools became established—and the great majority of them were financial failures—could they become 'independent' in the modern sense of deriving their income mainly from the pupils' fees. Two exceptions to this general statement were Wellington College, which was financed from the public subscriptions collected in memory of the great duke, and the Woodard Schools, whose founder used almost twentieth-century techniques of fund-raising (and personally raised £250,000 on behalf of his main foundations at Lancing, Ardingly and Hurstpierpoint).

Educationally, the main 'selling-point' was the revival or perhaps invention of the idea of a boarding school education as a valuable experience in itself, with the opportunities this offered for character training and (later in the century) organised games. Equally strong was the desire for a new style of education which broke away from the old tradition of crowded communal living. It is true that Victorian headmasters had much to say about *esprit de corps* : but they also insisted on much more civilised conditions of work and play. Apart from a more careful classification of the pupils into separate classrooms, which was necessitated by the introduction of new subjects and new teaching techniques, greater privacy was also secured by building separate cubicles for sleeping and individual studies for private work.[6] Houses run by 'dames', which had a long history in such places as Eton, Harrow and Rugby, were taken over by assistant masters—a development that helped to tighten up discipline and obviate rebellions of the kind which featured in the histories of many schools in the late eighteenth and early nineteenth centuries.

Some of the public schools were hampered—architecturally speaking—by their subordination to larger institutions, as at Winchester, Eton and Westminster, which were only freed from the control of the Warden, Provost and Dean of their respective foundations by the Public Schools Act of 1868. Even the schools which had been founded to express new educational and social ideas at University College and King's College, London, were circumscribed by occupying only part of the buildings founded primarily for other purposes. (University College School did not move to Hampstead till 1907 and King's College School to Wimbledon Common in 1897.) A few embryonic public schools were also founded in association with training colleges (as at Chester and Lincoln) but were fairly soon squeezed out of existence.[7]

The Victorian period was, nevertheless, pre-eminently one in which the founders of schools were ready to think of building or rebuilding on the grand scale. Even in those cases where the buildings took many years to complete, the new conceptions were present either in the minds of the founders or first headmasters.

This is the reason for my earlier reference to the first half of Victoria's reign as the 'heroic' period of school architecture, since distinctive educational philosophies can be associated with particular men who personally influenced the design of the schools which were to embody their ideas.

Both the speed and manner in which architectural expression could be given to these ideas again depended on financial resources. Broadly speaking, the school buildings inspired by the Victorian reformers may be classified into two main groups : what may be called the 'nuclear' development, by which new buildings were added to an older nucleus, and the 'quadrangular' development, by which elaborate buildings were planned *ab initio* on an ambitious scale. Both methods of expansion had occurred in a few places in earlier periods : for example, Winchester, Eton and Shrewsbury had exemplified major school foundations, initially planned on an extensive scale. On the other hand, during the seventeenth and eighteenth centuries, Rugby and Harrow had grown piecemeal and established their reputations more gradually.

However, in relating architectural style and form to ideas current in the Victorian period, it is the new foundations that are of the greatest interest. Without an existing school building from which to expand, they had either to find some other centre or design the school entirely from scratch. Since funds were usually very limited at first, several schools which later became well known began in country houses with large estates which were only gradually filled up. Notable examples of this category of school are Marlborough (*Plate* 20), which began in an early eighteenth-century mansion, later a coaching-inn made redundant by the coming of the railways; and Rossall, which occupied Rossall Hall, formerly the home of Sir Hesketh Fleetwood. Similarly, Radley occupied the family seat of the Bowyer family, and Bradfield the manor house of Thomas Stevens, the lord of the manor and rector of the parish. Most of the new buildings erected at these places were in Gothic style, which is to be expected in view of the strong Anglican conviction of the founders. An interesting exception here, however, is Marlborough, where the architect, Edward Blore, who had earlier been noted for his Perpendicular Gothic façades (as with the Pitt Building at Cambridge and Bedford Modern School), built in William and

Mary style. He may conceivably have been influenced by the classical design of the original house, though this did not inhibit the architects at Rossall and Radley.

Of the new foundations which began with a virgin site, probably the most notable from the architectural point of view are Wellington and Lancing. They form an interesting contrast. Both schools, it is true, were designed on the quadrangular plan, but the spirit of their architecture and educational outlook are quite different. Wellington, which opened in 1859, owed much to the Prince Consort, who influenced the decision to build a college instead of a series of equestrian monuments with the funds donated in memory of the Duke of Wellington, who had died in 1852. He also helped to choose the site, the architect, John Shaw (the younger), and the first headmaster, E.W. Benson. Shaw had worked on extensions at Christ's Hospital and Eton and had designed the Royal Naval School at Deptford (now Goldsmiths' College). Prince Albert wanted a college which would develop 'those branches of scientific knowledge which have a special application to the arts, commerce and industry of the country', and he disliked the Gothic style because of its 'monastic' associations.[8] At any rate, Shaw's design is in a style composed of Wren's Hampton Court and Louis XIII (*Plate* 21), a combination which, as Pevsner remarks, was later to emerge as the so-called Queen Anne fashion. Benson, for his part, wanted a public school of Arnoldian type, which he secured, as Arnold and others had done, by limiting the number of foundationers and increasing the number of fee-payers. He also managed to persuade the governors to engage George Gilbert Scott to build a Gothic chapel in preference to Shaw's design. However, in spite of this modification and some later building, Shaw's main design has survived.

Lancing and the other Woodard schools were equally based on a distinctive educational and social philosophy. Here the model was quite consciously monastic; hence the cloisters and, above all, the chapels, which formed an integral part of Woodard's vision of Education as the handmaid of Religion. The sites chosen by Woodard are all magnificent, and his architect son, Billy, together with Slater and the Carpenters (father and son), did their best to exemplify Woodard's dictum that 'No system of education would be perfect which did not provide for

25 Dulwich College Great Hall.

26 New Quadrangle at Rugby.

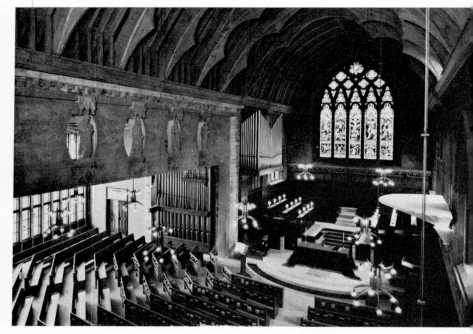

27 Uppingham College Chapel.

28 St Paul's School, Hammersmith.

the cultivation of the taste of the pupils through the agency of the highest examples of architecture.'[9] The architectural climax of the Woodard colleges is the chapel at Lancing (*Plate* 22), built in French Gothic style and higher from floor to vaulting than any nave or choir in the country except Westminster Abbey, York Minster and the Anglican Cathedral at Liverpool.

So far as the teaching arrangements were concerned Wellington and the early Woodard schools were relatively traditional both in the subjects taught and in the important place still given to the big schoolrooms and dining halls. More up to date in this respect were the major foundations of the 1860s, though they also usually adopted quadrangular plans in versions of the Gothic style. Most notable were Clifton (*Plate* 23) and Malvern Colleges, designed by Charles Hansom, and Framlingham and Elstow College, Bedford, designed by Frederick Peck. In Scotland a spiky baronial Gothic was used for Fettes College, near Edinburgh, which was designed by David Bryce and opened in 1870 (*Plate* 24).[10]

The chief breakthrough of the 1860s was, however, at Dulwich, an ancient foundation which carried out a major rebuilding with the proceeds of the £100,000 which came as compensation from two railway companies whose lines crossed the school estates. The architect, Charles Barry (the younger), broke almost fiercely from the conventional Gothic and also avoided the quadrangular plan. The building was in a style called 'North Italian Renaissance', but Ian Nairn describes it as showing 'fragments of all styles and scales' and as 'a fair candidate for the wildest nineteenth-century building in the whole of London'.[11] The design consisted of three blocks : two consisting of classrooms, and the third containing a lecture theatre and laboratory, a library and the Great Hall, which was the traditional big schoolroom reduced in status to the modern assembly hall (*Plate* 25).

This was by no means the end of Gothic, however. Vaughan had made much use of George Gilbert Scott at Harrow, and when Temple and his succesors at Rugby extended the Hakewill buildings, it was Butterfield who was called in and whose architecture now dominates the school and its surroundings (*Plate* 26). Thring at Uppingham chose G.E. Street as his architect, and the somewhat gloomy effect of his buildings was only relieved later by the Jacobean science block of Sir Thomas Jackson built

N

in the 1890s, the hall range of 1923 designed by Ernest Newton, and more recently by the modernisation of the chapel by the architectural firm of Seely and Paget (*Plate* 27). St Paul's, when it moved to West Kensington in 1884, employed Waterhouse as architect, and the effect he produced in purple brick and orange terra-cotta was certainly not lacking in boldness (*Plate* 28). As Pevsner observed before the buildings were demolished, 'there is an odd inability to age gracefully', and St Paul's moved—perhaps without regret—to its fifth set of new buildings, overlooking the river at Barnes, in 1968.[12]

After 1870 there were fewer new foundations and after 1900 fewer major buildings. Those few tended to be built on more conventional lines, and on the whole it seems that the public schools had, from the architectural point of view, ceased to be pioneers by the end of the Victorian period. Most of the new thinking in architecture for academic buildings since 1900 has come from central and local government architects and from those private architects who have contributed to the striking designs of some of the post-war universities.

Notes

CHAPTER 1 (pp. 1–18)

1. Frederic Harrison, *Autobiographic Memoirs*, London 1911, I, 14–54.

2. *Ibid*, 64–5.

3. Staunton, xix-xxi.

4. Newsome, *Godliness and Good Learning*, 4, 25, 34–5.

5. Bamford, *The Rise of the Public Schools*, 16ff.

6. Staunton, xxvi.

7. Mack, I, 334–6.

8. *Ibid.*, 337–8.

9. Quoted in Brian Simon, *Education and the Labour Movement, 1870–1920*, London 1965, 100. The alienation of grammar schools from their locality in the drive for 'public school' status is discussed in Ch. 3 of this work.

10. For a more detailed account of the effects of this act on aspiring grammar schools, see Brian Simon, *Studies in the History of Education, 1780–1870*, London 1960 (retitled The Two Nations and the Educational Structure), 318-36.

11. B.W.T. Handford, *A History of SS Mary and Nicholas College, Lancing, 1848–1930*, Oxford 1933, 98.

12. Parkyn, *Life and Letters of Edward Thring*, 178.

13. G.G. Coulton, *A Victorian Schoolmaster: Henry Hart of Sedbergh*, London 1923, 80.

14. Many endowed grammar schools suffered from divided control (of master and usher) written into the original school statutes.

15. Quoted by J.E.C. Welldon in 'Harrow School Chapel', in *Harrow School*, ed. Howson and Warner, 126.

16. *Ibid.*, 125.

17. Goulburn, *The Book of Rugby School*, Rugby 1856, 219, 239–40.

18. Bradley, Champneys and Baines, *A History of Marlborough College*, 183.

19. G. Lowes Dickinson, *Autobiography*, ed. Dennis Proctor, London 1973, 49, 57, 81.

20. Virginia Woolf, *Roger Fry*, London 1940, 38.

21. Newsome, *A History of Wellington College*, 264.

22. Michael T.H. Sadler, *Michael Ernest Sadler*, London 1949, 188; see also Lynda Grier, *Achievement in Education*, London 1952, 65ff.

23. Eric Eaglesham, 'Implementing the Education Act of 1902', *British Journal of Educational Studies* XI, 2 (1962–63).

24. Phyllis Grosskurth, *John Addington Symonds*, London 1964, 30–41.

25. Wilkinson, *The Prefects*, x-xi.

CHAPTER 2 (pp. 19–33)

1. Honey, *Tom Brown's Universe*, Ch. I, forthcoming.

2. For the development of this infrastructure, see D.P. Leinster-Mackay, 'The English Private School, 1830–1914' (Ph.D. thesis, Durham University, 1972). (Institute of Education Library.)

3. T.W. Bamford in *Educational Review* X, 1 (1957), 26.

4. T.J.H. Bishop and R. Wilkinson, *Winchester and the Public School Élite*, London 1967, 93–4.

5. Newsome, *Godliness and Good Learning*, Ch. IV.

6. W.J. Ong in *Studies in Philology* LVI, 2 (1959); repr. in P.W. Musgrove, ed., *Sociology, History and Education*, London 1970, 223–31.

7. If the lists in Table 1 (or in Tables 1 and 2 together) are accepted as a reliable guide to public school status, it follows that the published versions of the HMC list around 1902 are correspondingly misleading by their inclusion of schools like Boston Grammar School or the soon defunct Godolphin School, which were not members of a self-recognising community, and by their omission of schools like Hurstpierpoint, Loretto and Blair Lodge (a school that drew on the very privileged classes), which very definitely were. So already by 1902 the HMC list was, it may be suggested, a highly suspect basis of analysis.

8. The Headmasters' Conference doubled its numbers by the 1960s and underwent many other significant changes since 1902. Some of the schools which it took in had, in fact, been part of the public schools community before 1902 as delineated in the present analysis, but many of the schools which it later incorporated, though existing before 1902, had not previously been part of that community. I have counted more than eighty schools existing before 1902 which have been included in HMC lists from 1927 onwards used as the basis of the classification 'public school' by various analysts, but which we may assume had no trace of any such status

during the school years of their Victorian alumni, since they are outside the 164 which, as argued in my classification, is the very widest possible estimate of the public schools community by 1902. Add to these the schools which *were* among those 164 (and even more significantly those among the 64 of Table 1) yet which were not in key HMC lists from 1927 onwards (schools like Bath College, Blair Lodge, Forest, Weymouth, Ardingly, Derby and Westward Ho) and it can be seen that half a century of change in the character of the public schools community has had important and disastrous consequences for such analyses.

9. Thus by 1950 or 1960 HMC lists which were used as the basis of the classification 'public school' for the education of élite members analysed must have misrepresented the status of the schools attended by a very considerable proportion for those members who went to those schools before 1902, as very many did. Anyone who turns up in an élite in (say) 1944 as archbishop or viceroy or field-marshal or chief justice will typically be in his sixties or seventies, which means he entered his 'public school' (at the age of thirteen) before 1898, or even before 1888. A classification which reflects the public schools community of 1944 or later, rather than that of 1898 (or 1888) will therefore be a very misleading one.

This becomes serious when one considers the arguments which this kind of arithmetic is used to bolster up. The connection between attendance at public schools and entry into élites is so well known that the reclassification of a proportion of schools in specific analyses is unlikely to upset a conclusion generally applicable to the period from 1870 to 1970, which is that good proportions of public school products turn up in almost every type of élite group. It is when further generalisations are made, and precise percentages of public school men in any group in any period are calculated, that basic errors of classification become crucial.

Laski was almost certainly right about the élite character of British government in the period 1801–1924, but his conclusions depend little on the precise percentages of public school men he claimed to find in his analysis of cabinets. Statistics derived from a similarly fallible exercise are used to support Tawney's conclusions about the relative inaccessibility of élite positions in the 1920s for those outside what he called the 'closed educational system' of the public schools : there would be a good case for re-doing Tawney's analysis, which might then produce a more sophisticated set of conclusions about access to élites in that period. This sort of arithmetic has also been used to illustrate the 'democratisation of the ruling class in the twentieth century', and to show that public school boys had ten times the average chance of becoming managers in the 1950s (regardless of the fact that a third of the sample studied may have been at their 'public schools' before 1902). Yet another scholar has set out to 'ascertain *more or less exactly* the percentage of members of the liberal professions educated in the public schools' on the basis of 1940s assumptions about the public schools applied to a sample of whom 40 per cent entered secondary school before 1902.

10. No difficulties are likely to arise if the examination is restricted to one or two schools like Eton and Harrow. However, 'Social Class of Cambridge Alumni' (*British Journal of Sociology* I, 2, Jun. 1950) is an analysis by two sociologists, Hester Jenkins and D. Caradog Jones, who claimed to identify the top 23 public schools for purposes of classifying the previous schooling of men who were at Cambridge in the period 1751 to 1899. Up to a quarter of the 23 schools they allege were top public schools (throughout that entire period!) are open to question in comparison with the 22 schools of my Group I (and, to a lesser extent, even with the schools of my Group II). There seem to be no good reasons behind the choice of their top 23, which presumably reflect the two sociologists' own impressions about the relative standing of schools in a much later period; indeed, one is driven to suspect that they assumed that schools which were successful in projecting their pupils into élites must therefore be élite schools.

Unfortunately, this very arbitrary list of 23 allegedly leading public schools in the Victorian period has been made the basis of several other analyses of élites in terms of attendance at top public schools, all of which are therefore highly suspect in so far as they deal (as most of them do) with the products of Victorian schools. The most notable of them is the otherwise useful study by W.L. Guttsmann in 1963 of the British political élite from the mid-nineteenth century onwards. Nearly all his various classifications of public schools, and especially his lists of allegedly top public schools, are highly suspect when applied to the late Victorian period, and throw doubt on several of his conclusions about the nature of, and recruitment to, political élites for most of the period of his study.

11. Honey, *Tom Brown's Universe*. Forthcoming.

12. W.R. Lawson, *John Bull and his Schools*, Edinburgh 1908, 43, 49.

CHAPTER 3 (pp. 34–57)

1. See W.E. Winn, '*Tom Brown's Schooldays* and the Development of "Muscular Christianity"', *Church History* XXIX (1960), 64–73; A.J. Hartley, 'Christian Socialism and Victorian Morality:

the Inner Meaning of *Tom Brown's Schooldays, Dalhousie Review* XLIX (1969), 216–28; Bruce E. Haley, *The Cult of Manliness in English Literature*, Ann Arbor 1965. For a general survey of the genre, see P.G. Scott, 'School Novels as a Source Material', *History of Education Society Bulletin* 5 (1970), 46–56.

2. Mack and Armytage, *Thomas Hughes*, 294–5.

3. Macmillan MSS, 6 Aug. 1857. Quotations from the Hughes-Macmillan correspondence are from the British Museum, BM Add. MSS 54917 and 54918 (Vols CXXXII and CXXXIII of the Macmillan papers). Quotation is made by permission of the Trustees of the British Museum, and of Macmillan, of London and Basingstoke.

4. *British Quarterly Review* XXVI (Oct. 1857), 513.

5. *Times*, 9 Oct. 1857.

6. [Richard Ford] in *Quarterly Review* CII (Oct. 1857), 343; author identifications from the *Wellesley Index*.

7. [Fitzjames Stephen] in *Edinburgh Review* CVII (Jan. 1858), 172.

8. *Christian Observer* LVIII (1858), 491. For precursors in the genre, see Margaret Maison, 'Tom Brown and Company : Scholastic Novels of the 1850s', *English* XII (1958), 100–3.

9. *Dublin University Magazine* L (1857), 653.

10. E.g. Harold Child in *The Public Schools from Within*, 295; W.R. Hicks, *The School in English and German Fiction*, 19.

11. Hartley in *Dalhousie Review* XLIX (1969).

12. Kenneth Allsop, 'A Coupon for Instant Tradition', *Encounter* XXV (1965), 63 : see also the reply by A.L. Le Quesne, in *Encounter* XXVI (1966), 93–5.

13. Alasdair Campbell, *The School Novel*, London 1970, 3.

14. P.G. Wodehouse, 'The Tom Brown Question', in his *Tales of St Austins*, London 1903, 273–82; repr. from *The Public School Magazine*. The point about the cricket team selection is also raised by Child.

15. J.M. Ludlow, 'Thomas Hughes and Septimus Hansard', *Economic Review* VI, 3 (Jul. 1896), 306.

16. [Thomas Burbidge] in *North British Review* XXVIII (1858), 139; *Times*, 9 Oct. 1857; *Dublin University Magazine* L (1857), 656; *Christian Observer* LVIII (1858), 500.

17. Mack and Armytage, 14.

18. [Thomas Burbidge], 'George Esling', *Rugby Magazine* I (1835), 81–8, based on Carteret, a boy in Anstey's house (see *Correspondence of A.H. Clough*, ed. F.L. Mulhauser, Oxford 1957, I, 34); J.P. Gell, 'A Schoolboy's Story'. *Rugby Magazine* I (1835) 23–7,

109–20. P. Veyriras, *Arthur Hugh Clough 1819–1861*, Paris 1964, 52, gives J.N. Simpkinson as author of the second piece, but it is signed 'P', Gell's usual pseudonym in the magazine.

19. [W.D. Arnold], *Football. The First Day of the Sixth Match*, Rugby [1851].

20. [A.J. Arbuthnot ?], "[Football]", *The Rugbaean* 1 (1840), 22–4; [C.H. Newmarch], *Recollections of Rugby*, London 1848, Ch. XIV, especially pp. 132–3. Cf. Arbuthnot's hexameters on cricket in *Haileybury Observer* 11 (Sep. 1840).

21. E.M. Goulburn, ed., *The Book of Rugby School*, Rugby 1856, Ch. V. There are no football records of particular matches before 1850 : see Sir Alexander Gibb, *Football Records of Rugby School, 1823–1929*, Rugby 1930.

22. Arnold's essay is reprinted in his *Miscellaneous Works*, London 1845, 363–79.

23. There were at least two major clashes between Boughton-Leigh's keeper and Rugby boys in Arnold's time, in 1833 and 1837. The *Tom Brown's Schooldays* incident is closer to the second one; see T. Hughes, *Memoir of a Brother*, 2nd ed., London 1873, 26–7; A.J. Arbuthnot, *Memories of Rugby and India*, London 1910, 34–5; Sir John C. Dalrymple Hay, *Lines from my Logbooks*, Edinburgh 1908, 12–13; [Newmarch], *Recollections of Rugby*, 27; W. Edward Oswell, *William Cotton Oswell, Hunter and Explorer*, 2 vols, London 1900, I, 44; Bamford, *Thomas Arnold*, 71–3, 114–16.

24. Sydney Selfe, *Notes on the Characters and Incidents depicted by the Master Hand of Tom Hughes in* Tom Brown's Schooldays, *etc. etc.*, Rugby 1909, 17–18.

25. [William Gover] in *The Parent's Review* VI (Jan. 1896), 833–4.

26. Bamford, *Thomas Arnold*, 163.

27. E.E. Kellett, *As I Remember*, London 1936, 203.

28. G.T. Fox, *A Memoir of the Rev. Henry Watson Fox*, London 1840, 29, 72; W.R. Fremantle, *Memoir of the Rev. Spencer Thornton*, London 1850.

29. [Gover] in *Parent's Review* VI (Dec. 1895), 756; and VII (Mar. 1896), 35. Cf. A.P. Stanley, *Life and Correspondence of Thomas Arnold*, 5th ed., London 1845, I, 164–5.

30. Cf. P.G. Scott, 'The School Novels of Dean Farrar', *British Journal of Educational Studies* XIX (1971), 163-82.

31. Stanley, *Life of Arnold*, I, 88.

32. Arnold, *Miscellaneous Works*, 377.

33. Stanley, *Life of Arnold*, I, 314.

34. [A.P. Stanley], 'School a Little World', *Rugby Magazine* I,

2 (Oct. 1835), 105, Cf. W.D. Arnold's pamphlet *Football* (1851), and Melly, *School Experiences*, 231.

35. The stages, developed from Goffman's work on asylums, are described in John Wakeford, *The Cloistered Élite*, 128–59.

36. R.K. Merton, 'Social Structure and Anomie', *American Sociological Review* III (1938), 672.

37. *Saturday Review* IV (3 Oct. 1857), 313.

CHAPTER 4 (pp. 58–71)

1. Letter dated 4 March 1835 in Stanley, *Life of Arnold*, London 1901, 000.

2. The six other schools were : Marlborough, Rossall, Radley, Lancing, Brighton and Hurstpierpoint. All these were Church of England. In addition there were two day schools (Liverpool College and Berkhamstead) and at least six other schools, including those of other denominations (Mount St Mary's, Ratcliffe, Taunton, Llandovery, Wellington, and Eltham).

3. A convenient synthesising reference would be C. Norwood, *The English Tradition of Education*, London 1929. Born in 1875, Norwood was a Victorian product and headmaster of Marlborough and Harrow. He began to write about the schools early in the century and produced a major work (with A.H. Hope) in 1909.

4. Arnold himself was a critic and so was C. Norwood—see reference 3 above.

5. E.g. *Sermons*, London 1878, III, 137–8.

6. See T.W. Bamford, 'Public Schools and Social Class, 1801–1850', *British Journal of Sociology* XII, 3 (Sep. 1961), 224–35.

7. Stanley, *Life of Arnold*, 460–1.

8. Arnold, *Miscellaneous Works*, 1845, 213.

9. Stanley, *Life of Arnold*, 554.

10. *The Englishman's Register* 2, 14 May 1831.

11. See C.H. Sisson, *The Spirit of British Administration and Some European Comparisons*, London 1959.

12. For some discussion and Chinese parallels, see Wilkinson, *The Prefects*.

13. This has been commented upon in many school histories, e.g. Newsome, *A History of Wellington College*, 264.

14. See C.J. Vaughan, *A Letter to the Viscount Palmerston on the Monitorial System of Harrow School*, London 1854.

15. See B. Russell, *On Education*, London 1926. He also claims that Arnold's system was aristocratic, designed to train men for positions of authority and power, whether at home or in the Empire.

16. See, for example, Arnold's language in 'The Oxford Malignants and Dr Hampden', *Edinburgh Review*, Apr. 1836.

17. For the underlying differences, see W.B.D. Heaney, 'The Established Church and the Education of the Victorian Middle Classes: A Study of the Woodard Schools, 1847–1891' (D.Phil. thesis, Oxford University, 1961).

CHAPTER 5 (pp. 72–94)

1. O.F. Christie, *A History of Clifton College, 1860–1934*, Bristol 1935, 34.
2. *Ibid.*, 25.
3. Temple, *Life of Bishop Percival*, 57.
4. Hammond, ed., *Centenary Essays on Clifton College*, 12.
5. *Ibid.*, 13.
6. Temple, *Life of Bishop Percival*, 51.
7. Frank Fletcher, *After Many Days*, London 1937, 78.
8. *Ibid.*, 76.
9. 'Cambridge High Local Examinations' and 'Oxford and Cambridge Locals'. The names given to these examinations, which dominated the pre-university stage of education for so many decades, needs some explanation. They were neither connected with a university curriculum or residence, nor were they the product of a locality; they were devised, with papers set and corrected by examiners (from schools as well as colleges) appointed by a university for the specific purpose of examining candidates who were *not* attending a university. The candidates were usually, though not always, of school age. The examinations took place in a 'Local Centre', such as a school or hall, and were supervised by a responsible citizen of the locality. (In the case of schools recognised as 'centres', this was usually the headmaster.) The 'University Board', consisting of the examiners, published the list of results.
10. *The Wellingburian* XXV (1905).
11. *Ibid.* XXIV (1904).
12. William Whitehead, *Tripe and Onions*, Rushden 1954, 6.
13. This term is used in the Taunton Report to refer to those schools whose pupils left at the age of sixteen.
14. Walker, *History of the Oundle Schools*, 362.
15. *Ibid.*
16. H.G. Wells, *The Story of a Great Schoolmaster*, 2nd ed., London 1924, 44.
17. *Ibid.*, 4.
18. *Ibid.*, 33.
19. *Ibid.*, 26.

20. *Ibid.*, 36.
21. *Ibid.*, 325.
22. *Ibid.*, 146.
23. *Ibid.*, 109.
24. *Ibid.*, 108.

CHAPTER 6 (pp. 95–114)

1. F. Darwin, ed., *Charles Darwin: his Life*, 2nd ed., London 1902, 10–11.
2. E. Copleston, *A Reply to the Calumnies of the Edinburgh Review against Oxford*, Oxford 1810, 133.
3. *Report of HM Commissioners . . . [on the] Revenues and Management of Certain Colleges and Schools, Parliamentary Papers* (Irish University Press reprints, *Education General*: Vol. 10, Session 1864), pp. 42–3. (All subsequent references to this source are abbreviated to *Clarendon Report*.)
4. *Clarendon Report*, Vol. 10, 23.
5. *Ibid.*, Vol. 9, 217.
6. *Ibid.*, Vol. 9, 146.
7. *Ibid.*
8. *Ibid.*
9. *Ibid.*, Vol. 9, 146–7.
10. W.M. Thackeray, *The Irish Sketch Book*, London 1911, 368–9.
11. *Clarendon Report*, Vol. 9, 86.
12. T.H. Huxley, 'A Liberal Education : Where to Find It' (1868), in *Science and Education* (*Collected Essays*, Vol. 3), 79.
13. *Clarendon Report*, Vol. 12, 377.
14. *Ibid.*, Vol. 9, 32.
15. *Ibid.*, Vol. 9, 253.
16. Tyndall correspondence (Royal Institution Archives) : J.M. Wilson to John Tyndall, 15 Mar. 1867 [f.1787].
17. See P.H.J.H. Gosden, *How They Were Taught*, Oxford 1969, 122.
18. *Clarendon Report*, Vol. 9, 16.
19. Commission on Scientific Instruction and the Advancement of Science, *Sixth Report, Parliamentary Papers* (Irish University Press reprints, *Education Scientific and Technical* : Vol. 4, Session 1875), p. 58. (All subsequent references to this source are abbreviated to *Devonshire Report*.)
20. *Clarendon Report*, Vol. 9, 12.
21. *Devonshire Report*, 59.
22. *Ibid.*

23. *Clarendon Report*, Vol. 9, 33.
24. *Devonshire Report*, I.
25. *Ibid.*, 10.
26. *Ibid.*, 137
27. Staunton, *The Great Schools of England*, xix.
28. *Clarendon Report*, Vol. 9, 30.
29. *Ibid.*, Vol. 10, 311; compare Thomas Arnold's Lecture to the Mechanics' Institute at Rugby (*Miscellaneous Works*, 423).

CHAPTER 7 (pp. 115–28)

1. F.W. Farrar, *In the Days of thy Youth*, London 1876, Sermon 37 : 'School Games', 369.
2. The question of the relationship between chivalric idealism and social class is discussed in M. Valency, *In Praise of Love*, New York 1958, 42–7.
3. M.C. Battestin, *The Moral Basis of Fielding's Art*, Middletown, Conn. 1959, Ch. 2; Isaac Barrow, *Theological Works*, ed. A. Napier, Cambridge 1859, II, Sermon 35 : 'Of Walking as Christ Did', 524–45, esp. 539.
4. H. Brooke, *The Fool of Quality*, revised ed., London 1859, with preface by Charles Kingsley, I, xlv, 3, 5–6, 66–9, etc. Another influence upon this book, and on the sentimental-benevolent idea of manliness, was Rousseau, whose *Émile* had appeared in 1762 and had encouraged many to look to nature and primitive society to find man at his noblest and best.
5. See, for example, Rev. H.R. Heywood, *Manliness: A Sermon . . .*, Manchester 1877, Rev. H.S. Brown, *Manliness, A Lecture*, London 1858; S.S. Pugh, *Christian Manliness*, London 1867.
6. *Clarendon Report* : Rugby Evidence, Vol. IV, 295, paras 1,966–71; Shrewsbury Evidence, Vol. IV, 351–2, para. 1,041; General Report, Vol. I, 44–5.
7. S.T. Coleridge, *Aids to Reflection* (1825), Bohn ed., London 1884, 22–3, 143, 126–9.
8. Stanley, *Life and Correspondence of Thomas Arnold*, London 1844, I, 165.
9. Arnold, *Sermons*, II, London 1832, 122.
10. Arnold, 'On the Discipline of Public Schools', *Quarterly Journal of Education*; repr. in *Miscellaneous Works*, 369–70; *Sermons*, II, 1832, 126; *Christian Life, its Course, its Hindrances and its Helps*, London 1841, 18–19, 30–1; Stanley, *Life of Arnold*, I, 99–100, 125–6.
11. Stanley, *Life of Arnold*, I, 146; Arnold, *Christian Life, its Hopes, its Fears and its Close*, London 1842, 66ff.

12. Farrar, *Eric, or Little by Little* (1858), 24th ed., Edinburgh 1890, 167, 88; *St Winifred's, or The World of School* (1862), ed. of London 1912, 143–62; *In the Days of thy Youth*, Sermon 34 : 'The Courage of the Saints Possible in Boyhood', 343; *Words of Truth and Wisdom*, 3rd ed., Edinburgh, n.d., 136, 30.

13. Newsome, *Godliness and Good Learning*, 37.

14. For example, by Fitzjames Stephen in the *Edinburgh Review* CVII (Jan. 1858), 172–93. The first appearance of the phrase in print seems to have been in T.C. Sandars's review of Kingsley's novel, *Two Years Ago* in the *Saturday Review* III (Feb. 1857), 176.

15. Kingsley alludes to this idea in a letter to Hughes reprinted in *Charles Kingsley: his Letters and Memories of his Life*, edited by his wife, London 1877, II, 27. Plato discusses this concept in the *Laws* V, 731b, c, and in the *Republic* IV, 440a–441b.

16. *Clarendon Report* : Eton Evidence, Vol. IV, *passim*; O. Browning, *Memories of Sixty Years at Eton, Cambridge and Elsewhere*, London 1905, esp. 181–4.

17. Charles Wordsworth, *Christian Boyhood at a Public School*, London 1846, I, 117–20.

18. The following brief account of the rise of athleticism in the schools owes much to C. Rigby, 'The Life and Influence of Edward Thring' (D.Phil. thesis, Oxford University, 1968), and J.R. de S. Honey, 'The Victorian Public School, 1828–1902' (D.Phil. thesis, Oxford University 1969).

19. R.J. Mackenzie, *Almond of Loretto*, London 1905, *passim*. The reference to Spencer is to *Education Intellectual, Moral and Physical* (1861), ed. F.A. Cavenagh, Cambridge 1932, Pt. IV : 'Physical Education', 159. Almond expressed his educational ideas from time to time in print, notably in *Christ the Protestant*, Edinburgh 1899, esp. 153, and 'Football as a Moral Agent', *Nineteenth Century* XXXIV (Dec. 1893), 899–911.

20. 'E.E.B.', 'Games', *Journal of Education* N.S. VI (Feb. 1884), 69–72.

21. Herodotus, I, 30–2, trans. G. Rawlinson, London 1867, I, 142. Arnold's casual reference is recorded in Stanley, *Life of Arnold*, I, 117; cf. Plato, *Republic* III, 411.

22. J.A. Symonds, *Studies of the Greek Poets*, 3rd ed., London 1893, I, 339, 343.

23. W.J. Cory, *Ionica* (1858), 3rd ed., London 1905, 'Mimnermus in Church', 5–6; 'Academus', 28; 'A New Year's Day', 71. It should perhaps be mentioned that this kind of Hellenism, with its exaltation of the young and beautiful male form, sometimes accompanied and

expressed strong homosexual feeling. E.F. Benson's *David Blaize* (1916), a reflection of school life in the 1880s, celebrates passionate but chaste boyhood friendships and also includes an enthusiastic discussion among the protagonists of the athletic and aesthetic achievement of the Greeks. It would, however, be a mistake to assume that this was ever an 'official' institution in the schools comparable to the emphasis on 'moral earnestness'.

24. See, for example, Austin's 'Is Life Worth Living?' reprinted in W. E. Henley's interesting anthology *Lyra Heroica*, London 1892. This book was often prescribed for the certificate examinations at the turn of the century, with the result that the patriotic or imperialist verse of Kingsley, Kipling, Cory and Newbolt, which it contained, was made known to a wide audience of schoolboys.

25. E. Marsh, 'Memoir', prefaced to Rupert Brooke, *Collected Poems*, 3rd ed., London 1928, xii, xiv; Rupert Brooke, *Poetical Works*, ed. G. Keynes, London 1946, 'Vanitas' (Mar. 1906), 170–1; '1914 : Peace', 19. Brooke was well acquainted with the hyperaesthetic writing of the 1890s : he was given a copy of Oscar Wilde's *De Profundis* when he was at school, and at about the same time he also wrote a brief but brilliant parody of the jewelled prose of the 'decadence'. See G. Keynes, ed., *Letters of Rupert Brooke*, London 1968, 16, 22–3.

26. Alec Waugh, *The Loom of Youth*, London 1917, esp. Pt IV, Ch. VI : 'The Things that Seem', which describes a school debate on the value of athleticism in which the philistines are finally routed. Mr J.A. Mangan reminds me, however, that the games cult survived the 1914–18 war, sometimes in a very vigorous form, and has perhaps waned generally only since the last war. But it is true to say that manliness as a games-playing ideal saw no further development after the Great War.

CHAPTER 8 (pp. 129–46)

1. W.L.C. von der Goltz, *The Nation in Arms*, London 1887, Ch. 1, sec. 3.

2. John Warder and Reg Wilson, 'The British Borstal Training System', *Journal of Criminal Law and Criminology* LXIV (1973), 118, 127.

3. Winston S. Churchill, *My Early Life*, London 1930, Ch. 3.

4. Maclean, *The Public Schools and the War in South Africa*.

5. *Parliamentary Papers* (1904), XXX-XXXI, Questions 11,342ff.

6. *Ibid.*, Questions 11,491ff.

7. *Parliamentary Papers* (1907), XLIX, Question 64.

8. I owe this qualification to Mr John Keegan of the Royal

Military College, Sandhurst, whose careful reading of this chapter has also enabled me to make a number of other minor corrections.

9. *Lorettonian*, 21 Feb. 1900.

10. *Ibid.*; *Fettesian*, Apr. 1900.

11. *Glenalmond Chronicle*, Nov. 1906.

12. Erickson and Mommsen in *Marxism, Communism and Western Society*, New York 1972.

13. Olive Anderson, 'Christian Militarism', *English Historical Review* LXXXVI (1971), 46–72.

14. For the public schools' contribution to economic strength and industrial progress, see Barnett, *The Collapse of British Power*, Ch. 2.

15. F.N. Maude, *War and The World's Life*, London 1907, 381.

16. See *Loretto's Hundred Years, 1827–1927*, London 1928.

17. *Parliamentary Papers* (1904), XXX-XXXI, Question 11,581.

18. Introduction to H.V. Hesketh-Prichard, *Sniping in France*, London 1919.

19. *Lorettonian*, 20 Dec. 1915.

20. *Glenalmond Chronicle*, Aug. 1888.

21. *Ibid.*, Nov. 1905.

22. Paul Jones, *War Letters of a Public School Boy*, London 1918, 3–4.

23. Newsome, *Godliness and Good Learning*, 238.

CHAPTER 9 (pp. 147–67)

1. Charles Kingsley, *Health and Education*, London 1887, 85.

2. F.W. Farrar, *In the Days of thy Youth*, London 1889, 373.

3. Denis Brailsford, *Sport and Society*, London 1969, 25.

4. Edward Lockwood, *Early Days of Marlborough College*, London 1893, 66.

5. Leslie Stephen, 'Athletic Sports and University Studies', *Fraser's Magazine* II (Dec. 1870), 695.

6. F.A.Y. Brown, *Family Notes*, Genoa Royal Institute of Sordomum, 1917, 89. (Marlborough College Archives.)

7. Bradley, Champneys and Baines, *History of Marlborough College*, 106.

8. Quoted from Cotton's letter to parents dated June 1853. (Marlborough College Archives.)

9. There is uncertainty about the precise extent of the discontent under Wilkinson in 1851 and how far it contributed to his resignation in the early part of 1852. Bradley and his colleagues (*History of Marlborough College*, 156–62) paint a picture of grave insubordination leading to revolt. Mr L. Warwick-James, an Old Marlburian

who has closely studied the Wilkinson era, has suggested to the present writer that the *History* exaggerates the extent of the troubles and that Wilkinson's resignation had nothing to do with pupil discipline but was the consequence of his unpopular religious views (he was a High Church Anglican). However, Mr Warwick-James has stated that he has no proof of this. If the indiscipline under Wilkinson has been exaggerated, it nevertheless seems to have been serious. Boscowen Somerset, for example, in his diary which covers this period, refers to two pupils 'sent away', windows smashed, the desks of assistant masters broken into and Wilkinson's chairs broken up. The timing of Wilkinson's resignation is certainly interesting. It seems not unreasonable to suppose that it could have been the outcome of three factors—religious bigotry reinforced by troublesome pupils and the unhappy financial position of the school at the time. As regards this latter point, there is general agreement that in Wilkinson's last years and Cotton's early years the college was in serious financial difficulties due to unrealistic appreciation of the cost of maintaining the establishment coupled with a desire to charge small fees so as to enable the sons of relatively poor clergy to become 'gentlemen and scholars'.

10. *Marlburian* XLI, 624 (22 May 1906), 59. Other notable sporting masters under Cotton were George Cranston, something of a sporting eccentric, who hurled himself into rugby 'squashes' wearing a tall hat; Henry Richard Tomkinson, Cotton's brother-in-law, a fine all-rounder who had been educated at Rugby in Cotton's house; and the already mentioned John Sowerby, who, as assistant master under Wilkinson, organised games of cricket on half-holidays.

The *Marlburian*, with its self-appointed task as chronicler of Marlborough life and its continuous history from 1865 to the present, is a particularly useful barometer of the school climate of opinion and serves as a valuable index of the history of consensus and dispute surrounding the athleticism ideology.

11. G.E.L. Cotton, *Sermons and Addresses Delivered in the Chapel of Marlborough College*, Cambridge 1858, 406.

12. *Ibid.*, 43.

13. *Ibid.*, 220–1.

14. Quoted in G. Kitson Clark, *The Making of Victorian England*, London 1962, 271.

15. Barnett, *The Collapse of British Power*, 97.

16. Cheltenham College, established in 1841, was the first public school to develop a 'modern side'. Marlborough's 'modern side' (called in this instance the 'modern class') was created by Cotton in

1854. For details of this public school development, see Bamford, *The Rise of the Public Schools*, 25; J.W. Adamson, *English Education, 1789–1902*, Cambridge 1930, 156–7.

17. John McCunn, *The Making of Character*, Cambridge 1912, 76.

18. For a detailed discussion of this point, see J.R. de S. Honey, 'The Victorian Public School, 1828–1902' (D.Phil. thesis, Oxford University 1969).

19. Perkin, *The Origins of Modern English Society, 1780–1880*, 435.

20. S.T. Curtis and M.A. Boultwood, *An Introductory History of English Education Since 1800*, 3rd ed., Oxford 1964, 302.

21. *Marlburian* II, 17 (4 Oct. 1867), 202.

22. *Ibid.* II, 18 (18 Dec. 1867), 210.

23. *Ibid.* III, 3 (1 Apr. 1868), 37.

24. Farrar in *The Fortnightly Review*, 1 Mar. 1868, 237. (Published lecture delivered to members of the Royal Institute on 31 Jan. 1868.)

25. Farrar, *In the Days of thy Youth*, 289.

26. McIntosh, *Physical Education in England since 1800*, 70.

27. R. Wilkinson, 'The Gentleman Ideal and the Maintenance of a Political Élite', *Sociology of Education* XXXVII (Fall 1963), 21.

28. J. Wellens, 'The Anti-Intellectual Tradition in the West' in P.W. Musgrove, ed., *Sociology, History and Education*, London 1970, 59–60.

29. Between 1870 and 1914 there were over forty articles and letters containing details of life in Afghanistan, Australia, Bengal, Burma, Canada, Ceylon, Egypt, Gibraltar, Natal, New Zealand, The Punjab, South Africa, Tasmania, West Africa and the West Indies. After the Great War they ended abruptly.

30. See Hofstadter, *Anti-Intellectualism in American Life*.

31. Farrar, *Objects of School Life*, London 1875, 10. This statement of Farrar's, of course, does not contradict the point made about his alternative ideology of 'intellectual endeavour'. He continually regretted the low intellectual effort of the majority of the boys. 'Do not think', he told them in another of his sermons, 'that I disparage the physical vigour at which I daily look with interest but it is impossible to repress a sigh when one thinks that the same vigour, infused also into intellectual studies which are far higher and nobler, would carry all success and prosperity in life irresistibly before you.' (*In the Days of thy Youth*, 112–13.)

O

32. Harold J. Laski, *The Danger of Being a Gentleman and Other Essays*, London 1939.

33. C. Barnett, 'A Military Historian's View of the Great War', *Essays by Divers Hands* XXXVI (1969), 7.

34. Debating society topics, lecture attendances and correspondence in the *Marlburian* during this time suggest that the comments of J.W.D. Harrison (undated manuscript in Marlborough College Archives entitled 'Marlborough in the Sixties') to the effect that the boys were parochial and insular in their interests remained broadly valid until the twentieth century.

35. *Marlburian* VIII, 136 (22 Oct. 1873), 155. It has tentatively been suggested by E.G.H. Kempson, a former assistant master at Marlborough, that Trebla was John Albert Babington, housemaster of C3, 1869–75.

36. J. Llewellyn Davies, *Sermon in Marlborough Chapel, Feast of St Michael and All Angels*, Marlborough 1874, 5.

37. *Marlburian* XXV, 393 (10 Feb. 1890), 5.

38. *Ibid.* XXV, 394 (24 Jun. 1890), 94–5.

39. *Ibid.* XXVI, 419 (7 Oct. 1891), 156. For the response, see *ibid.* XXVI, 421 (4 Nov. 1891), 161.

40. *Ibid.* XXXI, 493 (3 Dec. 1896), 180.

41. *The Centenary Cavalcade*, 22. (Marlborough College Archives.)

42. The Education Act of 1902 created local education authorities which were empowered to grant financial aid to the traditional endowed grammar schools, set up municipal or county secondary schools, provide scholarships for poor but able pupils and award scholarships to the ancient and modern universities.

43. F. Fletcher, *After Many Days*, London 1937, 123–5.

44. *Marlburian* LXXVII, 1,065 (Winter 1954), 51.

45. F. Fletcher, *After Many Days*, 7.

46. *Marlburian* LXXVII, 1,001 (Feb. 1943), 7.

47. *Ibid.* XCIX (Lent Term 1964), 30.

48. See, for example, *Marlburian* L, 750 (7 Jun. 1915), 81; L, 757 (8 Jul. 1915), 92.

49. *Marlburian* LI, 769 (19 Dec. 1916), 191. Poem entitled 'In Memory of Captain R.O. Lagden' by 'R.B.' This poem is reproduced by kind permission of Mr Roger Ellis, headmaster of Marlborough College.

50. This is not to say, of course, that there were not steady and sound academic successes and that the 'intellectual endeavour' ideology was abandoned. To put the situation in some sort of perspective, the Marlborough College Register (1952 edition, 966–75)

records 474 Oxford and Cambridge exhibitions between 1880 and 1920. As indicated in the present discussion, it is a matter of relativity of emphasis and values.

51. J.H. Simpson, *The Public Schools and Athleticism* (Educational Times Booklets, No. 1), London 1923, 3.

CHAPTER 10 (pp. 168–76)

1. For the non-evaluative concept of a 'civilising process' in mind here, see Norbert Elias, *Uber den Prozess der Zivilisation*, 2 vols, Berne and Munich 1969. The folk antecedents of modern football are discussed in Norbert Elias and Eric Dunning, 'Folk Football in Medieval and Early Modern Britain', in *The Sociology of Sport: a selection of readings*, ed. E. Dunning, London 1971, 116–32. See also R.W. Malcolmson, *Popular Recreations in English Society 1700–1850*, Cambridge, 1973.

2. Fisher, *Annals of Shrewsbury School*, 313, 404.

3. F. Markham, *Recollections of a Town Boy at Westminster*, London 1903, 92–5; E.P. Eardley-Wilmot and E.C. Streatfield, *Charterhouse: Old and New*, London 1895, 92–5; A.H. Tod, *Charterhouse*, London 1900, 154; 'Rugby Football in the Sixties', *Cornhill Magazine* (Nov. 1922), 571–81; A.C. Adams, *Wykehamica: A History of Winchester College and Commoners*, London 1878, 366–7; J.B. Oldham, *A History of Shrewsbury School*, London 1952, 231.

4. A.W. Merivale, *Family Memorials*, London 1884, 330.

5. N. Wymer, *Dr Arnold of Rugby*, London 1953, 119; McIntosh, *A History of Physical Education in England since 1801*; and *Sport in Society*, London 1963, 64.

6. T. Walrond, 'Arnold, Thomas' in *Dictionary of National Biography*.

7. W.D. Arnold in *The Book of Rugby School*, ed. E.M. Goulburn, Rugby 1856, 151; Rouse, *A History of Rugby School*, 246; Francis J. Woodward, *The Doctor's Disciples*, London 1954, 183. A copy of *The Laws of Football as Played at Rugby School*, Rugby 1845, may be found in the library of the school.

8. The analysis here rests on that of K.G. Sheard in 'Rugby Football: A Study in Developmental Sociology' (M.Phil. thesis, University of Leicester, 1972).

9. G. Green and H. Fabian, ed., *Association Football*, London 1959, I, 140.

204   *The Victorian Public School*

CHAPTER 11 (pp. 177–86)

1. Published in R. Ackermann, *History of the Colleges of Winchester, Eton and Westminster, etc.*, London 1816.

2. Cf. N. Carlisle, *A Concise Description of the Endowed Grammar Schools in England and Wales*, London 1818, II, 148.

3. A plan of Rugby School as rebuilt by Hakewill is given in Seaborne, *The English School*, 170.

4. There is a good series of photographs of the former Christ's Hospital buildings before they were demolished, in the National Monuments Record, 23 Savile Row, London, W.1.

5. For the plan of the former King Edward's School, Birmingham, see Seaborne, *The English School*, 176. The rival Anglican and Nonconformist schools, with their contrasting architectural styles, may still be seen at Leicester (Collegiate School, 1836, and Proprietary School, now the Public Museum, 1837), Sheffield (Collegiate School, 1836, now part of the City College of Education, and Proprietary School, 1837, later part of King Edward VII School) and Liverpool (Liverpool Institute School, 1837, and Liverpool Collegiate School, 1843).

6. Cf. *Clarendon Report*, Vol. I, 287. For the cubicle system at Radley, see Seaborne, *The English School*, 252 and Plates 208–9.

7. At Chester the first principal of the training college, established in 1839, set up a flourishing science school which prepared boys for the universities and for the home and Indian civil services (see F.E. Foden, 'The Rev. Arthur Rigg : Pioneer of Workshop Practice', *Vocational Aspect* XXIII (1959)).

8. For Wellington, see Newsome, *A History of Wellington College*; J.L. Bevir, *The Making of Wellington College*, London 1920; *The Builder* (1856), 85–7; (1859), 55–7.

9. See K.E. Kirk, *The Story of the Woodard Schools*, revised ed., Abingdon-on-Thames 1952, Ch. 8.

10. For plans, elevations and descriptions, see *The Builder* (1864), 80–3 (Framlingham); (1864), 845–7 (Fettes); (1865), 46–8, 448–9 (Malvern); (1869), 765–7 (Elstow College, Bedford, now demolished). See also *The Building News* (1861), 856 (Clifton); (1864), 902–4 (Framlingham); (1868), 47–9 (Bedford).

11. I. Nairn, *Nairn's London*, London 1966, 196. See also *The Builder* (1868), 521–2, 530–1.

12. N. Pevsner, *London*, London 1952, II, 177. St Paul's was rebuilt twice on its original site near St Paul's Cathedral, then moved to Hammersmith and finally to Barnes.

The Contributors

T.W. BAMFORD
Director of the Institute of Education, University of Hull; author of *Thomas Arnold* (1960), *The Rise of the Public Schools* (1967) and editor of *Thomas Arnold on Education: A Selection from his Writings* (1970).

G.F.A. BEST
Professor of History, School of European Studies, University of Sussex; author of *Temporal Pillars: Queen Anne's Bounty, the Ecclesiastical Commissioners and the Church of England* (1964) and *Mid-Victorian Britain 1851–75* (1971).

IAN BRADLEY (joint editor)
Harold Salvesen, Fellow of New College, Oxford (1972–74). Author of *The Call to Seriousness* (1975).

W.H. BROCK
Reader in the History of Science and Director of the Victorian Studies Centre, University of Leicester; author of *H.E. Armstrong and the Teaching of Science, 1880–1930* (1973).

E.G. DUNNING
Senior Lecturer, Department of Sociology, University of Leicester; editor of *The Sociology of Sport: A Selection of Readings* (1971).

J.R. de S. HONEY
Professor of Education and Head of the Department of Education, University of Rhodesia; author of *Tom Brown's Universe: The Development of the Victorian Public School* (forthcoming).

J.A. MANGAN
Senior Lecturer in Education, Jordanhill College of Education, Glasgow; editor of *Physical Education and Sport: Sociological and Cultural Perspectives* (1972).

A.J. MEADOWS

Professor of Astronomy and Head of the Department of Astronomy and the History of Science, University of Leicester; author of *The High Firmament: A Study of Astronomy in English Literature* (1969) and *Science and Controversy: A Biography of Sir Norman Lockyer* (1972).

A.C. PERCIVAL

Author of *The Origin of the Headmasters' Conference* (1969) and *Very Superior Men* (1973).

P. SCOTT

Lecturer, Department of English Literature, University of Edinburgh; editor of *Victorian Poetry, 1830 to 1870: An Anthology* (1971).

M. SEABORNE

Principal, Chester College of Education; author of *Recent Education from Local Sources* (1967) and *The English School: Its Architecture and Organisation 1370–1870* (1971).

B. SIMON (joint editor)

Professor of Education, University of Leicester; author of *The Two Nations and the Educational Structure, 1780–1870* (1960), *Education and the Labour Movement, 1870–1920* (1965) and *The Politics of Educational Reform, 1920–1940* (1974).

N. VANCE

Harold Salvesen Fellow of New College, Oxford (from 1974).

Select Bibliography

There is an immense literature concerned with the Victorian public school. This bibliography is limited to books directly relevant to the present work.

Noel Annan, *Roxburgh of Stowe*, London 1965. (Chapter 1 covers the development of public schools in the nineteenth century.)

Gillian Avery, *Nineteenth-Century Children*, London 1965.

T.W. Bamford, *Thomas Arnold*, London 1960.

T.W. Bamford, *The Rise of the Public Schools*, London 1967.

Correlli Barnett, *The Collapse of British Power*, London 1972.

A.K. Boyd, *A History of Radley College, 1847–1947*, Oxford 1948.

A.G. Bradley, A.C. Champneys and J.W. Baines, *A History of Marlborough College*, London 1893.

Asa Briggs, 'Thomas Hughes and the Public Schools', in *Victorian People*, Harmondsworth 1965.

Harold Child, 'The Public School in Fiction', in *The Public Schools from Within*, London 1906.

Lionel Cust, *A History of Eton College*, London 1899.

F. Ferriday, ed., *Victorian Architecture*, London 1963.

J. d'E. Firth, *Winchester College*, London 1949.

G.W. Fisher, *Annals of Shrewsbury School*, London 1899.

W. Furness, ed., *The Centenary History of Rossall School*, Aldershot 1945.

John Gloag, *Victorian Taste*, London 1962.

A.B. Gourlay, *A History of Sherborne School*, Winchester 1951.

N.G.L. Hammond, ed., *Centenary Essays on Clifton College*, Bristol 1962.

Ian Hay, *The Lighter Side of School Life*, London 1914.

Brian Heeney, *Mission to the Middle Classes: The Woodard Schools, 1848–1891*, London 1969.

W.R. Hicks, *The School in English and German Fiction*, London 1933.

Richard Hofstadter, *Anti-Intellectualism in American Life*, London 1964.

J.R. de S. Honey, *Tom Brown's Universe: The Development of the Victorian Public School* (forthcoming).

J.B. Hope Simpson, *Rugby since Arnold*, London 1967.

R.D. How, *Six Great Schoolmasters*, London 1904.

Patrick Howarth, *Play Up and Play the Game: The Heroes of Popular Fiction*, London 1973.

E.W. Howson and G.T. Warner, ed., *Harrow School*, London 1898.

C. Kingsley, *Letters and Memories of his Life*, ed. by his wife, 2 vols, London 1877.

Harold J. Laski, *The Danger of being a Gentleman and Other Essays*, London 1939.

A.F. Leach, *A History of Winchester College*, London 1899.

E.C. Mack, *Public Schools and British Opinion, 1780 to 1860*, London 1938.

E.C. Mack, *Public Schools and British Opinion since 1860*, New York 1941.

E.C. Mack and W.H.G. Armytage, *Thomas Hughes: The Life of the Author of* Tom Brown's Schooldays, London 1952.

A.H.H. Maclean, *The Public Schools and the War in South Africa, 1899–1902*, London 1903.

Margaret Maison, 'Tom Brown and Company : Scholastic Novels of the 1850s', *English* XII (1958).

H.C. Maxwell Lyte, *A History of Eton College, 1440–1875*, London 1877.

P.C. McIntosh, *Physical Education in England since 1800*, London 1952; London 1968.

Geneva Mae Meers, *Victorian Schoolteachers in Fiction*, 1953.

M.C. Morgan, *Cheltenham College: the First Hundred Years*, Chalfont St Giles 1968.

Stefan Muthesius, *The High Victorian Movement in Architecture, 1850–1870*, London 1972.

Henry J. Newbolt, *The World as in My Time*, London 1932.

David Newsome, *A History of Wellington College, 1859–1959*, London 1959.

David Newsome, *Godliness and Good Learning*, London 1961.

E.M. Oakeley, *Bishop Percival*, Oxford 1919.

Vivian Ogilvie, *The English Public School*, London 1957.

Alicia C. Percival, *The Origins of the Headmasters' Conference*, London 1969.

Alicia C. Percival, *Very Superior Men: Some Early Public School Headmasters and their Achievements*, London 1973.

G.R. Parkyn, *Edward Thring, Headmaster of Uppingham School:*

Life, Diary and Letters, 2 vols, London 1898; 2nd ed., abridged, London 1900.

Harold J. Perkin, *The Origins of Modern English Society, 1780–1880*, London 1969.

John R. Reed, *Old School Ties: The Public Schools in British Literature*, New York 1964.

W.H.D. Rouse, *A History of Rugby School*, London 1898.

P.G. Scott, 'School Novels as Source Material', *History of Education Society Bulletin*, 5 (1970).

Malcolm Seaborne, *The English School: Its Architecture and Organisation, 1370–1870*, London 1971.

A.P. Stanley, *The Life and Correspondence of Thomas Arnold*, 2 vols, London 1844.

Howard Staunton, *The Great Schools of England*, London 1865.

William Temple, *Life of Bishop Percival*, London 1921.

Bernard Thomas, ed., *Repton, 1557 to 1957*, London 1957.

Paul Thompson, *William Butterfield*, London 1971.

E.S. Turner, *Boys Will Be Boys*, London 1948.

John Wakeford, *The Cloistered Élite: A Sociological Study of the English Public School*, London 1969.

W.G. Walker, *A History of the Oundle Schools*, London 1956.

Rupert Wilkinson, *The Prefects: British Leadership and the Public School Tradition*, London 1964.

Index

KING ALFRED'S COLLEGE
LIBRARY